THE TELEVISION ENTREPRENEURS

The Television Entrepreneurs
Social Change and Public Understanding of Business

RAYMOND BOYLE
LISA W. KELLY
University of Glasgow, UK

R Routledge
Taylor & Francis Group

LONDON AND NEW YORK

First published 2012 by Ashgate Publishing

Published 2016 by Routledge
2 Park Square, Milton Park, Abingdon, Oxon OX14 4RN
711 Third Avenue, New York, NY 10017, USA

First issued in paperback 2017

Routledge is an imprint of the Taylor & Francis Group, an informa business

British Library Cataloguing in Publication Data
Boyle, Raymond.
    The television entrepreneurs : social change and the
    public's understanding of business.
    1. Mass media and business. 2. Businessmen on television.
    3. Television viewers--Attitudes. 4. Business--Public
    opinion.
    I. Title II. Kelly, Lisa W.
    302.2'345-dc23

Library of Congress Cataloging-in-Publication Data
Boyle, Raymond, 1966-
    The television entrepreneurs : social change and public understanding of
    business / by Raymond Boyle and Lisa W. Kelly.
        p. cm.
    Includes bibliographical references and index.
    ISBN 978-1-4094-0322-7 (hardback)
    1. Businessmen on television. 2. Mass media and
    business--Great Britain. 3. Television programs--Social aspects--Great
    Britain. I. Kelly, Lisa W. II. Title.
    PN1992.8.B87B89 2012
    791.450941--dc23

                                                                        2011039523

ISBN 13: 978-1-138-11071-7 (pbk)
ISBN 13: 978-1-4094-0322-7 (hbk)

Contents

Acknowledgements

This book comes out of a research project funded by the Arts and Humanities Research Council (AHRC) entitled *Public Understanding of Business: Television, Representation and Entrepreneurship*. ID No: AH/F017073/1. Some of the early interviews were carried out with the kind support of the Wincott Foundation, thanks to David Crook for his help with this funding. A number of people helped guide us as we navigated our way through the project, these include, Philip Schlesinger, Christine Geraghty and Gillian Doyle. Thanks are also due to those people who offered comments and input at differing stages of the project including, Karen Lury, Annette Hill, John Corner, Ian Drummond, Katie Lander, Simon Down, Janine Swail, Emma Jones and Mark Hart.

Organizationally thanks are due to Samantha Emmanuel at CCPR, Vanessa Lampert at Focus Force, Maureen Kettle at Elite Secretarial Services and Laura Ross at Shoreditch Studios. A big thank you to all of the focus groups participants in both Glasgow and London who engaged so enthusiastically with the project. A number of busy people gave generously of their time to speak with us, it was much appreciated. They were, Andrew Davidson, Andrew Mackenzie, Chris Gorman, Claire Young, Daisy Goodwin, Danny Cohen, Dominic Bird, Doug Richard, Evan Davis, James Harding, Jeff Randall, Julie Meyer, Luke Johnson, Michele Kurland, Peter Grigg, Robert Thirkell, Roly Keating, Ruth Pitt and Sarah Beeny.

Material from the project has appeared as Business on Television: Continuity, Change, and Risk in the Development of Television's 'Business Entertainment Format' in *Television and New Media*, 12(3), May 2011, and The Celebrity Entrepreneur on Television: Profile, Politics and Power, *Celebrity Studies*, 1(3), November 2010. The book has extensively developed and expanded this material.

Thanks also to Neil Jordan at Ashgate, who was keen to commission the book. For Raymond, the support and understanding of Noelle remains important in allowing me to get this type of work done, thanks, once again. For Lisa, thanks to my husband Tiernan for always being there for me, I couldn't have done it without you. Thanks also to all of my wonderful family for their help and support, especially you Mum, and to my baby boy Saul for changing everything. Who knows what I did with my time before you came along.

Raymond Boyle
Lisa W. Kelly
Glasgow

Please leave any preconceived ideas you have of entrepreneurs at the door.
They're plain wrong.

Steve Parks, *How to be an Entrepreneur* (2006: 1)

Introduction

For most of its half-century of media dominance, TV has not had much truck with business programming.

> Virginia Matthews, Docu-soap can get in your eyes. *Management Today*, 7 February 2006, 40–45.

I was very impressed when I first saw the opening title sequence of the programme, showing the sweeping views of London and the Thames, together with the distinctive music. It was all very exciting stuff.

> Lord Sugar discussing *The Apprentice* (2010: 522).

Since the BBC launched *Dragons' Den* (BBC2, 2005–) and *The Apprentice* (BBC2, 2005–2006, BBC1, 2007–) in 2005, the profile of business and entrepreneurship has never been higher on British television screens. For example, alongside the annual appearances of the investor Dragons and budding apprentices, audiences have been introduced to philanthropic millionaires in *The Secret Millionaire* (Channel 4, 2006–), potential restaurateurs in *The Restaurant* (BBC2, 2007–2009), covert CEO's in *Undercover Boss* (Channel 4, 2009–) and fledgling product designers and suppliers in *High Street Dreams* (BBC2, 2010) and *Britain's Next Big Thing* (BBC2, 2011). This is in addition to the numerous successful entrepreneurs offering advice to a range of failing businesses across the property, catering, retail, hotel and manufacturing sectors of the economy. These include Sarah Beeny (*Property Ladder*, Channel 4, 2001–); Gordon Ramsay (*Ramsay's Kitchen Nightmares*, Channel 4, 2004–2009); Heston Blumenthal (*Big Chef Takes on Little Chef*, Channel 4, 2009); Mary Portas (*Mary Queen of Shops*, BBC2, 2007–2010, *Mary Portas: Secret Shopper*, Channel 4, 2011–); Ruth Watson (*The Hotel Inspector*, Channel 5, 2005–2007, *Country House Rescue*, Channel 4, 2008–); Alex Polizzi (*The Hotel Inspector*, Channel 5, 2008–); Sir Gerry Robinson (*Gerry's Big Decision*, Channel 4, 2009) and Hilary Devey (*The Business Inspector*, Channel 5, 2010).

This list is by no means exhaustive but it begins to demonstrate how the entrepreneur has moved into the mainstream of British popular culture while also highlighting that business and entrepreneurship can provide material for entertainment-led factual productions that move beyond the arena of news and current affairs. It is the understanding of these two issues that forms the basis of our research. First, we seek to examine the ways in which the worlds of business and entrepreneurship are represented in British factual entertainment television and how this has changed over the years. In particular, we are interested in the rise of the 'business entertainment format' and its relation to the development of a more commercial, competitive and entrepreneurial television marketplace both in the United Kingdom and around the world. Second, we are concerned with the role and impact that this type of factual entertainment television plays in shaping and circulating particular ideas about entrepreneurship and business more generally in wider public discourse. We argue that television remains a site of great cultural significance in the United Kingdom despite the emergence of social and online media. We also examine how audiences engage with business entertainment formats and consider whether popular entertainment television can articulate or indeed influence changing social and cultural attitudes to both the position and function of business and entrepreneurship in contemporary British society.

With this in mind, this book is divided into two parts. Part I is primarily concerned with television as an industry and the types of factual entertainment programming it produces. It also acknowledges however that television does not operate in isolation but is part of a wider matrix of media discourses through which people acquire ideas and knowledge about society more generally. Chapter 1 considers this further by setting out the broader context in which this study is located. It provides an overview of academic debates around changes within factual television, approaches to genre and questions of cultural value before moving on to examine issues relating to the definition and role of entrepreneurship in society and its representation within popular culture.

Chapter 2 then seeks to understand the broader economic and institutional framework that has helped shape patterns of television production in the United Kingdom since the beginning of the 1990s. As such, this chapter is concerned with a relatively neglected area of television studies, namely the production process. By drawing on interviews with channel controllers, commissioners, producers and presenters from across the BBC, Channel 4 and the independent sector, this chapter highlights the key individuals and the decision-making processes that have shaped the development of the business entertainment format. It also locates this within the broader socio-economic context in which the television industry has structurally changed during this period.

Chapter 3 is textual in focus, looking specifically at the programmes themselves. It is worth noting here that by 'factual entertainment television' we are referring to the move away from traditional documentary and current affairs approaches to representations of business and entrepreneurship towards 'business entertainment formats' that seek to engage and inform audiences in a number of ways. By this we mean the introduction of a visual aesthetic alongside the use of drama, emotion, personality and competition within an overall narrative structure. There has been a distinct lack of academic work carried out on such programming, with business entertainment formats tending to be subsumed within the category of reality television. This is something we aim to address in this chapter by offering a sustained analysis of a number of the programmes mentioned at the beginning of this introduction and by investigating the range of narratives around the entrepreneur and entrepreneurial culture that television represents.

Chapter 4 then seeks to place debates about television and its role in shaping cultural attitudes within a broader framework by considering the political and socio-economic position of business and entrepreneurship within the British experience. This involves examining some of the key narratives, myths and discourses that frame how politics, the media and entrepreneurs themselves view business and entrepreneurial activity. We argue that the structural changes to the television industry discussed in Chapter 2 need to be viewed in the context of the political and cultural shifts in attitudes to wealth and enterprise that have occurred in Britain since the early 1990s.

Part II of the book moves on to 'ask the audience' through the use of audience focus groups. In this section we are interested in the ways in which the wider viewing public understand both business entertainment formats and the concept of entrepreneurship more generally in society. Thus, Chapter 5 looks specifically at how members of the audience engage with a range of business entertainment formats *as* television and considers issues relating to the representations of business and entrepreneurship that television constructs. We focus on how members of the audience may respond to and make meanings from what they see on screen and how this impacts on their knowledge and understanding of the worlds of business and entrepreneurship.

Chapter 6 is concerned with audience engagement with the entrepreneur on television and explores how the range of representations offered on television connects with the experiences that viewers may bring to these programmes. It considers debates around the issue of role models with regards to business entertainment formats and looks at the representation of gender in particular.

Running throughout the book is the concept of the 'celebrity' entrepreneur and Chapter 7 considers this in detail. Specifically, this chapter is interested in understanding the role played by key business celebrities in converting media capital into various forms of political capital and also analyzes the perceptions of the celebrity entrepreneur that exist amongst audiences of business entertainment formats. In so doing, we argue that the shift in public profile of key entrepreneurs through television has also had political and public policy implications that go beyond the confines of the media industries.

A Note on Methods

The audience focus groups examined in Part II were carried out in September 2009 in both Glasgow and London to allow for a comparison between a regional (Scottish) audience with those based in Britain's business and financial capital. In total, 96 respondents between the ages of 18 and 60 took part and were divided into 12 groups. A diverse ethnic mix was sought across all sessions and participants came from a wide range of occupations. While the majority of groups were of mixed gender and occupation, there was one all-male and one all-female group conducted in each city alongside one group consisting solely of participants who defined themselves as business owners or entrepreneurs and another of employees or unemployed participants with no business experience. All respondents were required to be familiar with at least one example of a business entertainment format to allow them to draw on their personal viewing experience of such programming when taking part in discussions. Further information on the design of the focus groups is included in the Appendix.

This work comes out of a project funded by the Arts and Humanities Research Council (AH/F017073/1) which started in January 2009 and was completed by September 2011 and certain sections of the book draw on material that has appeared elsewhere (Boyle and Kelly 2010, Kelly and Boyle 2011). As stated at the beginning of this introduction, we take British broadcasting and programming as our focus, particularly with regard to the industry and audience research carried out, but the business entertainment formats discussed are largely global in nature. For example, *Dragons' Den* and *The Apprentice* originated in Japan and the United States respectively before being sold to numerous countries around the world while *Ramsay's Kitchen Nightmares* and *Undercover Boss* have both been adapted for the American market. Thus, while we outline the economic and institutional frameworks of British broadcasting and speak specifically to British audiences about their experiences, the rise of the business entertainment format is nevertheless part of a larger global phenomenon that demonstrates both the interconnectedness of the media industries, as well as the culturally specific context of local reception of content.

This books then brings together concerns around the production context of television, the narratives and representations that television produces and their reception by the audience. In this context the book can be placed within a broad communications studies tradition interested both in process and context as well as understanding the narratives of television texts. While we now live in the digital age of mobile screens and always-on content, we are convinced that television, and its attendant culture, will remain a central element of both popular and public culture for many years to come.

PART I
Industry, Text and Media Discourse

Chapter 1

Television, Representation and Social Change

The life-lessons learnt from watching *The Apprentice* or listening to a former contestant or reading the gospel of Donald [Trump] does, in my view, subtly affect the 'reality' of business.

Alf Rehn (2008: 780).

I think programmes such as *Dragons' Den* have brought ideas about enterprise to a wider audience. I base that on the reaction from the public and particularly younger people to the show. Among say 14 to 22-year-olds, they are interested in the programme and television has helped shape that climate of opinion.

BBC broadcaster and economist Evan Davis (interview with authors, 12 January 2007).

Television continues to matter in British popular culture. At the core of this book then is a concern with understanding the role that television plays in shaping public knowledge and understanding. We are interested in how ideas gain currency in society and the role that the media plays in this process. While we are focused on television in this study we are acutely aware that the medium does not operate in isolation but is part of a wider network of sources through which people acquire ideas and knowledge about society more generally. In an age of converging media, where the boundaries between online and offline worlds are increasingly nebulous, it is all the more important that recognition is given to interaction across media platforms of differing forms of content (Jenkins 2008); not least because an integral part of evolving television commissioning is to advocate a 360 degree commissioning policy that creates content across platforms and allows parts of the audience to more deeply engage with particular programmes or programming strands.

We are also concerned with understanding the broader economic and institutional framework that has helped shape the patterns of television production in the United Kingdom since the beginning of the 1990s. Throughout, we argue that television, as an industry, is crucially shaped by an uneven combination of economic, political, technological and institutional factors that are often enacted in practice and policy through key individuals in broadcasting organizations. At the core of this complex process are competing discourses about the role and function of television in contemporary society, which in a British context inevitably leads us to engage with debates around public service and more market orientated visions of television's role in the lives of audiences.

The range of discourses and representations that television produces are not ideologically neutral. They spring from key television professionals working in and across a range of media organizations, themselves shaped by their understandings of what they perceive are the needs and wants of both the industry that they work within and the range of audiences they wish to attract or engage. In other words, while broader structural factors such as media policy, the economics of the industry and technological innovations all create the climate (and indeed may set the parameters) within which these media professionals operate, this is only part of the cultural production process. Key decisions are then taken (and televisual trends created and shaped) by individuals across the industry that fundamentally define the content of television and the nature, scale and scope of the range of representations it may offer. Often specific industry practice and custom are informed by particular histories, traditions or institutional narratives that are reproduced in various ways through professional culture (see Nelson 2007, Steemers 2010 and Bennett 2011). It is this combination of structure and agency that makes television, as both an industry and a cultural form, such a compelling and often complex site of analysis.

In this book we aim to investigate the relationship between the broader political economy of the United Kingdom television industry and how this framework, in combination with institutional and individual practices and policies, helps shape the range and types of factual television focusing on issues around business and entrepreneurship. As such, this book extends the work by Boyle (2008, 2009) and Boyle and Magor (2008) that began to map out the relationship between representations of business and factual television in the United Kingdom. Of course for audiences, these industry and institutional processes remain largely obscure or even irrelevant as at the core of the relationship between audiences and television are the programmes themselves. Thus a strong textual dimension runs through the book as we seek to make sense of and map out the structures, narratives and range of representations that factual television offers around the core areas of business, work and entrepreneurship. In so doing we place them within a broader framework of television's own sense of its history, both in terms of the types of programmes it makes and the relationship it has with audiences. To this end, we would suggest that the reconceptualizing of audiences and their likes and dislikes or needs and desires has come to play an increasingly important role in shaping the nature of the television industry since the beginning of the 1990s, as we have moved from a supply-led model of media provision to one that increasingly views itself as being shaped by the demands of the audiences it seeks to connect with.

The first section of this chapter addresses the relationship between factual television and the range of forms and formats that have helped shape its engagement with audiences. At the core of this are debates about the nature of the relationship between the changing economics of television, television and social change and indeed the ways in which the audiences addressed by television are conceptualized and thought about in television research. The following section then examines how definitions and ideas about entrepreneurship and entrepreneurs have been framed more broadly in academic and public discourse. Given the centrality of the representations of entrepreneurial activity throughout this book, we highlight the ways in which *discourses* around this activity are framed and made sense of and begin to think about how television and the media more generally play a key role in this process.

The final section lays out the conceptual framework for this study. It focuses on the role of the audience and examines previous engagements with attempts to conceptualize the relationship between the public and television both as an industry and as a media text. In so doing we open up debates about the role that forms of journalism and entertainment play in shaping aspects of public knowledge and understanding on a range of issues and areas of public life. In the light of these discussions, we will revisit the overarching aim of this book and position this study within a framework that advocates the importance of connecting the production context, within which media content and texts get produced, with the increasingly complex ways in which audiences makes sense of television in contemporary society.

Television, Form and Formats

Academic work on factual television formats has tended to be concerned either with news and current affairs (Jenson 1987, Langer 1998) or the various modes of documentary on offer (Nichols 1991, Corner 1996). Hill (2007) explains that 'factual' is itself a value-laden term that evokes associations with truth, information and knowledge about the real world, thus it is perhaps for this reason that academic scholarship has historically taken as its focus content that can be understood in relation to the 'discourses of sobriety' put forward by Nichols (1991: 3). With non-fiction entertainment formats generally being prefaced with the term 'light', the more commercial or populist examples of factual television have attracted less critical analysis; although both Dyer (1973) and Lusted (1998) have considered light entertainment in relation to the popular culture debate whilst Bonner (2003) and Holmes (2008) have more recently taken 'ordinary' television and the quiz show as their respective objects of analysis.

Since the emergence of reality television formats however, questions have been raised about the traditional binaries between serious news and documentary and more entertainment-led programming. Not only has the industrial landscape of television changed in relation to this but so have popular and academic understandings of what counts as factuality. With the blurring of boundaries between the public and private, the real and the fictional, and information and entertainment, Hill (2007: 2) sees hybridity as being the distinctive feature of reality television and explains how 'popular factual genres are no longer stable, self-contained, or "knowable" entities but rather have migrated, mutated, and replicated in recent years'. While this has called for audiences to engage in more complex viewing strategies, it has also led scholars to rethink much of the work that has been carried out on documentary and factual programming, in addition to examining the proliferation of programmes classified as reality television (see Dovey 2000, Friedman 2002, Holmes and Jermyn 2003, Biressi and Nunn 2005, Austin and de Jong 2008, Ouellette and Hay 2008, and Murray and Ouellette 2009).

Reality Television Research

As Biressi and Nunn (2005: 10) point out, the term reality television is a broad one, encompassing a range of formats that are mainly hybrid in nature, such as docusoaps, real crime and emergency programming, talk shows, talent shows, video diaries, dramatic reconstructions, and 'gamedocs' or group challenge formats. Reality television can in turn be understood as a subset of factual entertainment, which also includes quiz shows, game shows and lifestyle programming. The particular focus of this book is the rise of the 'business entertainment format', which again is a term that encompasses a wide variety of texts, only some of which are understood as reality television.

Indeed the range of available formats and categorizations provides an insight into some of the changes that have occurred within the television industry as new forms of factual programming expand across the schedule. In a crowded digital landscape, in which any channel now competes with numerous rival free-to-air or pay digital channels for an increasingly fragmenting audience, Dovey (2000) suggests that shifts in form and tone within factual television have resulted in broader audiences being sought. In essence, there has been a move from factual programming being equated with seriousness and traditional understandings of public service broadcasting in the United Kingdom towards entertainment-led factuality broadcast across public service and commercial channels. Moreover, with regards to scheduling, the type of lifestyle formats traditionally confined to daytime slots have been transformed and transferred to the evening, replacing a range of genres in the process.

This latter development was first noted in work carried out by the Midlands TV Research Group (Brunsdon et al. 2001) looking at changes taking place during the 1990s within the 8 to 9 p.m. weekday slot on British terrestrial television. At the expense of serious documentaries, current affairs, sitcoms and light entertainment (such as variety and quiz shows), the group documented a significant increase in 'factual entertainment', a term that in this instance is described as the following:

> This has two main strands, 'docu-soap' and the range of programmes using real people that John Corner has called 'documentary lite' (2000) and lifestyle programming. It is the latter which originally sparked [the authors'] interest in the slot, and includes programmes about fashion, gardening, cookery, home decorating and DIY (Do-It-Yourself home improvement) (Brunsdon et al. 2001: 31).

Recognizing also the emergence of real crime and emergency programming during this period, the group acknowledges that the reasons for these changes are complex, involving supranational and national factors, such as the proliferation of cable and satellite broadcasting and the requirement in the 1990 Broadcasting Act that 25 percent of British terrestrial programming should be produced by independent companies.

While the broader political economy of these developments will be considered in more detail in Chapter 2, it is worth emphasizing here that the emergence of factual television is neither limited to the formats described above, nor to the 8 to 9 p.m. scheduling slot during the 1990s. For example, along with the emergence of business entertainment programmes during this period (a term and format absent from the aforementioned research), an Ofcom (2005) report on British television revealed general factual output to be the largest growth area across the five main channels during peaktime. This is in addition to general factual being the second most dominant genre in daytime, after news, and accounting for a quarter of all broadcast hours on multichannel television. Thus, this type of programming has gone on to have an even greater impact than that considered by the Midlands TV Research Group.

Despite this interest in factual programming, there has been a distinct lack of work carried out on how television deals with the world of work, business, finance and entrepreneurial activity, along with the emergence of business entertainment formats in particular. Often considered simply in relation to or as a subset of reality television (Hill 2007, Couldry and Littler 2008, Ouellette and Hay 2008, Hendershot 2009), there has been no sustained analysis of the shift from business as it exists within the realm of news journalism and the reporting of industrial and economic issues (areas that have been dealt with by Gavin 2000, Jensen 1987, Philo 1995 and Richardson 1998) to becoming a central focus in hybrid factual entertainment formats. This is something that Boyle (2008, 2009) and Boyle and Magor (2008) have made initial attempts to redress and in this book we substantially develop this research further.

Along with seeking to document and analyze the various forms of business entertainment programming, this research also heeds Dovey's (2000: 2) call for work in this area to 're-establish the idea of television as a material process in which real people make real decisions within particular and precise contexts'. This involves talking to key people involved in the commissioning and production processes of business entertainment formats in an attempt to examine whether television's developing interest in work, business, finance and entrepreneurial activity can be understood as primarily a response to wider social and economic change in society or to the developments that have occurred within the television landscape since the beginning of the 1990s.

Another aim of this work is to investigate how changes to the ways in which audiences have been conceptualized by the industry have shaped the nature of television programming during the same period. Related to this is a concern with the impact that business entertainment formats have had on public understanding of the worlds of work and business along with patterns of knowledge about entrepreneurship and the role of the entrepreneur in society. Conceptually, it is important that we examine how the idea of genre in television has been adapted and also how debates around the cultural value of the medium and issues of representation have been positioned within research carried out both in the United Kingdom and United States.

Television, Genre and Public Knowledge

Due to the hybridity exhibited in these programmes many of the texts appear to defy easy classification, thus it would be ineffective to try and produce what Neale (1990) refers to as an exhaustive list of characteristic components that would undoubtedly throw up exceptions. Instead, it is more helpful to apply what Mittell (2001: 9) describes as a cultural approach to genre, in which the aim is not to arrive at a concrete definition but 'to explore the material ways in which genres are culturally defined, interpreted, and evaluated'. This involves conceiving of genres as discursive practices and attempting to map out 'as many positions articulating generic knowledge as possible and situating them within larger cultural contexts and relations of power' (Mittell 2004: 13).[1]

With this in mind, this book seeks to consider not just the textual characteristics of business entertainment programming but also the particular production and programming decisions that arise within specific contexts and the various expectations and interpretations of factual television as experienced and understood by audiences. For example, it is interesting to map out how within differing institutions, such as the BBC and Channel 4, there are a number of departments and commissioning editors listed under the heading factual, such as 'documentaries and contemporary factual', 'specialist factual', and 'factual entertainment'. While these nuances within the production context may not be recognizable or of interest to the audience, Hill (2008) asserts that viewers are not only aware that changes are taking place in factuality but that they also respond to the various mix of styles within one programme in multiple ways. Thus, when examining the emergence of business entertainment formats within the industry and their subsequent impact on the viewing public, it is important to be aware of the complexities of both the production and reception context.

The move towards entertainment-led factual programming in the United Kingdom has also impacted on debates around the cultural value of television in terms of providing a public service or adopting a more market-oriented approach, with the latter generally conceived as a 'dumbing down' of the medium. There has also been a definite blurring or in some cases breaking down of the boundaries between the public and the private in factual and reality programming in particular. In her discussion of the restyling of factual TV, Hill (2007: 12) considers these changes with reference to what she regards as the two dominant

---

1   See also Frith (2000) and Couldry (2010).

arguments in factual television, namely 'the role of factual content in furthering or undermining modern democratic practices', and connects this to Corner's (1998) earlier consideration of questions of reception in relation to the 'public knowledge project' and the 'popular cultural project':

> Traditional factual genres can inform viewers about political, economic and social issues, and can help in their development as citizens who take part in democratic processes. The counter argument is to see factual content as undermining democracy through an overemphasis on entertainment. Commercial factual genres are thought to be infotainment, producing poor quality, overly stylized, ratings-driven programmes that work against the knowledge project. The increased commercialization of factual content has also infected public service factual genres, subverting the goal of these genres to inform citizens, treating them instead as consumers of 'tabloid TV'.

While the power of factual programming to inform and potentially influence the viewer is one of the central concerns of this research, it is not necessary to adopt such a binary approach to knowledge function and, in fact, Hill herself goes on to offer other models. This includes van Zoonen's (2005: 151) assertion that popular culture 'needs to be acknowledged as a relevant resource for political citizenship; a resource that produces comprehension and respect for popular voices that allows for more people to perform as citizens' and Dahlgren's (2005) notion of civic cultures, or rather the five cultural prerequisites of the public sphere in the form of 'knowledge and competence', 'values', 'affinity and trust', 'practices' and 'identities'. Along with Corner (1999), Dahlgren (2005: 416) also points to Scannell's (1996) consideration of the contribution that television has made to the 'democratization' of everyday life by continually expanding 'the topics and perspectives that can be aired and uttered in public, rendering more and more terrain as familiar and accessible to larger audiences, to be talked about and interpreted by them'.

With factual programming and reality television continually working to blur the distinction between the public and private, it can be argued that television has the potential to extend the public sphere to those who have been previously excluded from communicative and participative entitlements. Moreover, while there is anxiety around factual television's increasing emphasis on appearance, feeling, personality and mood, Dahlgren (2005: 419) adopts a more positive outlook, noting how in our everyday lives we make sense of our experiences of the world and ourselves through 'a combination of using our head and our heart', thus suggesting that television and the public sphere need not be any different. Just as Dahlgren calls for a rethinking of the Habermasian notion of the public sphere, Dovey (2000: 23) similarly highlights how traditional ways of seeing the world (rationality, objectivity, and masculine notions of identity) have been discredited and replaced with the personal, the subjective, and the particular, which he refers to as 'the feminisation of public life'. This is something that can be applied to factual programming as there has been 'a decisive move away from the traditions that strive for "objective" rendering of the world towards approaches that underscore the personal, sensational, the subjective, the confessional, the intimate' (Dahlgren 2005: 416).

Indeed, with regards to the personal and subjective, notions of identity formation and representation are central to work on the new television landscape and its various forms of factual programming. For example, in his analysis of the changes that took place in the British television industry during the 1990s, Murdock (1994: 155) outlines the shift from understanding 'broadcasting' as 'a public service whose prime responsibility is to develop the cultural rights of modern citizenship' to seeing 'television' as being 'just another appliance'. Explaining how the cultural rights of citizens comprise information, knowledge, representation and communication, he (1994: 159) goes on to describe representation as involving 'the right to have ones' experiences, beliefs and aspirations adequately and truthfully represented in the major forms of public culture'. For Murdock, there is an anxiety that a retreat from public service broadcasting to the production of programmes determined by market forces will not be able to adequately provide a range of representations. Yet, as Corner (1999) has noted, the market logics of the 1990s have often resulted in niche demographics being better served by commercial cable and satellite rather than terrestrial networks.

Developing out of this area of work, and something we want to explore in this book, is an interest in the ways in which particular television formats appear to get mobilized in wider articulations of the changing role and function of public service broadcasting in the multi-channel digital environment. In other words, business entertainment formats such as *The Apprentice* or *Dragons' Den* have been framed by the BBC as exemplars of contemporary public service content. They are not simply about entertaining but serve broader educational and public knowledge provision functions, which a multi-platform BBC can exploit as part of what it views as its public service remit (Boyle 2008).

Representing Entrepreneurship on Television

The notion of representation is interesting in relation to business and entrepreneurship. For example, Williams (2004: 61) explains how 'in popular television drama and comedy, businessmen and entrepreneurs have often been represented as suspect, untrustworthy or figures of fun' and goes on to suggest that this is bound up with British attitudes to wealth and materialist values; although the negative representation of businessmen on television is something that Lichter, Lichter and Rothman (1994) have also considered in relation to prime time American programming. As Boyle and Magor (2008) point out however, British cultural attitudes to business and entrepreneurship appears to have shifted significantly since the 1990s, not least within the television industry itself, which has had to become increasingly entrepreneurial as the broadcasting industry and the independent production sector has developed. Thus, this research seeks to not only consider the ways in which, as a subset of factual entertainment programming, business programming offers up 'representations of reality' that programme makers and audiences have to negotiate, but to also examine how the range of representations of entrepreneurship have changed in relation to race and gender, as well as issues of trust and integrity.

Before moving on to discuss the notion of entrepreneurship in more detail, particularly with regards to how definitions and ideas about entrepreneurial activity are broadly framed in academic and public discourse, it is worthwhile highlighting some of the similarities and differences in examples of American and British programming and also in academic work carried out on factual and reality television. One of the main attractions of these kinds of formats is the capacity for overseas sales. In this sense, global formats are adapted and reworked for a local audience, creating branded programming that produces handsome profits (Steemers 2004). While the flow for fictional programming has tended for the most part to travel one-way, from the United States to the United Kingdom, Britain has experienced overseas success with the creation of business entertainment formats like *Ramsay's Kitchen Nightmares*, which has been remade in the United States. In contrast, *The Apprentice* and *Dragons' Den* originated in the United States and Japan respectively before being bought by the BBC. Despite the same formats existing on both sides of the Atlantic, academic approaches to these types of programming tend to differ. Most notably, as the preceding discussion about public knowledge suggests, scholars in the United Kingdom have traditionally focused on the notion of public service broadcasting and the cultural value of television as a medium.

As the television landscape has developed however, many conventional understandings have had to be revised and reworked in order to account for more market-led approaches to programming; although as already detailed, this does not mean that new forms of factual and reality shows fail to engage with the public sphere completely. In the United States, on the other hand, there is less of an emphasis on television as a public service or its cultural value due to the commercial nature of the industry from its inception.

Nevertheless, scholars such as Ouellette and Hay (2008) and McMurria (2009) have considered factual entertainment and reality television in relation to neoliberal ideology and the move towards governing at a distance. According to Ouellette and Hay (2008: 2–4), as American society has entered a period in which the state has increasingly withdrawn from certain sections of public life (such as welfare provision), so television has filled the void, endorsing the neoliberal notion of 'governing at a distance'. Television and reality programming in particular has begun to offer viewers 'informal guidelines for living', acting as a 'resource for inventing, managing, caring for, and protecting ourselves as citizens'. This concern with citizenship is similar to much of the British work carried out in this area and indeed Couldry and Littler (2008) have examined the British version of *The Apprentice* in relation to neoliberal politics.

What becomes clear is the crucial role that a range of *contexts* plays in understanding the position and impact of television. For example, as we will discuss in Chapter 3, the original American version of *The Apprentice* is very different in style, tone and content from the BBC public service adaptation. Indeed, interviews with key BBC executives for this book reveal the significant transformative process that was required in adapting the format for a British audience. Thus we have industry and institutional contexts, which clearly differ between the British and American television industries; audience contexts, as specific cultural and social attitudes across the United Kingdom differ; and professional and genre contexts, where style and industry norms are always shifting and reinventing television forms and formats. For example, programming in the United Kingdom at the end of the noughties appears to have signaled a move away from the highly-formatted television of the early part of the decade towards more traditional 'lightly-constructed' observational documentaries (two strands of factual entertainment that will be analysed in detail in Chapter 3). Indeed, Dan Adamson (cited in Bell 2009), Executive Producer on the first three series of the British version of *The Apprentice*, argues that there has been changes in factual entertainment that, in some ways, have resulted in the genre beginning to return to its observational documentary roots:

> Viewers will watch something if it's well made and it gives them information as well as entertainment. We've gone through a cycle where everything has to be about confrontation and jeopardy and I think we're coming out of that. Audiences are smart and can see when you're trying to over-egg the pudding. As factual and factual entertainment producers, we have to work harder to make sure our ideas are built on content.

This also suggests a perception among producers that audiences are constantly changing at some pace and that the organizational pressure in such a competitive television marketplace requires the continuous development of new versions or upgrades of existing formats.

The Media and Entrepreneurship

In this section of the chapter we want to discuss some of the research that has engaged with debates around the definition and role of entrepreneurship in society. For the purposes of this book we are particularly interested in identifying research around entrepreneurship that engages with the media in its various forms and with television in particular. In addition, we are concerned with investigating the ways in which public discourse around entrepreneurship and, by association, the entrepreneur has been articulated through governmental and public policy. We recognize that the literature around entrepreneurship and business activity is extensive and it is not our aim to systematically cover this vast area; although as we argue below the work of Elizabeth Chell (2005, 2007) provides a useful entry point to key debates around how entrepreneurship gets framed in society. Rather, we want to provide an overview of some of the shifts in thinking about this area and suggest how it plays a role in providing a broader conceptual framework for the book. To this end, the work of Anthony Sampson (1996) provides a useful entry point into this discussion.

The Entrepreneur, Image and Metaphor

Throughout the *Company Man*, Sampson (1996) is concerned with examining the broader cultural images that have shaped the narratives and self-images that have surrounded the 'company' or corporate worker from the nineteenth century through to the 1990s. He identifies the crucial role that myths play in sustaining particular patterns of economic development and legitimizing the dominance of specific modes of political and economic thinking. In the 1980s across both the United States and United Kingdom he argues (1996: 168) that the corporate culture which had been attacked from the left for its linkages with the military and 'for manipulating society' came under a more sustained attack from the political right, who attacked it for complacency and for being overly bureaucratic in the face of an increasingly global economy.

Sampson views the new entrepreneurs of this period as the 'raiders' who, encouraged by the neoliberal political right in both countries, attacked the old structures and the so called 'captains of industry' who found themselves increasingly blamed, along with 'big government', for the decline of economic competitiveness. Against the larger backdrop of concerns about the ability of western businesses to compete in a global markets, a rush to deregulate and 'roll back the state' was a new political philosophy that positioned enterprise as the key driver of wealth generation and helped facilitate a culture clash as the collectivist business model clashed with the new champion of popular capitalism. As Sampson (1996: 169) argues:

> The capitalist was reinterpreted as an heroic life-force, a bringer of growth, innovation and riches to others as well as himself ... the champions of the new entrepreneurs reverted to the older mythology of the late nineteenth century, which was influenced by Herbert Spencer, Social Darwinism and the 'survival of the fittest'. Capitalists once again adopted the metaphors of the jungle and ocean – lions, eagles or sharks pursuing and devouring their prey.

As we argue in Chapter 4, the issue and importance of metaphor and its relationship to making sense of both entrepreneurship and the role of the entrepreneur in society is a recurring one within what might be called contemporary entrepreneurial studies.

Indeed, defining entrepreneurial activity is in itself highly problematic. As noted by Boyle and Magor (2008), there are various definitions relating to the term entrepreneurship in circulation (see Shane and Venkataraman 2000: 218) but Henderson and Robertson (2000: 279) helpfully suggest that in the twenty-first century, 'narrow concepts of enterprise as 'business entrepreneurialism' mainly identified with small business activity, are likely to be less relevant than the broader view of entrepreneurship as a set of qualities influencing behaviour and enabling individuals to be flexible and creative in the face of change'. However even this does not capture the shifting political nature of the term, as Chell (2007: 11) explains how entrepreneurship has become interlinked with other concepts such as enterprise: 'Enterprise is thus a highly malleable construct subject to the vagaries of the political climate and institutional influences that attempt to shape the meaning for particular social and political ends'. She discusses the attempts by governments to facilitate more enterprise-orientated societies but argues that too much attention and emphasis has been placed on a rather crude economic valuing of the entrepreneurial process rather than understanding its much complex interplay with social and cultural aspects of society.

Simon Down (2006, 2010) suggests that the terms enterprise, entrepreneur and entrepreneurship are indeed all highly flexible concepts often used and mobilized by politicians for particular ends at specific historical moments and that seeking to absolutely define these areas is not a particularly helpful task. Rather it is more useful to examine how these terms have been mobilized by key economic and political actors and by entrepreneurs themselves in the narratives they construct around their own self identities to make sense of their lives and occupations (Down 2006). This more open-ended approach is explored in some detail in Chapters 3 and 4 of the book when we examine the narratives factual television constructs around the entrepreneur and how society more generally understands these terms. Indeed within academic studies of entrepreneurial activity it has become more recognized that approaching the area through the importance of narrative can be insightful and 'open new perspectives' (Johansson 2004: 285). Of course the extent to which television has helped frame how these terms and narratives are understood, constructed and reproduced will be the focus of the later chapters that investigate how audiences engage with television's discourses of business.

To this end, it is perhaps helpful to see how other terms such as creativity, for example, have been picked up in policy terms and moved from what Schlesinger (2007) in his study of creative industries policy calls from 'discourse to doctrine'. With creativity becoming such a ubiquitous term used across the arts, industry and education, it has become almost meaningless in terms of content. Ironically, given his role as one of Britain's most famous entrepreneurs, Lord Sugar, star of the BBC's version of *The Apprentice* has similarly argued against the over-use of the term entrepreneur by the media:

> You can't go into Smith's and buy a book and just become an entrepreneur. You've got to have some killer instinct in you ... People shouldn't be allowed to use the word entrepreneur. It's used too frequently, it should be illegal. I

can't call myself a lawyer or a doctor, because I don't have the qualifications (*Management Today* 1 May 2001).

Throughout the following decade however, the term entrepreneur experienced its highest ever media profile in the United Kingdom, in no small part thanks to programmes like *The Apprentice* fronted by Lord Sugar. Research that has examined the role the media plays in shaping debates around entrepreneurship is the area we now direct our attention to in the next part of the chapter.

Popular Media Culture and the Entrepreneur

Nicholson and Anderson (2005) provide evidence of how between 1989 and 2000 the metaphors used to describe entrepreneurial activity in a very particular section of the British national press changed. In their albeit limited study of the London-based *Independent* newspaper, they identify a significant increase in stories that address or discuss the entrepreneur in society and highlight how, during this period, the entrepreneur was overwhelmingly presented as male (for example, only one female was mentioned in 1989 while this had risen to 12 in 2000). Echoing Sampson's (1996) findings, Nicholson and Anderson (2005: 161–162) also state how coverage in 1989 presented the entrepreneur as a heroic figure, with an attendant set of metaphors: 'The entrepreneur is magician, royalty or giant. He is a hero conquering disability or economics, at the pinnacle of the political evolutionary scale. The entrepreneur is saviour of floundering economies, prosperity, companies, and blushing women … and advises as revered guru'. By way of contrast, Nicholson and Anderson argue that by 2000, the metaphors became less idolatry although they continued to nurture the mythology at the core of entrepreneurial activity. A degree of potential hostility was also found from journalists wishing to challenge rather than simply uncritically reproduce the self-serving myths around entrepreneurs.

 This study has severe limitations however; not least because it starts by suggesting it will examine media changes before focusing solely on one newspaper and making few connections with broader shifts in media representations of business during this period. It also fails to acknowledge public relations practice in enhancing public profile through media coverage and the increasingly important role that public relations also plays in journalistic discourse, or what Schlesinger and Tumber (1995) call 'promotional culture' within which a massively expanded media sector developed between 1989 and 2000. Despite this however, the research does highlight the ways in which language and representation more generally works to make sense of activity that is often diverse and at times abstract. It also positions these changes against the broader context of the rise in 'enterprise culture', which became a central discourse in so much governmental policy from education to the creative industries during this period.

While Nicholson and Anderson (2005) capture the increased newspaper usage of the term 'entrepreneur', they never fully outline the range of activities that this is used to describe. These may include, for example, the traditional business definitions of entrepreneurship to its increasingly ubiquitous usage across a range of sectors of the economy from the arts to education and the emergence of the 'social entrepreneurs' discussed in the work of Clark (2009) and Mawson (2008). The latter is a growing international movement that has at its core the notion of mobilizing entrepreneurial skills for broader social and community good and the extent to which this aspect of entrepreneurial culture is represented through television is discussed further in Chapter 6.

This explicit linking of perceptions of the entrepreneur to media discourse is more directly addressed in the work of Radu and Redien-Collot (2008) who examine how the French newspaper industry has represented entrepreneurship since the turn of this century. At the core of what they conceive as a three-part ongoing project is an interest in the interplay between the media, public and political discourse around the role and function of the entrepreneur in the French economy. Drawing from a social psychological background, Radu and Redien-Collot (2008: 260–261) identify their key research objectives as being,

> the issue of the social representation of entrepreneurs in the French press and its potential impact on desirability and feasibility beliefs. Our premise is that the social representation of entrepreneurs in the French press may play a fundamental role in shaping the perception of both entrepreneurship's desirability (entrepreneurship as an *attractive* career option) and social feasibility (entrepreneurship as an accessible and realistic career option).

Arguing that the press is being used to sell the idea of a more entrepreneurial French economy to a largely resistant French public, they also suggest that two competing models of employment in the French economy are being articulated in newspaper coverage. One is characterized by more 'risky' entrepreneurial activity (a position increasingly articulated by political elites) and the traditional (often State) employee paradigm that is viewed as less risky by the public, but increasingly perceived by political elites as incompatible with the needs of the French economy.

Radu and Redien-Collot's engagement with work that examines the role of the media in shaping and influencing public opinion is drawn from a relatively narrow strand of communications and social psychology. Moreover, their findings are at this juncture restricted to looking at the range of representations that appear across the French newspaper and magazine sector; although they hope to next examine the production processes that produce these discourses and interestingly view the manner by which entrepreneurs themselves use and mobilize the media for lobbying and network purposes as a significant gap in the existing research agenda. What they do find however is a doubling in the number of stories around entrepreneurship carried in the French press between 2001 and 2005. Again, the dominant representation of the entrepreneur is overwhelmingly male and, in this case, usually between 30 and 40 years of age. As such, they find not only an absence of women but also of very young and older entrepreneurs.

The key discourses surrounding these range of representations include the centrality of entrepreneurial activity as an increasingly important driver of economic growth; the regionally rooted nature of many French entrepreneurs; the association of entrepreneurship with notions of economic freedom and creative expression; and interestingly, a perception that 'in becoming entrepreneurs (sic), an individual fulfills objectives that are at the same time collective and personal. French entrepreneurship must then lead to tempered individualism that focuses equally on public utility and on personal projects and drives' (Radu and Redien-Collot 2008: 277). In other words there appears to be an attempt to construct a particularly distinctive French national model around the role of the entrepreneur that is both attempting to shift public perception while politically reassuring the public that the larger collective ideals of France have not been abandoned. While the research at this stage has not examined the production or audience contexts within which these discourses are constructed and consumed, it does highlight the importance placed on the media in raising public discussion around the role and function of the entrepreneur in society, while at the same time serving to remind us of the continuing importance of the local and the national in shaping specific media discourses.

The role of the media in shaping, either intentionally or more discursively, the profile of entrepreneurship is of course one of the central interests of this book. Down (2010) argues that the role of the media has probably been under researched with regard to its influence in shaping the discourses around enterprise and suggests that the rise of what he calls 'entre-tainment' formats such as the BBC's *Dragons Den,* have helped to give prominence to a particular cultural stereotype relating to the entrepreneur. Down (2010: 187) goes on to explain how this representation of the entrepreneur does not easily map onto the more complex and diverse reality of entrepreneurial identities but nonetheless acknowledges that making sense of why business related content has become so popular in television terms will tell us much about shifting social attitudes towards 'material success, self-fulfilment and social mobility'. He also argues that the intersection of enterprise and culture is not well researched, echoing the point made by Rehn (2008) about the benefits of taking a more holistic view of the role played by popular culture in constructing narratives and discourses around enterprise and entrepreneurial activity.

Even when major pan-European attempts to look at the relationship between the media and social change have been instigated (specifically around the impact of television in shaping business behaviour), the lack of research in this area is noted (Media Management and Transformation Centre 2007, European Commission 2007). The European Commission (2007: 34) report concludes that more research into the attitudes of television viewers towards entrepreneurial representations 'could be a first step towards closing the present gap in the research'. The Commission report set out what it views as the key questions around media representations of entrepreneurship that should form part of a European research agenda. Underpinning this report are a number of assumptions however. The first is that entrepreneurial activity is probably misrepresented on television and needs to offer a more realistic range of discourses, while the second is that this type of activity is unquestionably a good thing and the media needs to be used to better promote entrepreneurship. Finally, the report illustrates the political significance given to this area within the wider European economy, a recognition that more needs to be done economically to stimulate entrepreneurial activity and an implicit sense that television and the wider audio-visual sector can possibly play a key role in this process.

In this book we address a number of these issues, although from a differing starting point than the European Commission report. We are not interested in finding out ways to better promote entrepreneurship for example, as this is not the primary function of television in the United Kingdom. Rather we are interested in understanding the role factual television plays in shaping public knowledge and understanding of business and entrepreneurship and, in so doing, uncover what this tells us about the changing nature of both television as a firstly a cultural form – through its relationship with Corner's (1998) 'public knowledge project' – and also as an industry in the United Kingdom.

Framing the Project: A Multi-Disciplined Approach

This work then is firmly rooted within a broader tradition concerned with issues that are central in media and communication studies; including the political economy of the media, the importance of representation in creating meaning and reception studies of the audience. However, given the particular focus of the study, it clearly engages with and draws from an eclectic range of sources and influences from other disciplines, such as television studies and a broader sociological-approach to the media and culture more generally. As we have noted above, the subject matter of business representations has also been of interest to other business and managerial disciplines. For example, Rehn (2008), writing from within management and organization studies, has made a plea for a more hybrid and flexible approach to be taken to the study of the relationship between popular cultural representations of business and organizations. He argues that management and organization studies increasingly recognize that a relationship exists between the discourses that generally circulate around business in popular culture and more intricate and significant organizational cultural shifts. He also makes the point that traditional concerns about investigating aspects of the popular or 'lowbrow culture' which have existed within managerial and organizational studies is no longer a sustainable position.

Rehn (2008: 755 – and quoted in the epigraph above) argues that among the audiences for these popular cultural forms, be they television programmes such as *The Apprentice* or computer games such as *Prison Tycoon* (ValuSoft 2005), are managers and decision makers who are 'doing real things in real organizations [and] are also affected by what popular culture does'. What is being suggested is that the range of popular media outlets which engage with business related content (however constructed and framed around entertainment or dramatic values they are) help construct various discourses that potentially help and reshape perceptions across both public and business professionals. Interested in the notion of business knowledge and its production, Rehn (2008: 778) argues that across these popular culture forms, from books to television, 'we simply cannot see where the entertainment ends and the serious "formation of business knowledge" begins, or even if we can uphold the idea of there being a difference'.

For Rehn then, what is required is for the field of managerial and organizational studies to set aside its rather lofty and disdainful attitudes towards the study of popular culture and begin to recognize that it can instead bring a level of empirical knowledge to business and organizational cultures. He (2008: 780) therefore tentatively argues for the emergence of a field around 'the cultural studies of organisations', a hybrid two-way study around the 'social effects of organizational life'. Of course there is also evidence that across management and business schools, particularly in the United States that popular programmes such as *The Apprentice* are being mobilized in the teaching of business-related programmes (see Eisner 2006) but, for us, the recognition by Rehn (2008) of the benefits that a more open, hybrid and muti-disciplined approach brings is useful.

Nevertheless, we would argue that we want to locate this research within a media and communication studies framework, as opposed to a cultural studies field of enquiry. Thus, this book is shaped by sociologically informed approaches to the study of the creation of media power and knowledge, such as that displayed in the work of Seale (2002) in his analysis of the role that the television plays, across news, current affairs, drama and documentary, in shaping public attitudes and understanding around health and health related issues. At the core of this process is the ability of the media to impose narratives on often complex issues and to frame issues around particular recognizable discourses, often reinforcing them in the process. This is in addition to highlighting particular aspects associated with certain professions, as demonstrated in the work of Kilborn, Hibberd and Boyle (2001) looking at the possible impact television representations of vets and veterinary practice may have on recruitment patterns into that industry.

This approach views the broader political, economic and cultural contexts within which television gets produced as being central in understanding how particular discourses are constructed. In addition, the empirically grounded communication studies concern around understanding how audiences, in all their complexity, actively engage and make sense of these discourses and how in turn that audience is framed by broader social and cultural forces, is an important part of the conceptual framing of this work. This also echoes the observation made by Carrabine (2008: 99) in his study of media representations of crime and the media, that the distinction between informing and entertaining the public (if it ever truly existed) has certainly been significantly blurred in recent years. Indeed, as argued by both Carrabine (2008) and Seale (2002), audiences move between and across differing media and genres within particular media: 'This is not to suggest that people are incapable of distinguishing between the real and the imaginary, but to insist that media audiences commute on a daily basis between books, magazines, newspapers, computers, television, cinema, radio and so forth in ways that veer from vague distraction to fierce concentration' (Carrabine 2008: 99). To that end, while this book is focused on television, we are acutely aware that other media play a key role in shaping the perceptions and the knowledge that audiences bring to their engagement with television and, in our field of study, entrepreneurs regularly appear across media in complex ways.

Drawing on work from both Britain and Sweden, Hill, Weibull and Nilsson (2007) argues that while the public knowledge project has not disappeared, public service broadcasters are nevertheless under pressure. Their audience research (Hill, Weibull and Nilsson 2007: 39) suggests that while *public* factual genres are associated with importance and prestige among audiences 'this does not mean that they are regularly watched'. However, by way of contrast, *popular* factual television, framed by entertainment, scores less well in terms of importance but is watched more. Given our focus on business related content and factual entertainment formats or 'business entertainment', this raises the question as to what extent this hybrid might achieve popularity while also carrying an element of importance or prestige relating to the public service element of broadcast television. Evan Davis (interview with authors, 12 January 2007), the BBC broadcaster and presenter of *Dragons' Den* suggests that,

> *Dragons' Den* is an entertainment programme and its worth remembering that. It comes from BBC Entertainment. However part of the entertainment value of the programme derives from a sense that what is going on matters and is authentic. So it doesn't work if it feels like a TV entertainment show. Its entertainment value derives from the perception that it isn't all just for entertainment. That's why it is important that while these programmes may have pantomime elements it also has what might be called *high fibre* discussions of what might be called a business kind. In truth that enhances the entertainment value [our emphasis].

In this context, the next chapter examines the shifting institutional, economic and cultural nature of British television in its engagement with business content since the beginning of the 1990s. This historical analysis of the rise of business television aims to identify some of the key drivers of change in the range of representations offered by television around business and entrepreneurial activity and looks at some of the debates and tensions that exist around the relationship between television, formats, entertainment and journalism.

Chapter 2
Continuity and Change in the Development of Television's 'Business Entertainment Format'

Business people [on television] were either dry boring people in suits, or shifty characters up to no good. Sir John Harvey-Jones was a rare individual who could make that leap. He was a high powered industry figure who could make business accessible. The language of business when it was being discussed in the papers or in the news, it was discussed in a jargon that kept people out. There was a great mystery about business. Sir John Harvey-Jones went into businesses and humanized it [sic], by focusing on the people behind the business.

> TV producer Michele Kurland discussing the BBC series *Troubleshooter*
> (interview with authors, 11 January 2007).

So many things in TV production are around individual talent [as much as] sociological change. So a person in a position of power can change and shape programming. At the BBC, Robert Thirkell [producer of *Troubleshooter*] had a dynamic and skilful way of filmmaking.

> Danny Cohen, then Head of E4 and Channel 4 Factual Entertainment, 2006–2007
> (interview with authors, 7 March 2007).

The aim of this chapter is to trace the historical development of the depiction of business on British television and explain the shift that has seen business issues not only informing television news journalism and current affairs but also being incorporated into the realms of entertainment-led factual programming from the beginning of the 1990s onwards. In doing so, we acknowledge that the television industry has itself developed into a business during this time, with the result being that rather than operating primarily within creative terms, broadcasters and programme makers have come to view themselves as [creative] entrepreneurs. As the television writer, director and independent producer Michael Darlow (2004: 541) argues, 'By 1993, most independent producers as much as broadcasters, saw themselves as businesses which made programmes, not as they had a decade earlier, as programme makers who also ran businesses'. Since the 1990s, these two shifts have run parallel to one another and it raises the issue of whether the development offscreen of a more commercial, competitive and entrepreneurial TV marketplace has impacted on the way the medium frames its onscreen engagement with business, entrepreneurship, risk and wealth creation.

Central to these developments within business programming is the increasing importance of television formatting within the industry and the way in which public service broadcasters, such as the BBC and Channel 4, have moved away from the notion of business content as supposedly dry and inaccessible to what can be described as more relevant and engaging 'business entertainment formats' epitomized by programmes such as *Property Ladder*, *Ramsay's Kitchen Nightmares*, *Mary Queen of Shops*, *Dragons' Den* and *The Apprentice*. Drawing on interviews with channel controllers, commissioners and producers from across the BBC, Channel 4 and the independent sector, this chapter calls attention to a number of key individuals involved in this process whilst also examining some of the tensions that arise from combining entertainment values with more journalistic or educational approaches to factual programming.

As Matthews (2006: 43 – quoted in the epigraph to the introductory chapter) notes, for many years television had little engagement with business programming. Significantly, there has been a lack of research carried out on in this area by both television scholars and those within the field of media and communications. While some research has taken a specific interest in both the United States and United Kingdom versions of *The Apprentice* (Couldry and Littler 2008, McGuigan 2008), we noted in Chapter 1 how work on factual television has tended to focus on the move from current affairs and serious analytical documentary to docusoaps, lifestyle and reality TV. This means that the development of business entertainment programming (a related but distinct genre) has remained a largely hidden and unexamined area of television history.

In an attempt to begin to address this situation, we begin by looking at the representations of business on British television and in particular its problematic status within the BBC. We then examine the key personnel involved in the production of BBC2's *Troubleshooter* (1990–1995) before outlining how the series established a template for future generations of business programming in the United Kingdom by placing an emphasis on drama, risk and the casting of an accessible business expert. We also focus on the evolving nature of public service broadcasting, particularly in relation to Channel 4's adaptation of the business format for its own viewers through an initial combination of lifestyle, property, entrepreneurialism and expert opinion.

Finally, we examine the rise of the global entertainment format and consider both its importance to an increasingly competitive and entrepreneurial television marketplace and the way in which certain international business formats have been successfully adapted by the BBC for a public service audience. Throughout this chapter there is an awareness of the changes that have occurred within the industry and the subsequent impact on how television functions as a business and what is understood by factual programming. However, there is also an emphasis on aspects of continuity that run throughout television culture with regards to personnel, networks, production companies and the updating and reworking of particular formats. This continuity not only results in programming that continually references aspects of television history but it also seeks to reduce risk in what has become an ever more competitive and precarious multichannel digital landscape.

Engaging with Business in the Factual Arena

The Problem of the BBC

Prior to the 1990s, British factual television's engagement with the world of business, finance and enterprise tended to be restricted to news journalism and current affairs. While the latter is typified by the long-running BBC2 series *The Money Programme* (1966–), it is significant that with regards to its news output the BBC did not have a Business Editor until 2001 when journalist Jeff Randall was appointed by then Director-General Greg Dyke to the role. Broadcasting institutions have historically been comprised of dedicated departments commissioning news, documentary and drama programming, alongside arts, science and history-related content. However this has not extended to the realm of business, meaning that the types of formats and range of representations on offer within factual television have been limited. Fictional programming, on the other hand, has regularly featured businessmen (and it has traditionally been men) in key roles. Yet, as we highlighted in Chapter 1, a number of academic studies (Lichter, Lichter and Rothman 1994; Williams 2004) have revealed how portrayals have tended to be negative with popular drama and comedy presenting businessmen and entrepreneurs as 'suspect, untrustworthy or figures of fun' (Boyle and Magor 2008: 126). A report by the Washington-based Media Institute (Theberge 1981) refers to such characters as 'crooks, conmen and clowns' and indeed these fictional types are exemplified in a range of successful programmes from the 1980s, such as the crooked J.R. Ewing in the US prime time soap *Dallas* (CBS; BBC1 1978–1991), conman Arthur Daley of comedy drama *Minder* (ITV 1979–1994) and Del Boy Trotter, the lovable clown from sitcom *Only Fools and Horses* (BBC1 1981–2003). These representations have changed however with the development of reality television from the 1990s onwards. As Hendershot (2009: 244) notes, 'reality TV is a genre obsessively focused on labour' and this focus has opened up a wider range of business representations onscreen, allowing the traditional dichotomy displayed in fictional programming between comedy/foolishness and drama/criminality to dissipate.

Despite the capacity of business to provide fictional programming with both dramatic and comedic characters and scenarios, commissioners and producers within the factual arena have been slow to recognize its potential as a subject area. In part, this lack of engagement is bound up with wider British attitudes to wealth and materialist values (Williams 2004) and the way in which up until the 1970s, a dominant corporate culture consisting of large, paternalistic organizations meant that the image of the loyal 'company man' was instilled in the public consciousness while the risk-taking entrepreneur remained largely absent from the public's imagination (Sampson 1996). As we noted in the previous chapter, such cultural attitudes began to change however in the 1980s as the role of enterprise in shaping economic development and wealth generation became increasingly part of mainstream political discourse.

Nevertheless, this was not immediately reflected within television programming and, as a public service broadcaster, the continued absence of business and enterprise-related issues from the BBC's factual agenda has been particularly problematic. As explained by producer Robert Thirkell (interview with authors, 13 March 2009), who initially worked for the BBC's Science Department before going on to revolutionize business programming with the creation of more entertainment-led formats in the 1990s, the Science Department was the only place within the BBC making business-related content throughout the 1980s. Yet, he suggests that even then, the department

> really wasn't interested in making business programmes and didn't think they mattered ... nor was anybody else at the BBC ... I actually feel people in the BBC at the time hated money. It was that old British thing that had always been there, that it wasn't classy or intellectual to have anything to do with business or money. Whereas I was always really intrigued by it because it creates so much of what we see, it creates so much politically, it affects us so much.

Thirkell's perception of the BBC is one that continues to find echoes among a number of key individuals working within the television industry today.

For example, Luke Johnson (interview with authors, 20 March 2009), a successful British entrepreneur and Chairman of Channel 4 from 2004 to 2010, argues that the BBC's attitude to business is bound up with its status as a publicly-funded institution. This, he believes, differentiates the corporation's decision makers from independent producers who run their own companies and therefore have 'some sort of understanding of what it is like to be in business and to meet a payroll'. Furthermore, due to the organization's perceived left-of-centre sensibilities, Johnson also suggests that BBC employees are 'sceptical about capitalism and suspicious of the whole profit motive and so therefore their empathy with, and their understanding of what drives invention and entrepreneurship is limited'. The BBC's former Business Editor Jeff Randall (interview with authors, 11 January 2007) espouses a similar opinion, stating that prior to his arrival,

> the BBC was culturally and structurally biased against business. The evidence was that it had no business editor, never had one. It kidded itself that it did business because it had an economics editor. I had to convince people there that business sits on the crossroads of commerce and finance, and that economics sits on the crossroads of politics and economics.

It was not until the appointment of Greg Dyke as Director-General of the corporation in 2000 that a sustained effort was made to reverse the BBC's traditional antipathy towards business; an approach that gained the full support of the former banker and economist Gavyn Davies when he accepted the position of BBC Chairman a year later.

On joining the BBC, Dyke (2004: 140), who had spent many years running profit and loss companies and was thus used to operating within a different culture and ethos to that of the public service institution, delivered an attack on the corporation's track record of covering business issues by stating that mainstream news and current affairs programmes had 'ignored or failed to understand the real business agenda' and that the corporation must 'understand what profits are for' (Teather 2000). As well as the appointment of Randall, he installed Thirkell as creative director of the newly formed Business Unit, tasked with producing business features and reinventing the current affairs series *The Money Programme*. Transforming the latter from a traditional magazine format to a single-subject documentary series that continues to perform well within the multichannel television environment, it is nevertheless Thirkell's feature documentary work both within the Business Unit and prior to its formation that can be recognized as having a substantial influence in shaping the rise of the business entertainment format and transforming the BBC's relationship with business content.

The Troubleshooter Template: Drama, Risk and Expert Opinion

> Business is not, as commonly believed, about numbers and endless computer calculations. It is about people and their interactions and dealings with others (Harvey-Jones 1990: 10).

Thirkell's status as the man who revolutionized business programming was acquired somewhat by accident rather than design when an opportunity presented itself in 1987. While at the BBC's Science Department, Thirkell worked on *The Business Series* as a researcher but was planning on leaving the corporation to embark on his own entrepreneurial venture of running a stall on Portobello Market. Around the same time, Sir John Harvey-Jones, the industrialist and recently retired Chairman of Imperial Chemical Industries (ICI), expressed an interest to the BBC's Director of Television Michael Grade of working within the medium in some capacity. As explained by Thirkell (interview with authors, 13 March 2009), Grade's subsequent proposal to make a programme focusing on the challenges facing British manufacturing was met with considerable internal resistance, with the BBC's Documentary Department turning it down on the grounds that 'businessmen were boring and programmes on business were dreary' and therefore not suitable television material.

Due to his previous involvement with *The Business Series*, the project was passed to Thirkell, who became the eventual producer and director of *Troubleshooter*. However, Thirkell himself suggests that this was 'presumably on the basis that it would never work' given his limited experience and imminent plans for departure. Having never made a television feature before and coming from a family of novelists, his interests were literary based leading him to focus on narrative and character:

> When I got that first *Troubleshooter*, which was my first film, I just couldn't do anything but make it a story, because that is all I could see, that is the only way I could see of making it. I didn't understand how people made films. I only understood stories. So therefore I tried always to tell stories, which I still do.

It was this injection of narrative and focus on larger than life characters that transformed *Troubleshooter* from a supposedly dry and dreary prospect into a BAFTA-award winning series on its broadcast in 1990.

Discussing his own involvement with the programme, Sir John Harvey-Jones (1990: 10) emphasizes how he was 'certainly not interested in doing a propaganda job for industry' but rather his drive was to use television to reveal to the public the drama and excitement which he saw as integral to running a business. His other passions were manufacturing and the role that small businesses play in the economic wellbeing of the country, thus it was these types of companies that became the focus of the original series while the second instalment in 1992 also examined public sector organizations, including a National Health Service hospital trust and the South Yorkshire Police force. In each instance, Harvey-Jones was sent in to assess the organizational problems of the business and offer advice on how management could turn things around. This resulted in a lightly-constructed series that very clearly placed itself within the observational documentary mode. While the structure and visual aesthetic of the series is something that we will consider further in Chapter 3, Harvey-Jones (1990: 15) himself keenly points out how 'there were no "set ups" and everything that happened was filmed or recorded [and] shown as it happened'. What the series offered then was a dramatic narrative and characters viewers could empathize with through its focus on real people, the risks involved in running a business and the impact of this on their everyday lives.

As such, *Troubleshooter* worked to bring business to life for a wider audience than those historically attracted to current affairs. Producer Michele Kurland (interview with authors, 11 January 2007), who went on to work with Thirkell on a number of his later formats before becoming Executive Producer of *The Apprentice* for BBC1 in 2007, explains how the casting of Harvey-Jones was central to the show's success, as he was able to make the leap from the business world to mainstream television by humanizing the characters involved and making business accessible in the process. It was this combination of securing a suitable personality with relevant expertise alongside Thirkell's ability to craft a 'story' around a particular business issue that led to *Troubleshooter* not only securing another BAFTA for its second series but also acting as a template for future generations of business entertainment programming on both the BBC and Channel 4. Ironically both Thirkell and Harvey-Jones (Harvey-Jones 1996: 3) felt that by the third series they were 'disinclined to continue with that particular approach to business programmes. We felt that the programmes were beginning to follow a formula and we wanted to take a different, more elastic approach'. This meant that *Troubleshooter Returns* (1995) took a more expansive and discursive look at the world of business and how aspects of British national life had changed through retracing some of the key influences that had shaped Sir John's life.

The Rise of the Independent Production Sector: Businesses or 'Lifestyle Companies'

Following the success of *Troubleshooter*, Thirkell was specially commissioned to produce a one-off programme for the Edinburgh Television Festival in 1993 assessing the fortunes of the independent production sector (Darlow 2004). Crucially, the emergence of business programming onscreen occurred at a time when the business of television was experiencing dramatic changes, largely due to a deregulatory trend embarked on by the Thatcher government that had resulted in the growth of the independent production sector and the overall move towards a more business-focused medium.[1]

In 1991, this shift within the industry towards putting profits first saw Gerry Robinson, a former Coca-Cola Finance Director and Chief Executive of catering company Compass PLC, appointed Chief Executive of the Granada Group. Having no previous experience of broadcasting, Graham Murdock (1994: 155) explains how Robinson came with 'a reputation for controlling costs' and, as Darlow (2004: 532–533) highlights, while his appointment enraged programme makers, it was celebrated in the city as a positive response to 'shareholder discontent and a falling share price'. Robinson's arrival was followed by the departure of David Plowright in 1992, chairman of the group's television subsidiary, who Murdock (1994: 155) suggests was forced to resign after 'refusing to implement the measures asked for' in terms of cutting costs.

The furore that erupted within the industry following the appointment of Robinson and Plowright's replacement Charles Allen (who was similarly inexperienced in television but, like Robinson, had proved successful in business and would himself appear in an episode of *The Secret Millionaire* on Channel 4 in 2011) is particularly noteworthy considering that Robinson not only received a knighthood in the 2003 New Year's Honours List for services to the Arts and Business but that he also went on to have a career in front of the camera as a successor to Harvey-Jones's 'troubleshooter' character (a move we shall document further in the next section of the chapter). During his successful tenure at Granada therefore, it appears that Robinson sought to apply his own business techniques to the television industry itself, turning it into a business first and a producer of programmes second.

This shift towards a market-led industry provided the backdrop then to Thirkell's one-off *Troubleshooter* programme for the Edinburgh Television

---

1   See Darlow 2004, Sparks 1994, Murdock 1994 and Ursell 2000 for further details on deregulation, the rise of the independent sector, casualization of the workforce and move towards a market-led regime.

Festival. With Thirkell selecting three companies of varying sizes to represent a cross-section of the independent production sector, Harvey-Jones set about examining how each of them operated as a business. The exercise was tricky given that it was likely to reveal either that programme makers were bad at business, thus indicating the difficulties within the independent sector to secure profits and meet a payroll, or that they had achieved business success, thus jeopardizing the emphasis traditionally placed on television as 'a public service whose prime responsibility is to develop the cultural rights of modern citizenship' (Murdock 1994: 155). What Harvey-Jones concluded, however, was that they 'were not really businesses at all; they were, in his phrase, "lifestyle companies"' (Darlow 2004: 540).

As explained by business investor Modwenna Rees-Mogg (2008: 67), differing types of companies tend to be categorized within the business world as either 'lifestyle' or 'PEG', namely 'Potential for Explosive Growth', with the latter referring to companies that are able to be sold at a profit, usually to the benefit of not just the founder but also private investors who have supplied the capital required to take the business to the desired level. For many businesspeople however, this is neither an aim nor a feasible option, a situation that Rees-Mogg (2008: 52) helpfully outlines to prospective entrepreneurs:

> Are you prepared to try and build an explosively large business which you can sell quickly for millions of pounds or do you want to run a business for yourself that will give you a job for life and a great lifestyle? … private business investors do not want to invest in a business which you are going to run for yourself and your family. They describe this type of business as a lifestyle business and do not see enough potential for profit.

It was this latter category into which Harvey-Jones placed most independent television production companies in the early 1990s.

What Darlow (2004: 541) finds interesting about these findings is that while a decade earlier, he believes programme makers would have been content for their production companies to have been described in 'lifestyle' terms, by 1993 'the majority of independent producers saw Sir John's analysis as a damning indictment, a diagnosis of failure'. This is indicative of the newfound importance placed on business and profits within the industry and indeed Harvey-Jones's assessment was short-lived when the government lifted restrictions on takeovers within ITV the following year. As Darlow (2004: 542) points out, a number of senior executives in the companies that were subsequently taken over were made millionaires, having been previously offered generous share options in order for them to stay loyal to their companies during the Independent Television Commission (ITC) franchise bidding race.[2] For those who saw themselves as entrepreneurs or businesspeople

---

2   This included Greg Dyke at London Weekend Television who would go on to become Director-General of the BBC.

then, the deregulatory trend and subsequent opening up of the industry had suddenly made television very lucrative.

This was only for the privileged few however, as the franchise bidding wars and consolidation of companies ultimately impacted on overall profits, staff levels and the quality of programme output within the independent sector. In his analysis of the organization of work in the television industry during this period, Sparks (1994: 134) argues that such changes 'have not been as a result of technological developments, as is often supposed, but rather of economic and political pressures'. Spurred on by the creation of Channel 4, this saw a shift from the existence of a few, large organizations with a skilled, unionized workforce to a number of small, independent companies using casual labour and offering minimal training. Running a small business within the independent sector became increasingly difficult therefore with Sparks (1994: 151) arguing that the only way to secure profits and retain high quality programming using a reduced workforce is by making employees 'work harder, or longer, or more flexibly, for the same payment'. Notably, Sparks is writing just before the sudden explosion of docusoaps and reality TV formats on British television; a move that can be understood to have developed in part as a result of the problems facing television workers to produce high-volume, low-cost programming with minimal staff and skills. By producing unscripted, cheap reality programmes featuring ordinary people and using portable equipment, companies were able to further reduce their outlay and bypass writers, actors and the need for large crews.[3]

The Development of Docusoaps and Personality-Driven Factual Programming

Thirkell went on to develop a number of other business formats throughout the 1990s that continued to be broadcast on BBC2 to a relatively niche minority audience. Amongst these were the docusoap *Back to the Floor* (1997–2002) and the documentary series *Trouble at the Top* (1997–2004) and *Blood on the Carpet* (1999–2001), which focused on troubled bosses and business battles respectively. In this sense, it is important to note that Thirkell's formats were not developed in isolation from the wider television industry at this time but instead reworked many existing techniques within a business context. For example, *Back to the Floor*, which featured company bosses returning to the shop floor for a week to gain a different perspective on their business, consisted of 30-minute episodes in the aforementioned docusoap style that came to prominence on the BBC in the mid-1990s and which signalled a move away from documentary as a 'discourse of sobriety' (Nichols 1991) towards a lighter type of public service programming that prioritized entertainment over social commentary (Bruzzi 2000). This format has since been revisited in hour-long form with the Channel 4 programmes *The Secret Millionaire* and *Undercover Boss*, although both add a twist by keeping

---

3   See Raphael (2009) for a similar political-economic account of what he describes as the 'infotainment' tend in American television programming from the 1980s onwards.

the identities of the eponymous millionaires and CEOs secret as they respectively volunteer within deprived communities and work undercover in their own businesses.

It is interesting that Series 4 of *Back to the Floor* featured the aforementioned Luke Johnson, then Chairman of the restaurant group Belgo, as he returned to work in the company's flagship Covent Garden restaurant after being away from the customer-facing end of the business for 15 years. This was followed by an episode focusing on the Chairman of Millwall Football Club at the time Theo Paphitis, who has since gone on to become a 'Dragon' in BBC2's business entertainment series *Dragons' Den*. Thirkell's documentary series *Trouble at the Top* and *Blood on the Carpet*, which drew on the more traditional documentary modes (Nichols 1991) but with added voiceover narration, likewise brought to television screens for the first time businessmen and women who would go on to contribute to future business entertainment formats in a number of ways. This is indicative of the mutually beneficial relationship that can develop between broadcasters and businesspeople, as programme makers are able to utilize specialist expertise while professionals raise their media profile and boost their business brands in the process.

The first episode of *Blood on the Carpet*, documenting the hostile takeover by Granada of the catering and hotel business Trusthouse Forte, featured the Granada Chief Executive at the time Gerry Robinson outlining the key tactics used to secure the deal. As we have previously mentioned, on his departure from Granada, Robinson was approached by Thirkell's Business Unit to reprise the Harvey-Jones troubleshooter role in a reworked format entitled *I'll Show Them Who's Boss* (BBC2, 2003–2004) focusing on family businesses. Executive produced by Michele Kurland, the focus was again on drama, characters and a well-chosen business expert that viewers could engage with. Kurland (interview with authors, 11 January 2007) explains that the key to bringing special interest content such as business to a wider audience is to emphasize the human aspect: 'Business is about people and something I learned from Gerry Robinson is that there is no secret or mystery to business ... he demystifies it, strips it back to a number of core issues, one of which is listening to people'. Robinson's ability to pinpoint the core issues of struggling businesses allowed him to again follow Harvey-Jones's lead by tackling the bureaucratic National Health Service in the Open University series *Can Gerry Robinson Fix the NHS?* (BBC2, 2007). This time, however, the reference to Robinson in the title, as well as within later programmes *Gerry's Big Decision* (Channel 4, 2009) and *Can Gerry Robinson Fix Dementia Care Homes?* (BBC2, 2010), indicates the importance now placed on providing viewers with a reliable expert to guide them through the business world and who also, more importantly, is able to function as an appealing television personality.

This strategy of creating personality-driven factual programming based on the troubleshooter template has since been continued by both the BBC and Channel 4. This includes programmes such as *Mary Queen of Shops* (BBC2, 2007–2010), where retail expert Mary Portas attempts to turn around struggling fashion boutiques in the face of stiff competition from high-profile retail chains; *Mary Portas: Secret Shopper* (Channel 4, 2011–), which again sees Portas work with high-street chains and well-known brands to give shoppers better service; *Ramsay's Kitchen Nightmares* (Channel 4, 2004–2009), a series following Michelin-starred chef Gordon Ramsay as he tries to transform the fortunes of failing restaurants around the country; and *Beeny's Restoration Nightmare* (Channel 4, 2010), an account of property developer Sarah Beeny's attempts to save the Georgian stately home she purchased with her husband from ruin and turn it into a luxury events venue. By actively incorporating the name of the business expert in the title of each series, the result has been that Ramsay, Portas, Beeny and Robinson have become recognizable 'faces' for their respective channels by appearing across a range of lifestyle, current affairs and business entertainment programming. This has become complicate however as, apart from Ramsay, these personalities have begun to move between BBC2 and Channel 4 (with Beeny most recently making the move from Channel 4 to front the social enterprise series *Village SOS* broadcast on BBC1 in August 2011; although her name does not feature in the programme's title).

While this focus is bound up with the increasing importance placed on celebrity within both television programming and British society in general, it has also enabled the format to diversify using a variety of means, most notably through the use of personal investment and campaigning strategies.[4] The value of having business experts from specific fields attached to public service broadcasters became particularly evident during the credit crunch and subsequent recession which Britain experienced at the end of the noughties. For example, during this period Robinson, Portas and Ramsay hosted a series of current affairs programmes dealing precisely with the challenges facing businesses and consumers in an economic downturn. This included special editions of *The Money Programme* in the form of *Gerry Robinson's Car Crash* (2009) and *Mary Portas: Save Our Shops* (2009) for BBC2, as well as Gordon Ramsay's *Great British Nightmare* (2009) on Channel 4, in which the chef campaigned for viewers to support their local restaurants. Longstanding business entertainment formats were also reconfigured in 2009 to reflect ongoing changes within the economy, resulting in Portas's aforementioned BBC2 series becoming *Mary Queen of Charity Shops* and Channel 4's *Property Ladder*, featuring Sarah Beeny, being renamed *Property Snakes and Ladders*.

We would argue that business entertainment programming began to attract a wider audience once Channel 4 recognized its potential and embarked on a

---

4   Since his departure from the BBC, Robert Thirkell has also been involved in a number of programmes for Channel 4 in which the celebrity chef and successful entrepreneur Jamie Oliver has worked to spearhead various public campaigns and engage in social enterprise initiatives. These include *Jamie's School Dinners* (2005), *Jamie's Chef* (2007) and *Jamie's Ministry of Food* (2008), as well as *Jamie Oliver's Food Revolution* (2010–2011) for American network ABC, all programming that again features the business expert's name in the title.

commissioning process at the end of the 1990s to produce similar types of factual programming to BBC2. For Andrew Mackenzie (interview with authors, 20 March 2009), Head of Factual Entertainment at Channel 4 from 2007 to 2010, business has remained attractive to factual commissioners in recent years because it has 'natural jeopardy ... business is entertaining, it is full of jeopardy, and those are two things you need in a popular factual format'. This statement demonstrates how far the industry's understanding of business programming has come since the late 1980s when Grade, Harvey-Jones and Thirkell struggled to get *Troubleshooter* made. With entertainment producers now looking at business from a variety of perspectives, such as focusing on characters, emotions and the dramatic nature of the risks involved, business-related factual content had become an integral element of the television schedule in the United Kingdom.

Channel 4's 'Wall of Leisure' and the Evolving Nature of Public Service Broadcasting

In her account of the birth and development of Channel 4, Maggie Brown (2007) outlines how under the stewardship of Chief Executive Michael Jackson and Director of Programmes Tim Gardam, the channel moved away from its original mission to provide innovative and experimental programming towards a more predictable schedule populated by lifestyle-oriented formats, or rather the 'wall of leisure' that dominated from the end of the 1990s. Channel 4 was not alone in adapting its public service remit to meet the demands of an audience increasingly accustomed to entertainment-driven multichannel content and whose aspirational desires chimed with the New Labour rhetoric of the time. As previously mentioned in relation to docusoaps and indeed Thirkell's style of business programming, the BBC had been at the forefront of this trend for a number of years.

The BBC was initially surprised by the success in 1996 of docusoaps such as *Airport* and *Vet School* however. Indeed, Alan Yentob (interviewed in *Who Killed the British Sitcom?* Channel 4, 2006), who was responsible for commissioning the first docusoap at the BBC, describes how 'they were really a kind of "summer relief" and [then] they arrived in the schedule and looked like they were doing quite well. And it was a bit alarming ... it wasn't expected'. Despite the unexpected nature of this success, Dovey (200: 134) explains that it soon became apparent that it was 'not just the novelty of the format that appealed [but] rather the way it met network requirements; it was an idea who's time had come'. In essence, this type of light, factual entertainment responded to changing market conditions by being more economical to produce than drama, comedy or serious documentary and proving popular with a desirable audience. For Born (2004: 431), the BBC's Documentary Department can in this instance be praised for its attempts to diversify the genre by developing new styles of programming (unlike the environment described by Thirkell a decade earlier). While docusoaps tended to deal with the workplace and institutions, other lifestyle formats also developed around cookery, gardening and the home. Two key producers of this type of programming for BBC2 were Peter

Bazalgette, whose independent production company Bazal made the long-running trio *Ready Steady Cook* (1994–), *Changing Rooms* (1996–2004), and *Ground Force* (1997–2005), and Daisy Goodwin, who devised the early hit *Home Front* (1994–1998) and whom Brown (2007: 249) credits with possessing the 'knack of effortlessly thinking up new programmes as [easily as] others bake cakes'. Both went on to be involved in some of Channel 4's core successes with Bazalgette popularizing the *Big Brother* (Channel 4 2000–2010, Channel 5 2011–) reality format in the UK and Goodwin developing *Grand Designs* (1999–), *Property Ladder* and *Jamie's Kitchen* following her move to the independent company Talkback Thames. Brown (2007: 249) argues that with the BBC facing criticism by the end of the decade for its reliance on factual entertainment and BBC2 in particular being 'under pressure to move back to more serious fare, such as history, [this left] the yuppie lifestyle field open for others to exploit, at a time when incomes were rising and advertisers and sponsors were detecting a mood of change'.

While Channel 5 made an attempt at this with the Talkback-produced *House Doctor* (1999–), it was Channel 4 that really seized the opportunity to employ the 'wall as leisure' as part of a range of responses designed to entice and hold on to viewers in the face of fierce competition. Through a clever combination of lifestyle, property, expert opinion and entrepreneurialism, Channel 4 was able to offer viewers what then Head of Factual Programming Andrew Mackenzie (interview with authors, 20 March 2009) described as 'a connective point' in its programming, or rather something or someone they could relate. For example, following the success of *Property Ladder*, which followed ordinary people as they tried to make it as property developers, the channel produced a series of formatted programmes documenting various couples, families and friends as they attempted to ditch the nine to five urban existence for a new, more exciting lifestyle abroad. In *No Going Back* (2002–2004), *A Place in France – Indian Summer* (2004) and *Chaos at the Chateau* (2007), participants searched for a property abroad that would also function as a business, such as a ski resort in the Pyrennes, an Indian restaurant in the Ardeche and a luxury boutique hotel in Slovakia. In addition to the emotional turmoil of moving to a new country and the tensions inherent in living and working together, there were also problems around trying to conduct a business in a foreign language and, more significantly, securing finance for each project. The result was a highly dramatic and, in the case of the latter two, often comedic process in which the cameras captured the real-life ups and downs involved in starting a new life abroad.

Referring to a later production, *Willie's Wonky Chocolate Factory* (2008), which follows chocolate producer Willie Harcourt attempt to launch the produce from his Venezuelan plantation in the British market, Mackenzie makes an key point that can be applied to many of the participants of these shows: 'I don't think you think of him as an entrepreneur. You think of him as an idealistic man who is following his pipe dream'. Thus, although entrepreneurialism tends to be at the heart of such programmes, within this particular strand of lifestyle-oriented entertainment it is often disguised or masked in a way that makes it more accessible to a wider audience.

Perhaps more so than the BBC, Channel 4 was also able to benefit from its relationship with independent television producers during this time, many more of which had sprung up in recent years. Echoing Luke Johnson's argument about how having to meet the demands of a payroll impacts on the programme making decisions taken by independent producers, Bazalgette (2005: 42) explains that with regards to the development of new forms of factual and reality programming, 'entertainment producers, with no loyalty to the documentary tradition, would prove the most groundbreaking'. As advertising revenues began to be squeezed at the end of the 1990s due to the development of digital television and new media, Channel 4 had to find ways of maintaining its audience and advertising share with light factual entertainment that was economical to produce and easy to promote.

Much of this was achieved with the production of *Big Brother*, a long-running success for the channel in terms of advertising revenue and attracting the coveted 16 to 34-year-old audience demographic (Bulkley 2009). Yet Peter Bazalgette, who became chief creative officer of Endemol International after his company Bazal was absorbed by the *Big Brother* producer, was nominated as one of the Daily Mail's 'Worst Britons' for popularising the format in the UK. This highlights the tension that still exists both within the industry and British society more generally between television's public service obligations and the need for broadcasters and independent companies to work as businesses. Producer Ruth Pitt (interview with authors, 3 April 2009), who ran her own independent production company before first becoming Head of Documentaries at Granada in 1996 and then producing factual entertainment such as *Million Dollar Traders* (BBC2 2009) for the BBC, recalls how when chairing the Edinburgh Television festival in 1998, her decision to ask Bazalgette to deliver the prestigious McTaggart lecture was met with considerable resistance:

> At the time, a lot of people said 'why are you giving the McTaggart speech to a man that is changing our industry and giving us all of these horrible cheap programmes like *Big Brother*?' And my answer to that was, 'because he's a brilliant businessman and we need to learn how he approaches things' … He is just a fantastically clever man and I think he is an example of how to run a good business in the media.

Indeed Pitt expresses dismay at the fact that 'people in this industry still don't run [television] as a business actually. It is far too much a lifestyle industry', a statement that echoes Harvey-Jones's earlier assessment.

With regards to Channel 4 however, there are producers who continue to combine business and commercial acumen with programming that exhibits a public service ethos. For example, in addition to the aforementioned lifestyle and property shows, independent producer Stephen Lambert of RDF Media created a new strand of formatted reality documentaries with *Faking It* (2000–2004), which Potter

(2008: 240) describes as 'a variant on "fish-out-of-water" series like [the BBC's] *In at the Deep End* from the 1980s' and *Wife Swap* (2003–2009), a long-running success for Channel 4 that went on to sell around the world. This is in addition to the aforementioned *Secret Millionaire*, a business entertainment format that we will discuss throughout the book. Brown (2007: 255) explains the attractiveness of such programming by describing how these durable and more commercial strands 'started to elbow out the old style fly-on-the-wall documentaries which, while they chronicled life in all its awkwardness, did not necessarily produce a neat resolution or large audiences'. Moreover, such programming satisfied the growing need to find entertaining ways to present factual content to viewers, as explained by Danny Cohen (interview with authors, 7 March 2007), then Head of E4 and Channel 4 Factual Entertainment: 'One of the challenges for programme makers today is that you have to make everything entertainment because there is such choice out there. So you have to make interesting subjects entertaining and dynamic because otherwise people might go elsewhere'. This view was echoed by all of the producers we talked with while researching this book, whether they worked for Channel 4, the BBC or independent production companies.

This challenge continues to exist in an era that has seen the development of global entertainment formats become a key strategy within the television industry. Unlike the previous business programmes discussed, both *The Apprentice* and *Dragons' Den* have been adapted by the BBC from existing shows in foreign territories and, as such, are indicative of the importance placed on global entertainment formats within an increasingly competitive, interconnected and entrepreneurial television industry.

The Rise of the Global Entertainment Format

First broadcast by the American network NBC in 2004, *The Apprentice* revolves around a job interview that is presented in the form of a series-long challenge that sees the supposedly weakest candidate being fired in each episode. In this sense, it has much in common with the reality gameshow *Big Brother*, although instead of contestants facing a public vote their fate is decided by the entrepreneur Donald Trump, whose company provides the prize of the much sought-after apprenticeship. The link with *Big Brother* is unsurprising, given that the creator of *The Apprentice*, Mark Burnett, was also involved in the US version of *Survivor* (CBS 2000–), an earlier reality format developed by British producer Charlie Parsons who unsuccessfully sued *Big Brother* producers Endemol for 'theft of copyright' due to the similarities between the two programmes (Waisbord 2004: 366). This incident is indicative of a changing business model which places increasing importance on the world of 'vertically integrated transnational television companies with huge inventories of game shows and reality TV formats' (McMurria 2009: 183). As Steemers (2004 173–4) explains,

In the more competitive and fragmented broadcasting environment that emerged in Europe in the 1990s, the use of entertainment formats has a clear commercial logic. Faced with an expansion of transmission time and the loss to pay television of key sporting events, entertainment formats provide a more cost-effective way of filling schedules with local productions than locally originated drama.

Although there is not one agreed definition of formatted TV in use, Bodycombe (cited in Altmeppen, Lantzsch and Will 2007: 95) puts forward a useful description in which he explains that 'a format sale is a product sale. The product in this instance is a recipe for re-producing a successful television programme, in another territory, as a local programme'. The term 'recipe' is particularly significant here as it highlights that rather than exist as a stand-alone, 'canned' product, what is traded in these instances are actually '(successfully tested) concepts for producing entertainment content'.

Along with the aforementioned commercial logic and the political benefits related to the fact that by acquiring the rights to a television format and adapting it within a specific country it is then classified as a domestic production (Moran 1998), many scholars have placed an emphasis on the fact that one of the key advantages of this type of production is the way in which it is seen to reduce risk and promote predictability due to the fact that it has been 'successfully tested' elsewhere. As Waisbord (2004: 365; 378) notes:

> Besides lower costs, imported formats offer some measure of predictability based on their past performances in numerous countries. The constant and increasing pressures for turning profits means that there is little, if any, time for innovating or trying new ideas. All incentives are to reach out for proven ideas that can help diminish uncertainty. Formats, then, are the ultimate risk-minimizing programme strategy ... Formats are a form of McTelevision. Shorthand for the McDonald's fast-food chain, the prefix *Mc* stands for a business model characterized by efficiency, calculability, predictability, and control that caters products to specific local requirements, usually informed by cultural factors.

With regards to business entertainment formats, which draw on the 'natural jeopardy' of the business world to provide drama and tension, it is interesting that this new television business model works to eliminate risk as much as possible. Of course, as this is a creative industry in which there are no certainties with regards to which programming will be successful in differing national contexts, nothing is ever guaranteed. Thus, for every successful global format, there are many that have failed to sell or attract sufficient audiences in certain countries.

There are also different issues at stake within varying types of formats. For example, David Frank (cited in Rouse 2003) of RDF Media explains how the reality programming that his company specializes in, such as *Faking It* and *Wife Swap*, require very different skills to produce a successful adaptation than those needed when reproducing a gameshow. While the latter is about replicating a studio-based format, the skill in the former lies in the casting, filming and editing process. The British gameshow *Who Wants to be a Millionaire* (ITV, 1998–), which is owned by Celador, became the first format to offer not just a license to other broadcasters but a complete package incorporating production expertise and technical know-how such as computers, set, music, software graphics, titles and lighting (Steemers 2004). This allows buyers in different countries to replicate the style of the series using home-grown presenters and members of the public acting as both participants and audience. This is different from the process that the BBC embarked on in adapting both the American version of *The Apprentice* and the Japanese business entertainment format *Money no Tora* (Nippon 2001–2004), which was to become *Dragons' Den*.

The Problems of Adapting International Formats for a Public Service Audience: The Apprentice *and* Dragons' Den

According to Waisbord (2004: 368), the emphasis placed on extreme challenges and weekly elimination pioneered by early reality formats such as *Survivor*, means that such programming 'can be read as the global projection of capitalism, naked individualism, and competition'. This is a criticism that can similarly be ascribed to *The Apprentice*, in which participants take part in weekly challenges but this time with the objective of securing a six-figure appointment with one of Trump's companies. First broadcast during an economic boom, these aspects posed a challenge for the public service ethos of the BBC when the corporation purchased the format from FreemantleMedia to broadcast on British television. As explained by Roly Keating (interview with authors, 13 March 2009), the controller of BBC2 from 2004 to 2008,

> *The Apprentice* was a classic, extravagant exaggeration of American entrepreneurship, and we had big debates about could this possibly translate into the British landscape. Aren't we too sceptical for that? Do we really admire business people in the way that Americans seem to? Could we really take such an American format and then convert it into something that worked on a public service channel in the UK? And I think it could have gone very badly wrong, but we were lucky to have an exceptional team at Talkback who engineered a British version of the programme which is utterly different from the American [original] in all sort of key elements. Not least because it very actively added onto the original Donald Trump format, a British documentary tone of voice, observational tone of voice, not far from what Robert Thirkell was doing in the 1990s.

What is highlighted here are some of the challenges faced by broadcasters in adapting television formats for both a different broadcasting system and a particular national audience. In this instance, however, *The Apprentice* was not only able to reference Thirkell's programmes but it also presented a very timely opportunity for BBC2 as Keating's predecessor Jane Root had recently 'identified the role and impact of enterprise and entrepreneurship on British life as something she wanted reflected in the channel's output' (Boyle 2008: 419).

Root's vision for the channel had much in common with New Labour rhetoric of the time emphasising the need for a more enterprise-oriented culture, and indeed Born (2004: 172) explains how from the late 1990s onwards, 'BBC production departments strove to become intensely entrepreneurial'. As we discuss in more detail in Chapter 4, Fairclough (2000: 33–34) outlines how a number of commentators have accused New Labour of being 'fascinated with the glamour of business' and highlights some of the problems surrounding this type of government discourse:

> Calling industry or business 'enterprise' is sort of a semantic engineering, engineering of meaning – it seeks to attach the values of 'being enterprising' (taking initiative, being creative, etc) to a process that also has a less rosy aspect. There is also an attempt to re-value 'entrepreneur' – to encourage its use in such positive senses.

For the BBC, *The Apprentice* offered an opportunity to both reverse the traditional antipathy displayed by the corporation towards business, wealth and profits while at the same time capitalizing on the 'glamour of business' through a reality gameshow framework and the figure of Sir Alan Sugar; a supposed East-end barrow boy made good enough to secure first a knighthood and then a peerage following his appointment by Prime Minister Gordon Brown in 2009 as the government's 'Enterprise Czar'. As explained by Jane Lush (BBC Press Release 2004), the BBC's Entertainment Commissioner at the time of its initial production, *The Apprentice* was a 'breath-taking and original way of using entertainment to bring business to people who might not have thought it was for them' and indeed the project was extremely successful at attracting a wide demographic, transferring to BBC1 after its first two series.

Dragons' Den was a slightly different proposition having originated in Japan as a low-budget, late-night show targeting a cult, niche audience. Eschewing the group challenge aspect of the reality gameshow format, the premise of the programme involves aspiring entrepreneurs making a direct pitch for funding to wealthy investors, or rather the Dragons of the title. Essentially, it is based on existing 'business angels' initiatives that seek to facilitate investment into early stage businesses (Rees-Mogg 2008). Notably, given the emphasis placed on risk, jeopardy and drama in business entertainment programming, the term 'angels' is replaced with 'dragons', thus introducing a more ruthless, and some would say cruel, streak to proceedings. While the Japanese series took place in the boardroom of the television company in order to minimize costs, the BBC adaptation turned an empty warehouse into the 'den', stripping five multi-millionaires of all their trappings (except, of course, their cash, which sits on a table beside them) as each decide whether to invest their own money into any of the companies on offer.

Dominic Bird (interview with authors, 27 March 2009), executive producer of the programme, admits that for the first two series, the BBC adaptation was also something of a cult. However, since then, it has become the definitive version which has sold around the world. Explaining how Japanese company Sony own the format and act as guardian of the brand, Bird states that,

> [Sony], as far as I understand it, used the BBC programme as their template, and ... I am not even sure whether the people around the world would even look at the Nippon version. I think it is the BBC show that people use. I mean some of them, word for word, will use our Evan [Davis – presenter] script at the intro of the show.

While Sony, then, recoup the rewards of the success of overseas adaptations, the BBC have sought to diversify the format by launching an online version in 2009. With the television programme being broadcast for only eight weeks per year, Bird points out that this is not enough time to deal with the thousands of applications the BBC receive for each series. Thus, the online version not only increases the scale of the programme but it also satisfies the growing demand within the broadcasting industry to produce 360 degree content that operates across platforms (in the form of broadcast, web and mobile technology).

Attracting a 'Double' Demographic

Online content is also seen as a way of targeting a younger demographic but, along with *The Apprentice*, *Dragons' Den* has always been popular with young viewers. This is particularly interesting given that both shows were originally broadcast on BBC2, a channel that aims to attract a primarily upmarket ABC1 audience rather than teenagers or young adults. Executive producer Bird (interview with authors, 27 March 2009) attributes this to the way in which television, in the right circumstances, possesses the power to bring ideas about specialist issues to a wide audience by framing them in an entertaining and aspirational way: 'There is a younger generation who see being a Dragon or being a business person as a cool thing to do .. it is related to being on TV, the same way that often people aspire to, you know, the celebrity side of life'. Doug Richard (interview with authors, April 2009) however, an American entrepreneur who featured in the first two series of *Dragons' Den*, goes into more detail about the relationship between the show's content, television scheduling and what he describes as the 'double audience' of both adults and younger viewers.

In the first instance, Richard argues that broadcasting *Dragons' Den* at 8 pm rather than after the watershed helped attract a younger audience. He attributes this decision to the fact that the series was regarded as high-risk because executives were not sure if anyone would tune into a show about business. Of course, both the British and American versions of *The Apprentice* also attracted similar demographics in prime-time, but this is much more likely to be bound up with the reality gameshow format that is so favoured by younger audiences. Second, Richard believes that adult viewers understand the show differently from their younger counterparts and take different pleasures from it:

> It just always amazes me when two people can watch precisely the same thing and have comprehensively different experiences of that moment. To my mind what you are actually seeing is a difference of focus. The adult is emotionally tied to the entrepreneur's failure while the kid looks at the entrepreneur and thinks 'I could do a better job. I am empowered by it'. The adult looks at it and says 'oh my God, it is so embarrassing that somebody like me is failing in public'. The kid is saying 'somebody like them is failing, but I can do better'. And so it is hugely aspirational and empowering for these teenagers: 'Well it ain't that hard, I am going to go and do it' (interview with authors, April 2009).

For Richard then, *Dragons' Den* has become 'role model TV', not in the sense that either the investors or entrepreneurs act as role models to young viewers but that the series simply reveals both the process of pitching for investment and the standard that is required, thus taking much of the mystery out of business. As Down (2010: 185–186) argues, '"Reality" shows such as *Dragons' Den* … are essentially etiquette guides, about how to be and behave in particular social contexts. *Dragons' Den* shows people – both participant and viewer – what, and what not, to do in order to be a successful entrepreneur'.

This ability to combine a focus on entertainment with educational aspects while also attracting a wide demographic makes business entertainment formats particularly attractive to public service broadcasters. Presenter Evan Davis argued that there was enough 'fibre' in the entertainment content of *Dragons' Den* to allow people to feel that the programme was also doing them good (interview with authors, 12 January, 2007). Indeed, it is notable that attempts by the increasingly commercial ITV to create similar programming, such as *Tycoon* (2007) and *Fortune: The Million Pound Giveaway* (2007), proved too derivative and thus failed to achieve a balance between entertainment and insight.[5] The overtly commercial Channel 5 (which has some public service remit also) has, on the other hand, found success by adapting the troubleshooter format and narrowly applying it to specific industry sectors in the form of *The Hotel Inspector* and its subsequent spin-offs *The Business Inspector* and *The Restaurant Inspector* (2011–). We would argue that it is the more public service focused channels, BBC2 and Channel 4, that have viewed these programmes as a way of delivering entertaining factual content while also dealing with subject matter that bestows a Reithian element of seriousness.

---

5   *Tycoon* was based on *American Inventor* (ABC 2006–2007), a co-production between Simon Cowell and Peter Jones of *Dragons' Den*, while *Fortune: Million Pound Giveaway* also featured fellow Dragon Duncan Bannatyne as one of a panel of judges.

It is also important to note that although programmes such as *Dragons' Den* and *The Apprentice* succeeded in attracting a young demographic despite this not being their original intention, programme makers later capitalized on this with first a special 'Junior' version of *Dragons' Den* for Comic Relief in 2007 and then *The Junior Apprentice*, broadcast on BBC1 in 2010. Indeed, more educational approaches to business programmes also exist outside of the prime time schedule. These include *Tricky Business* (2006–2009) and *Teen Tycoons* (2009); both produced for Channel 4 Learning by the independent production companies IWC Media and Cheetah Television respectively. In the former, young entrepreneurs with a business problem are given advice and mentoring from multi-millionaire businessman John Boyle, while it is the eponymous 'teen tycoons' (three successful 19-year-old entrepreneurs) who take on the role in the latter. Moreover, CBBC (a BBC digital channel aimed at six to 10-year-olds) broadcasts *Beat the Boss* (2006–), in which Saira Khan, runner-up on the first series of *The Apprentice*, tasks three children and three business executives to design a new product in each episode.

Commissioners and producers of public service programming are quick to point out however that these programmes are most definitely grounded in entertainment, although Roly Keating (interview with authors, 13 March 2009) also suggests that,

> *Dragon's Den* and *The Apprentice* are not unlike Robert [Thirkell's] generation of business programmes. They are commissioned for entertainment but I think the penny has dropped that they are actually extremely potent tools to draw people, probably beyond the screen, into quite detailed information about how to set up a business or management techniques and so on. I think part of the attraction of *Dragon's Den* for the BBC is that it does have enormous potency beyond the screen as an idea that captures people's imagination, a frame through which they can think about questions [around] business ideas or how to pitch ideas and find out other things. But the programme itself doesn't pretend to be a documentary depiction of reality and never has. It is clearly an artifice that nonetheless accurately reflects a particular part of the value chain.

This analysis reflects on the trajectory of business-related content on television as it has moved from the more straightforward journalistic arena of news and current affairs towards documentary, lifestyle and finally factual entertainment programming.

Conclusion

As Hill's (2007) audience research indicates there is a strong correlation between reality formats being popular but not valued by the audience, while more traditional documentary forms are highly valued but not perceived as popular. The mobilization by both the BBC and Channel 4 of various popular formats using business-related content (in some cases more explicitly than others) signalled a step change in public service approaches to reach out to audiences in the digital age through increasingly popular forms, but remaining inflected with distinctive content. Indeed we argue that this begins to explain how public service broadcasters are reformulating their strategies toward factual content in order to attract and maintain audiences in a multichannel age. It is of course worth re-iterating that these shifting television representations of business are not ideologically neutral and may be indicative of the ways that particular notions of the role of the individual and their relationship to risk and business have become normalized in mainstream television over the last few decades.

What is clear is that a mapping of the development of these types of programmes offers an insight into wider television industry shifts as producers (both independent and in-house) have moved from addressing a fairly captive analogue audience towards engaging with a more restless viewership in the digital age. We also argue that while wider structural factors remain central in shaping the trajectory of television as both an industry and cultural form, television also remains shaped by key individuals working in particular genres at central moments in an organization's history. The legacy of Thirkell's *Troubleshooter*, and his continued role as a respected television producer almost two decades on, is indicative of the manner through which the history of television is continually recycled with themes such as business being presented for different audiences using a variety of styles over a sustained period. Thus we contend that by combining historical analysis, in-depth interviews with industry professionals and a wider examination of the changing television marketplace, the development of a previously overlooked television format can be traced, revealing that rather than simply being a subsidiary of reality programming, the business entertainment format has a distinct history. It also illuminates the shifting conventions of popular factual television in contemporary British society and changes the way in which business, entrepreneurship, risk and wealth creation has become represented on mainstream television.

In the next chapter we examine in more detail the range of narratives and representations around business and entrepreneurship that have become increasingly prominent on British television screens.

Chapter 3

Risking it All: Analyzing 'Business Entertainment Formats'

We had created a 'star' presenter in Sir John, a 'star' concept in making over firms, sacking bosses and transforming lives, as well as 'star' subject areas. Most important of all, we had identified strong stories within 'star' firms that were small enough to film.

Robert Thirkell discussing *Troubleshooter* (2010: 15).

I know [producers] struggled for a while doing business on telly because they couldn't work out how to make it visual and what format to do it in.

Property Ladder presenter Sarah Beeny (interview with authors, 4 March 2010).

The previous chapter traced the historical development of business programming on British television while also examining some of the developments to occur within the industry itself (both nationally and globally) that have resulted in programme makers becoming more aware of the business nature of the medium. The aim of this chapter is to now look more closely at the business entertainment formats to emerge on television in the United Kingdom since the broadcast of *Troubleshooter* in 1990 by first analyzing how the programmes are structured and second examining the range of narratives and representations adopted by the television entrepreneurs. We then outline the key visual characteristics pertaining to business entertainment formats before considering the use of emotive concepts such as risk, relationships and resistance.

As we have already pointed out, rather than continuously create original factual output in an era of 24/7 broadcasting, factual-based programming has begun to take on constructed elements that allow it to function as reproducible (and potentially lucrative) formats as opposed to more straightforward documentaries. In this chapter, we argue that this type of business entertainment programming can be placed within a continuum that features lightly-constructed documentaries at one end of the scale through to highly-formatted reality television at the other. This has resulted in two mains strands of business entertainment being established in the form of the 'troubleshooter' format, which has its roots in the documentary tradition, and the 'business gameshow', which is derived from the more recent emergence of reality television. It must be noted that although there is some crossover between these two types of programmes, each of these strands share specific elements that allow us to group them together into a larger category while also beginning to map out the various narratives, representations and visual characteristics on offer.

Creating a Narrative Structure

The Troubleshooter Template

As detailed in the previous chapter, *Troubleshooter*, the original business entertainment format, was created by producer Robert Thirkell for the BBC in the late 1980s and first broadcast on BBC2 in 1990. As suggested by the quotation that opens this chapter, rather than being asked to take a documentary approach to a specific business-related subject, Thirkell was given a 'name' first, in the form of recently retired industrialist Sir John Harvey-Jones, and tasked with creating a concept around him. This led to a constructed element being added to the resulting factual series that not only challenged previous documentary conventions but also set the template for future troubleshooter-based programming:

> Television always changes what it looks at, just by virtue of filming it, but at the time the convention was never to acknowledge this. I didn't realise this, so along with executive producer Richard Reisz I accidentally came up with a plan not only to accept that television changed what it looked at but, taking that to its logical end, to use television to try to change reality on a grand scale. Sir John Harvey-Jones, the hero, would charge into companies, see what was wrong and suggest changes – such as selling half the company or even sometimes sacking the boss (Thirkell 2010: 7).

The troubleshooter format thus takes an existing business that is experiencing trouble and brings in an 'expert' to assess the company and offer advice on how to turn things around. This relatively simple premise provides producers with a definitive structure in terms of a beginning, middle and end. For example, each opening segment introduces both the expert and the business to the audience and outlines their credentials and troubles respectively. The main body of each programme then follows the expert as he or she visits the company in question to obtain the perspective of management and staff, assess the everyday workings of the business and gain insight into what is going wrong. The process then reaches a conclusion with the expert delivering his or her verdict and putting forward a number of recommendations for management to decide whether or not to accept.

In terms of creating a reproducible format, the troubleshooter approach builds to a specific *outcome* by revealing whether those responsible for the company choose to implement or reject the advice offered and, more importantly, whether the troubleshooter's intervention achieves results. The latter is presented via a coda which details how the company is faring at a later date as a result of the overall process. In television terms, this can also be described as a 'makeover' or 'reveal'. This approach allows for potential *conflict* and *jeopardy*, along with adding a decidedly *human element* to proceedings, as the Chief Executives and Managing Directors involved face uncomfortable analyses and critique while the livelihood of each company's workforce is essentially on the line. The troubleshooter format therefore draws on the documentary tradition by filming real-life events that are occurring within actual businesses but, rather than document them in a straightforward observational or participatory manner, instead offers a lightly-constructed version that packages business into 'entertainment with a purpose', the phrase used by Andrew Mackenzie, then Head of Factual Entertainment at Channel 4, to describe successful factual entertainment formats (The Factual Commissioning Forum, 11 March 2009). With this framework in place, the suspense, frustration or excitement created in each episode is dependent on the characters involved, the conflicts to arise and, of course, the final outcome.

Once a reproducible format such as the troubleshooter approach is established, producers can adapt and modify it to satisfy a number of ends. Channel 4 was one of the first to replicate the *Troubleshooter* series with *Risking it All* (2004–2006), in which Martin Webb (a serial entrepreneur who is also behind the People's Pubs chain which donates its profits to local charities, community groups and individuals), follows the trials and tribulations of ten budding entrepreneurs as they attempt to start up their own businesses. As outlined in Chapter 2, Sir Gerry Robinson then became the BBC2's troubleshooter for a new generation with *I'll Show Them Who's Boss* and *Can Gerry Robinson Fix ... the NHS?* and *Dementia Care Homes* before also appearing on Channel 4 with *Gerry's Big Decision*. In 2010, Hilary Devey similarly sought to turn around struggling small businesses in Channel 5's *The Business Inspector* before becoming a Dragon in 2011 for the ninth series of the BBC2 show.

Thirkell was himself one of the first to tweak the format however with the BBC2 series *Back to the Floor*, in which bosses essentially find themselves acting as their own troubleshooter by returning to the sharp end of their business for a week in order to gain a new perspective on how the company operates. This was updated almost a decade later with *The Secret Millionaire* and *Undercover Boss*, two formats based on a similar premise by RDF Media for Channel 4. In the first instance, the eponymous millionaires volunteer within deprived communities around the country before revealing their true wealth and donating money to those they believe to be most in need. The latter, on the other hand, sees bosses working incognito within their own companies before revealing themselves to staff and recognizing the contribution of good employees with a promotion, pay rise or some sort of reward.

Shows such as these tend to focus on a range of businesses, such as toy manufacturers and shoe factories in *Troubleshooter*, holiday firms and football clubs in *Back to the Floor* and construction and waste management companies in *Undercover Boss*, to name but a few (along with the various community-based projects in *The Secret Millionaire*). However, there is also a trend for troubleshooter programmes focusing solely on certain sectors. This includes capitalizing on Britain's obsession with property in Channel 4's *Property Ladder* and, more specifically, highlighting service industries in the form of a series of programmes concerned with restaurants, retail and hotels; as seen in Channel 4's *Ramsay's Kitchen Nightmares* and *Mary Portas: Secret Shopper*, BBC2's *Mary*

Queen of Shops and Channel 5's *The Hotel Inspector*. While this is in part due to the increase in personality-driven programming that results in certain experts becoming recognizable 'faces' for broadcast channels (a trend we noted in Chapter 2), it can also be attributed to the fact that these are sectors that viewers are familiar with and interested in. As producer Robert Thirkell (2010: 8) notes, 'the audience love seeing behind the scenes of places we see and use every day, as long as they are seen from a new angle'. The result is that factual programming often returns to the same sectors over and over again within a variety of different formats: the restaurant trade, for example, has formed the basis of the docusoap *Boiling Point* (Channel 4, 1999–2000), troubleshooter formats *Ramsay's Kitchen Nightmares*, *Big Chef Takes on Little Chef* and *The Restaurant Inspector*, as well as the business gameshow *The Restaurant*. With this in mind, we will now go on to examine the structure of the business gameshow in more detail and outline how it differs from the troubleshooter strand of business entertainment.

The Business Gameshow

So far we have explained how the troubleshooter format offers a lightly-constructed version of real-life events by filming the everyday workings of a failing business and asking an expert to assess what has gone wrong. In contrast, the business gameshow revolves around an artificial situation that is created for the purposes of filming and which employs 'the framework of competition to capitalize on the spectacle of "ordinary" people under extreme (television) pressure – a staple element of the quiz and game show from its earliest days' (Holmes 2008: 25). We outlined in Chapter 1 the numerous forms that 'reality TV' can take, from real-crime and emergency programming to video diaries and dramatic reconstructions (Biressi and Nunn 2005). For the purposes of this analysis however we are employing a more narrow definition that understands reality television as those programmes that involve group challenge or game/quiz show elements. It is important to note that some of these programmes also contain more traditional documentary features, hence the use of the word 'gamedoc' by Couldry (2010), and this is something we will consider later in the chapter in relation to the learning process and visual aesthetic. On the whole, though, we argue that the troubleshooter format is more rooted in the documentary tradition while the artificial and competitive aspect of the business gameshow results in what can be understood as highly-formatted reality TV programming.

The business gameshow takes the form of a series of group or individual challenges in which contestants showcase either their general business ability or skills within a specific sector and are judged on their performances by an industry expert or prospective employer. Each week one contestant is eliminated until the winner is revealed and rewarded with some sort of employment contract. It is these gameshow elements that inform the narrative structure of each episode. For example, on introducing both the contestants and judge/expert, specific tasks or challenges are issued at the beginning of each episode. The main body of the programme then follows the teams or individuals as they formulate a strategy and put it into action within certain time-restrictions. Everyone is gathered together at the end of the process to be judged on their efforts and offered the opportunity to explain their decisions before the show culminates with that week's winner being revealed while the weakest performer is eliminated.

Once again, the result is a reproducible format that has a definite *outcome* and which is full of *conflict* and *jeopardy*, as the contestants argue over the best way to succeed in each task while continuously facing the prospect of being eliminated. There are however two key things to consider. First, unlike its troubleshooter predecessor, the business gameshow is cumulative in nature. While the troubleshooter approach is episodic, in that each episode stands alone, the business gameshow puts forward a serialized narrative that sees the eventual outcome (in the form of the overall winner) deferred until the final instalment. This makes the viewing experience very different as audiences are expected to tune in over a longer period of time and get to know the remaining contestants as they deal with the various challenges and pressures of showcasing their ability.

Second, while the troubleshooter format features actual companies in which livelihoods are under threat, the contestants in business gameshows are competing for a position that has been created in order to satisfy a television production. The prize in question is real (and very lucrative) and contestants may have indeed quit their jobs and left their families behind in order to take part, but essentially the series is based on an artifice and the focus is on individual achievement, the clash of personalities and working under pressure rather than what it takes to run a successful business over a number of years in the real world. In addition to its gameshow structure therefore, these features also work to satisfy its inclusion in the reality television genre and differentiate it from the troubleshooter format which we argue has its roots more firmly in the documentary tradition.

The Apprentice provides a useful template for the business gameshow and indeed the original American version has since been sold around the world with local versions having been produced to varying degrees of success in a number of markets. In a similar manner to the troubleshooter format, other business gameshows have tended to focus on one sector, such as the restaurant trade in *The Restaurant*, fashion and product design in *Project Catwalk* (Sky1, 2006–2008) and *Design for Life* (BBC1, 2009) respectively and, indeed, the modelling business in the *Next Top Model* (Sky Living, 2005–) franchise; the American version of which began broadcasting in 2003, thus preceding *The Apprentice* by a year and earning the title of the original business gameshow. The overall aim of these programmes is that the intense task-based structure of the series allows participants to learn and hone their craft so that they are then ready to enter the world of business within their own specific sector, something they share with the talent show format. Ouellette and Hay (2008: 133) point out that in the modelling industry, the successful model must sell themselves effectively as a brand or, as Tyra Banks, presenter and creator of *America's Next Top Model* describes it, become the 'CEOs of Me'. One departure from this is *Million Dollar Traders* (BBC2, 2009), a one-off series which set out to see how easy it would be to turn eight members of the public into City-traders capable of running their own hedge fund.

These examples of the business gameshow focus on playing an artificial game in order to win an actual job however there are other programmes that are more concerned with investing in existing businesses. The most notable of these is the BBC's *Dragons' Den*, which draws on real-life angel initiatives that offer investment to business start-ups. In one sense, key elements of the business gameshow are present in that there is a panel of judges who question contestants on their businesses within a certain amount of time before deciding whether to invest their own personal money. It also has much in common with the quiz show however, in that instead of carrying out tasks or taking part in challenges, participants are quizzed on sales figures, profit margins, equity offered and so on, and must deliver without access to their business plans and financial records. There is no formal elimination process but there are winners and losers as those that do not impress go home empty-handed (following each dragon declaring 'I'm out') while others shake hands on an investment deal. In terms of structure, the action is neither episodic nor serialized as each pitch and negotiation is condensed into bite-sized chunks throughout an hour long programme.

Other examples that highlight the diversity of the business gameshow format include series such as *Make Me a Million* (Channel 4, 2005), *High Street Dreams* (BBC1, 2010) and *The Next Big Thing* (BBC2, 2011), which are concerned with mentoring aspiring businessmen and women as they attempt to launch their own products onto the market and, indeed, *I'm Running Sainsbury's* (Channel 4 2009), which allows workers on the shop floor to conceive and implement new initiatives within the British supermarket chain. While there are still tasks and challenges issued on a weekly basis in these shows, they are related to the development of actual products and businesses and thus are more lightly-constructed than either *The Apprentice* or *Dragons' Den*. In contrast, BBC3's *The Last Millionaire* (2009) was a highly-formatted business gameshow that places successful young entrepreneurs in cities around the world before setting them tasks to see who can make the most money using their entrepreneurial skills. Exhibiting elements of the travelogue through its focus on foreign cities, a further twist is added in that it is the winners who are allowed to leave each week and thus able to go back home to their luxurious lifestyles while the last person standing is declared the overall loser.

In this section we have demonstrated the two main types of business entertainment formats on offer while also highlighting the diversity of programming available. What each of these examples has in common is an attempt to package business content into an entertaining structure that can be easily reproduced in variety of ways. We will now go on to examine the various roles adopted by television entrepreneurs in business entertainment formats and the ways in which *vocational* and *televisual* skills are required to transform a successful entrepreneur into a television personality.

The Television Entrepreneur

The term 'television personality' (Langer 1981; in Marshall 2006) has long been used within film and television studies to distinguish the type of fame granted to those who appear on the small screen from the theory of film 'stardom' first put forward by Dyer (1979); with both being considered to be different from that of 'celebrity' (Geraghty 2000). While one of the concerns of this research is how entrepreneurs that appear on television go on to become wider media celebrities (something that will be discussed in detail in Chapter 7), we first want to look at some of the problems related to the term television personality when applied to business entertainment formats. As Lury (1995: 117) has noted, television studies has often struggled with analyzing television performance, with the categories of personality (those who appear in factual programming) and actor (those who appear in fiction) often being entangled; although it is the case that 'the personality is also always in some sense "acting"'. Bennett (2008: 34) concurs by suggesting that many scholars simply 'conflate the wide variety of performers on television into one category: the television personality'. However, he (2008: 35) also highlights a more narrow understanding that posits the TV personality as those performers within the factual arena that essentially play themselves, 'making little distinction between onscreen and private personas: Jamie Oliver as "Jamie Oliver", for instance'.

This category includes everything from light entertainment performers to daytime magazine presenters, gameshow hosts, news anchors and the range of experts who appear on lifestyle programming covering cookery, gardening, fashion and interior design. It is this latter category that has received the most attention within television studies in recent years following what Brunsdon (2003) terms the 'lifestyling of British television' from the 1990s onwards (see also Brunsdon et al. 2001). The focus here has primarily been on various notions of the ordinary, including the 'ordinari-nization' of television itself (Brunsdon et al. 2001: 53), the transformation of ordinary people through makeover strategies (Lewis 2008, Weber 2009, Ouellette and Hay 2008) and the construction of the television personality or expert as 'ordinary/extraordinary' so as to position them as 'just like' the audience despite exhibiting certain levels of knowledge, control and power (Bonner 2003). Bennett (2008: 36) takes this further by distinguishing between *televisually* skilled and *vocationally* skilled performers and suggesting that those in possession of some sort of skill related to their professional status in a specific field have become increasingly visible on British television screens, particularly as progamme presenters. While such skills validate their appearances on television and give credibility to their authenticity of character (something that is important within the immediate and intimate world of television), vocationally skilled performers nevertheless also have to master certain televisual skills if they are to secure longevity onscreen and acquire wider fame (Bennett and Holmes 2010: 72).

The Entrepreneur as Presenter/Troubleshooting Expert

The category of vocationally skilled performer is thus central to the appearance of entrepreneurs as onscreen experts but, again, this consists of a diverse group of roles and performance styles. Discussing the aforementioned Jamie Oliver, De Solier (2005: 477) explains how the celebrity chef (who is often termed an entrepreneur by the British media due to his various business interests) portrays in his cookery programmes a 'leisure identity' as opposed to a 'professional identity' by reconfiguring cooking not as 'domestic chore' or 'professional labour' but as primarily a leisure activity. It can be argued that Oliver's onscreen identity has since changed due to his role in political campaigning shows such as *Jamie's School Dinners* and *Jamie's Ministry of Food*. However, entrepreneurs portraying a 'leisure identity' is certainly not the case in business entertainment formats, which often seem to have been subsumed within the realm of lifestyle and reality programming by the academy despite their differences in focus.

In Channel 4's *Ramsay's Kitchen Nightmares*, for example, another celebrity chef Gordon Ramsay imparts his professional skills within the kitchen and draws on his reputation as a successful restaurateur to act as troubleshooter to failing restaurants around the country. In this sense, Ramsay's expertise are very much validated by his professional offscreen status and, while it can be argued that he is playing an 'exaggerated' version of himself for the cameras, it is his ability to blend his professional identity with a televisually skilled performance (that consists both of direct address to camera and a distinctively aggressive and confrontational performance style) that has contributed to the long-running success of the series. We discuss this again in more detail later in the book when we consider audience reactions to Ramsay's onscreen persona.

Gordon Ramsay has the dual-role of both presenter and business expert in *Ramsay's Kitchen Nightmares* and this is a similar device employed in other troubleshooter formats such as BBC2's *Mary Queen of Shops* and Channel 4 *Mary Portas: Secret Shopper*. Sarah Beeny of Channel 4's *Property Ladder*, on the other hand, functions slightly differently as she adopts more of a mentoring role to the would-be property developers who appear on the show, remaining in control of the situation in her presenter guise but exhibiting a much less confrontational style when imparting advice to the ordinary people taking part who indeed regularly ignore her well-informed suggestions. By directly addressing the camera and, by extension, the audience at home, the television viewer is encouraged to identify with the presenter/expert in these programmes, a position that is supported due to the way in which their credibility is validated by their offscreen success within their respective restaurant, retail and property businesses. In this sense, they may be playing a heightened version of themselves on television, but they are nevertheless positioned as being authentic characters, or rather 'just-as-they-are' in real life, in relation to their business skills and knowledge.

The Entrepreneur as Judge/Investor

Just as the troubleshooter programme is only one type of business entertainment format, not all entrepreneurs who appear on television assume the dual presenter/ expert role. For example, Lord Sugar acts as a judge on *The Apprentice*, a reality gameshow in which he becomes the real-life employer of the winning contestant. Likewise the Dragons of *Dragon's Den* similarly make judgements regarding the quality of pitches and potential business opportunities put forward by aspiring entrepreneurs in the Den, although in this case they offer real-life financial investment rather than a one-year contract to those who succeed. In neither instance do the entrepreneurs assume the role of presenter or regularly address the camera and the audience at home. Instead, *The Apprentice* features a voiceover by Mark Halilley while the televisually skilled presenter Evan Davis acts as an intermediary in *Dragons' Den*. Through television's system of 'delegated looking' (Bennett and Holmes 2010: 74) however, the viewer is regularly aligned with the viewpoint of Sugar and the Dragons and thus encouraged to draw on the skills, knowledge and expertise put forward by these entrepreneurs before going on to judge the contestants and participants accordingly. It is also the case that these figures perform a certain 'nasty' role that has become appealing to audiences schooled in reality television and which is indicative of the televisual skills they have acquired. However this does not necessarily make them appear inauthentic, as their ruthlessness is again legitimized by their offscreen achievements within the demanding world of business.

Yet, while the public and private personas of these television entrepreneurs are presented as being almost indistinguishable, the identification process established between the audience and such personalities becomes more problematic. For example, as Bennett and Holmes (2010: 71) note, 'television's discourse of glamour allows its personalities to function as figures of identification and "reachable" ideals of wealth, extravagance and glamour' without breaching the 'boundaries of a middle-class taste culture of the period'. This notion of 'reachable' wealth is difficult to establish with prosperous entrepreneurs in general, not to mention those whose appearances on television have subjected them to the celebrification process and the subsequent lifestyle that accompanies it.

Again, it is important to point out that this occurs on different levels, so that nationally recognizable figures like Portas and Beeny become easier to identify with than Ramsay, who has achieved transnational fame as both a Michelin-starred chef and television personality on both sides of the Atlantic. Likewise, those experts who directly address the camera are able to establish a stronger rapport with the audience than those who sit solely in judgment of others due to their wealth and achievements. Indeed the opening sequence of *Dragon's Den* was toned down during the 2009 recession as images of the millionaire Dragons driving top-of-the-range cars, flying in private jets and relaxing aboard luxury yachts was no longer deemed appropriate by the BBC (interview with Dominic Bird, Executive Producer of *Dragons' Den*, 27 March 2009).

There is therefore a certain masking involved or disavowal in relation to the financial and cultural capital acquired by television entrepreneurs offscreen and their onscreen personas; although prior to the recession viewers were perhaps encouraged to *aspire* to be like these figures rather than *identify* with them per se. One way of negotiating this is by invoking a 'rags to riches' narrative that, as we examine in the next chapter, is both well-established within business reporting (Guthey, Clark and Jackson 2009) and easily recognizable to the audience. In this sense, an emphasis is placed on the way in which celebrity entrepreneurs have overcome some sort of adversity, typically in terms of class, background or lack of academic ability, to achieve wealth and success through sheer hard work. This narrative is then presented as something that is potentially 'reachable' to the television-viewing masses and these issues are something that we will discuss later in the book. In the meantime, however, we consider how business entertainment formats have found ways to make the 'boring' subject of business dramatic and visual while also connecting with audiences on an emotional level.

Going on a Journey

Movement, Location and the Reveal in the Troubleshooter Format

In his guide to storytelling in factual and reality forms of television and film, Robert Thirkell (2010: 6) relays an anecdote about the pre-production stage of *Troubleshooter*, when he made his first recce visit to see what Sir John Harvey-Jones actually did on a day-to-day basis:

> He took me with him to a heat-exchanger factory he was visiting in Hertfordshire. When we arrived all he did was say hello, look at the accounts for twenty minutes, and leave. It was even more boring than watching paint drying. My career was on the line. I vowed never to make films in an engineering subcontracting factory.

Earlier in the chapter we explained how this seemingly boring process was able to be packaged into an entertaining structure for television that had a definite beginning, middle and end and which created conflict before providing a final outcome. What was also required however was to provide this structure with visual impact that kept the programme moving along and held the interest of the viewer until the culmination of the episode.

The answer to part of this problem is *movement*. For example, rather than film Sir John sitting at a desk surveying the accounts of each company, *Troubleshooter* simply states his extensive paper research in the voiceover. The body of each programme is instead concerned with his *journey* to the company in question, beginning with him physically being driven there. He is then introduced to management and staff and taken on a visit around the factory or the shop floor where he is able to inspect the efficiency of the machinery and working practices.

This results in footage of his various encounters, shots of the assembly line and machinery in action, and close-ups of staff carrying out intricate tasks and of the resulting finished products. It is only when his final assessment and advice is to be delivered that all parties come together and sit down in what makes for a tense-filled moment. Most troubleshooter formats have since adopted this approach and indeed taken it further. Experts with big personalities and high energy levels, such as Gordon Ramsay and Mary Portas, are hardly ever filmed sitting down (except in the obligatory 'driving to their destination' shot or when Ramsay is sampling a meal, although he often tastes food while standing up) but instead are constantly moving around, inspecting things and pointing out areas of improvement. Likewise, business gameshows regularly issue challenges that require contestants to set up market stalls, sell goods door-to-door, film a commercial or put on a highvend event. These are tasks that require action and, as such, work to reverse the image of business people confined to a desk crunching numbers.

Another visual aspect of business entertainment formats is a focus on *location* or *place*. Again, due to the documentary approach of the troubleshooter format, cameras are always taken to a real-life business set in a particular city around the country. These regional cities offer a context for the company's troubles, whether it is the importance of a particular factory in terms of jobs for the community, a country house hotel aiming to attract tourists to the area or the decline of the high street and its impact on neighbourhood restaurants and shops. In addition to being presented with a very clear sense of location in terms of the surrounding area, audiences are also able to view the actual place of business and, more importantly, discover what goes on behind-the-scenes. It is here that the focus on specific sectors becomes clear, as viewers are more likely to have experience of clothes rails, lunch menus and hotel foyers than the abstract machinery employed within factories. Location and place is also important within the business gameshow but this is for reasons of aesthetics rather than business per se and as such we shall discuss it in more detail in the following section.

The moment of 'the reveal' is also crucial in providing the troubleshooter format with a narrative conclusion and visual impact. In its original incarnation, this was essentially a coda that followed the overall assessment of each company, in which it was revealed whether the management had taken on board Sir John's advice and its subsequent impact on the business. Essentially, the final images of the episode depicted either a scaled back factory with less machinery and staff or a renewed business with a sense of purpose. The successors to *Troubleshooter* have since taken this further. By focusing on particular sectors, the 'makeover' aspect of the format becomes fully realized as specific changes are made to the actual 'look' of the businesses in question. This was first demonstrated in *Property Ladder* (the business series with most links to home decoration shows) with the completed property being unveiled to the audience along with before and after shots of each room. Those programmes concerned with restaurants, retail and hotels went on to employ a similar technique, often by arranging a relaunch to showcase the visual changes that had been implemented and thus illustrate not only the overall transformation of the business at the hands of the troubleshooter but also the potential customer base. In these latter examples, television producers found a perfect way to make business visual while providing a satisfying conclusion to the troubleshooting process.

It can be argued that 'the reveal' occurs in the business gameshow too, although it generally takes the form of a decision being made to eliminate a contestant rather than a transformation taking place. As already noted, movement and location are also important in the business gameshow but this is employed in different ways. For example, series such as *Make Me a Million, High Street Dreams* and *Britain's Next Big Thing* have much in common with the troubleshooter format as they often begin by introducing contestants in their natural business habitat before going behind the scenes at shops, restaurants, and so on, as various meetings are attended in an attempt to launch new products onto the market. In this sense, there is often a focus on documentary features within an overall competitive structure. Movement and location are much more stylized in *The Apprentice* and *Dragons' Den* however and this is something that we will now consider in more detail, along with how these shows link to documentary practice.

The Learning Process and Visual Aesthetics in The Apprentice *and* Dragons' Den

Couldry (2010) and Couldry and Littler (2008) describe the British version of *The Apprentice* as a 'gamedoc' and 'aesthetically polished documentary' respectively. In both instances, the documentary aspect of the series is linked to the way in which it works as a learning tool for the audience. For example, while Couldry and Littler (2008: 261) understand the show as 'both an entertaining spectacle and popular education', Couldry (2010: 78) also quotes executive producer Daisy Goodwin's statement that *The Apprentice* is 'the first entertainment show to have a *real* point – to show what it takes to get ahead in business' [our emphasis]. The learning or educative aim of both *The Apprentice* and *Dragons' Den* is something that was regularly highlighted in our own interviews with producers and television executives involved in the production of both programmes: *Dragons' Den* presenter Evan Davis (interview with authors, 12 January 2007) notably referred to it as 'educational fibre.' Nevertheless, although former BBC2 controller Roly Keating (interview with authors, 13 March 2009) recognizes that both of these shows function as 'extremely potent tools to draw people, probably beyond the screen, into quite detailed information about how to set up a business', he goes on to say that a series such as *Dragons' Den* 'doesn't pretend to be a documentary depiction of reality and never has.' Thus, it is important to be aware of the constant negotiation that occurs between documentary and reality techniques within programmes such as *The Apprentice* and *Dragons' Den*; two highly-formatted business gameshows that are broadcast on public service channels and therefore aim to offer some educational content in addition to an entertaining narrative and distinctive visual aesthetic.

The learning and educational nature of business entertainment formats is something we will consider further in Chapters 5 and 6 when we discuss the findings of our audience research. For now, however, we want to focus more specifically on the formal elements of *The Apprentice* and *Dragons' Den* and consider how they differ from their troubleshooter counterparts. For example, as we have highlighted, rather than send cameras onsite to film existing businesses, both of these shows bring contestants to a central location that can be controlled, to a certain extent, by the production team. Again, the level of control exerted varies within each programme.

Dragon's Den, for instance, is entirely set-based, with the first few series having been shot in a disused warehouse before moving to Pinewood Studios, London. Retaining an industrial feel, the set changes slightly with each series but essentially features an exposed brick interior with stark wooden floors, a large bank of windows that suggest an unnamed urban landscape beyond, some strategically placed pillars and a steep staircase that contestants have to climb in order to enter the Den. A lighting rig is used to light each of the five dragons and, more importantly, the contestants, who have to deliver their pitch under the intense heat of the lights and glare of the cameras. This notion of being placed 'under the spotlight' brings to mind quiz shows such as *Mastermind* (BBC1, 1972–1997; BBC2, 2003–) and indeed the contestants are grilled on their business knowledge by the intimidating dragons without access to notes. However, unlike the two minutes of intense questioning the contestants on *Mastermind* are subjected to, the pitches in *Dragon's Den* are not time-restricted and thus can be filmed over a number of hours of which only a few minutes may make the final edit. In the short segments that are broadcast, electronic music is played as the contestants enter the den and during breaks in negotiation to add to the tension and create an increasingly ominous mood before the Dragons reveal whether or not they will invest.

Dragons' Den is the business gameshow that is furthest removed in style from the troubleshooter format. This is because, apart from a short interview contestants give to presenter Evan Davis, the series is only concerned with the moment of the pitch and thus provides very little contextual information about the budding entrepreneurs. It is only in the spin-off shows, *Dragons' Den: Where Are They Now?* (BBC2, 2007) and *What Happened Next?* (BBC2, 2010) that we see the businessmen and women in their natural business habitat discussing whether the deal they secured came to fruition (more often than not the investment falls through after filming). Yet, despite the omission of everyday working practices, *Dragon's Den* provides useful information on how to deliver a successful pitch (Down 2010) and can therefore be considered educative on this aspect of business.

In contrast to the purely studio set-up of *Dragons' Den*, the British version of *The Apprentice* combines both set-based and location filming within its game structure and, as such, has a complex relationship to the notion of place. In the first instance, *The Apprentice* equates success in business with the city of London, inviting all of the contestants to the capital and depicting them walking across Millennium Bridge in its opening sequence. London's architecture is central to the show's distinctive visual style, with sweeping aerial shots of the city showcasing the River Thames, the award-winning Gherkin building in the Square Mile and the City's other financial district of Canary Wharf (with the latter two functioning as symbols of the success of the City until the banking crisis that occurred at the end of the noughties). The show's contestants are housed in a luxury home and chauffeur-driven in premium cars, thus hinting at the type of wealthy lifestyle that may befall the eventual winner of the game. As described by former Channel 4 executive Andrew Mackenzie (interview with authors 20 March 2009), *The Apprentice* showcases London as a 'special place where people are rewarded in exorbitant ways'. Yet, the actual tasks are carried out in more everyday locations such as a street market, shopping centre or car showroom where contestants come into contact with both industry professionals and members of the public. The vérité feel of these scenes, which aim to reveal the often chaotic and haphazard way in which contestants approach the set tasks, are then contrast with the highly-constructed boardroom showdown that unfolds in the final third of each episode and where contestants have to justify their actions.

The boardroom scene in *The Apprentice* is filmed in a studio to allow for the cameras, lights and gallery housing the director and technical team.[1] This is obscured onscreen however in two ways. First, establishing shots of the Square Mile and Canary Wharf in East London appear before the contestants enter the boardroom and second, the person who is eliminated is filmed walking out of Lord Sugar's actual business headquarters (Amstrad headquarters in Brentwood, Essex, for Series 1 to 3 and the St Albans, Hertfordshire, base of Viglen Ltd thereafter). The onscreen implication is that the vérité filming of the tasks is carried into the boardroom despite the presence of two diverse locations. This again suggests an attempt by the production team to present the series as more of an 'aesthetically polished documentary' rather than signpost its constructed nature and explicitly align it with reality television. The use of voiceover in the show also adds to this, with Roly Keating (interview with authors, 13 March 2009) explaining that in an attempt to convert the 'extravagant exaggeration' of the American format into a suitable programme for the public service BBC, 'a British documentary tone of voice' was actively added. It is notable that in the voiceover, contestants are referred to as 'candidates' thus maintaining the overall conceit that they are simply taking part in an extended job interview as opposed to a televized business gameshow. Nevertheless, the use of music in the series works as a distancing device. For example, in addition to creating tension and suspense in a similar manner to *Dragons' Den*, a combination of classical, popular and original music is used to also accent the moments of humour that frequently occur. In combination

---

1   The reasons for filming the boardroom scene in a studio are discussed in an article on the BBC website entitled 'The Workings of *The Apprentice*'. Available at: http://www. bbc.co.uk/apprentice/series6/workings.shtml (Accessed 11 April 2011).

with the sometimes arch voiceover and the smooth camerawork, this allows viewers to step back and consider not only the overall constructed nature of the situation but also the relatively absurd conditions that contestants are asked to work under.

The distinctive aesthetic of *The Apprentice* is integral to its continuing success and many of its key elements have since been adopted by other business entertainment formats.[2] This includes BBC2's business gameshow *The Restaurant*, which features music by the same composer, Dru Masters, and Channel 5's *The Hotel Inspector*, a troubleshooter series with a voiceover by Mark Halliley, narrator of *The Apprentice*. Programmes such as *Property Ladder*, *Ramsay's Kitchen Nightmares*, *Mary Queen of Shops* and *Mary Portas: Secret Shopper* on the other hand, differentiate themselves by having Sarah Beeny, Gordon Ramsay and Mary Portas provide the respective voiceovers and directly address the camera, thus creating a more intimate connection with the viewer. In particular, *Mary Queen of Shops* can be considered a departure from the original *Troubleshooter* aesthetic through its use of loud pop music and quick-cut editing, two techniques that complement Portas's strong visual image and the fast-paced world of fashion retail she inhabits.

We have thus far demonstrated how the troubleshooter format uses movement and location to take viewers on a visual journey that culminates in the moment of 'the reveal'. We have also discussed the ways in which business gameshows combine the learning process with a distinctive visual aesthetic that again plays with the notion of location and place and which uses a range of formal techniques to create moments of tension, distance and intimacy. In the following section, we take this further by examining how business entertainment formats also aim to take the audience on another kind of journey, namely an emotional one, by using business as a framework through which to look at ordinary people and the emotive concepts of risks, relationship and resistance. As Thirkell (2010: 5) notes, 'it is hard to care about a subject, easy to care about a story' and business entertainment formats seek to offer stories about passionate people looking to either turn their businesses (and, by extension, their lives) around or establish their arrival on the business scene (the latter of which is neatly encapsulated in the title of the *Next Top Model* franchise where the next 'face' to look out for in the modelling industry is crowned each season).

---

2 By way of contrast, the original American version of *The Apprentice* (NBC 2004–) had to be revitalized with the broadcast of *The Celebrity Apprentice* for three seasons between 2007 and 2009. A return to the regular format for the show's tenth season again saw a dip in the ratings thus the celebrity version was reinstalled the following year. In Britain, a special celebrity edition of the show was broadcast in 2007 and 2009 to raise money for Comic Relief.

Establishing an Emotional Connection

Relationships

In our discussion of narrative structure in business entertainment formats, we highlight the ways in which conflict is created by bringing in an expert to assess a business or by pitting budding businessmen and women against one another for a prize position. This results in a tense and stressful situation as real people are quizzed, interrogated, challenged and judged in a process overseen by successful entrepreneurs who have been placed in a position of authority for the purposes of a television production and who, through their regular appearances onscreen, can also be considered celebrities. This results in a constructed hierarchy that undoubtedly creates conflict but, with business as a subject matter, it is important to note that the workplace also revolves around known hierarchies that determine how the various people involved relate to one another. This provides business entertainment formats with ample opportunity to uncover these relationships and display them onscreen for analysis.

For example, troubleshooter formats such as *Back to the Floor* and *Undercover Boss* are primarily concerned with the way in which staff members are often underappreciated by a senior management team far removed from the shop floor. They aim to reveal this through a conceit which sees bosses return to the sharp end of their businesses for a short period in an attempt to understand the work staff do and, in the case of the latter series, even reward them for their efforts.[3] Similarly, in an episode of *Mary Portas: Secret Shopper*, Portas uncovers that the Managing Director of the expanding British retail chain Pilot hires shop managers without meeting them first and when he finally visits one of his stores (accompanied by the camera crew), the astonished manager begins to cry due to the significance of the moment. These instances work as points of identification for viewers who are expected to not only recognize the problems created by the hierarchy of the workplace but also respond emotionally to the personal circumstances and reactions of the people onscreen.

Due to issues of access and filming constraints, large corporations tend to be avoided in business entertainment formats in favour of small to medium-sized enterprises that offer up the type of meaningful encounter described above. Another rich source of material for troubleshooter type programmes however are family businesses, which revolve around an entirely different set of relationships based on shared histories, sibling rivalry and family pecking order. Family businesses have thus formed the sole basis of certain series, such as *I'll Show them Who's Boss* and

---

3   It is notable that troubleshooter formats featuring bosses returning to the sharp end of their businesses never result in staff being fired onscreen. Instead, the focus is on the 'journey' taken by the boss and the rewards meted out to 'good' workers. This 'feelgood' approach is significant as it works to differentiate such formats from their more 'nasty' business gameshow counterparts.

Keep it in the Family (BBC2 2009), as well as featuring in programmes that look at a range of different companies. In most instances, issues of gender, favouritism and an inability to relinquish control feature heavily; all emotive subjects that are intended to be easily recognizable to audiences.

In contrast to the troubleshooter format however, the relationships in business gameshows are always highly constructed and the competitive structure leads to very different dynamics being played out than those within the everyday world of business. In *The Apprentice*, for example, the contestants are split into teams each week, originally according to gender, and must appoint a Project Manager. Again, this is an attempt to *impose* a hierarchy but, in this case, it is useful because it complicates the notion of competition. In order to win the task, the teams must demonstrate the ability to collaborate and work together, hopefully under the effective leadership of the Project Manager. However, to progress to the next level, they must also shine as individuals, a requirement that affects trust and social bonds between contestants and regularly leads to someone being set up for a fall (typically the Project Manager). As former contestant Claire Young explains, 'the psychology of *The Apprentice* is very interesting because you have to work as a team but constantly [try to] outshine each other' (interview with authors, 29 September 2009). Even when contestants enter a business gameshow as an already-established couple or team, such as in *Make Me a Million, The Restaurant* or *High Street Dreams*, the stress they are placed under can test even the strongest relationship with one partner often quitting as a result. Relationships are also put to the test in *Dragons' Den* when more than one person is pitching or when the creative drive behind a product has to interrupt negotiations in order to consult with whoever deals with the financial side of their business. This tends to reveal a tension between both parties that the investors seize on as a weakness before declaring 'I'm out'.

Risk

The pressure placed on existing relationships is only one example of the risks inherent in first, setting up your own business and second, taking part in a business entertainment format. As suggested by the title of the Channel 4 series *Risking it All*, people often leave the security of their jobs and put their homes and families on the line in order to pursue a dream of being their own boss and running a successful business. This presents a very attractive proposition for a television producer seeking to produce popular factual entertainment that engages a wide audience. Likewise, the contestants on business gameshows risk their existing way of life to take part in a televized competition in which they are afforded little security as they are continuously at risk of being eliminated depending on their performance. This is in addition to the fact that by appearing in a highly-formatted series, as opposed to the more documentary-based troubleshooter format, they open themselves up to intense media scrutiny. Risk and jeopardy make for compelling viewing however and when a business entertainment format is able to successfully convey what is at stake for the participants (in their real lives) it is more likely to connect with the audience emotionally.

Two such examples of this can be seen in the troubleshooting formats *Mary Queen of Shops*, broadcast on BBC2, and Channel 4's *Gerry's Big Decision*. In an episode of the former, Portas visits a struggling South London boutique run by a young couple, Becky and Max, who have three children and are currently around £10,000 in debt. Questioning Max's decision to give up paid employment elsewhere to help run the shop, Portas outlines the severity of the situation by stating 'You've got to make some money. A little bit of nothing is not going to feed your family.' As she goes on to explain that the business faces closure, the sequence ends with a close-up of Becky who wipes away tears and begins to break down as she states: 'I want to succeed. I've got three kids and I don't want to show them that the way is failure, cause it really isn't. And once I shut that door and put that closed sign up, I've failed.' Devoid of background music and quick cuts, the camera lingers on Becky as she explains the importance of her business to her and her family and contemplates their future. While it is impossible to say whether or not the business would have survived without the intervention of Portas and the production team, the suggestion is that this is the couple's only remaining option, an approach that seeks an emotional reaction from the audience.

The second example occurs in an episode of *Gerry's Big Decision* where Sir Gerry Robinson has to decide whether or not to invest some of his own money in Britain's oldest chair manufacturers, H J Berry & Sons, who are on the verge of going bust. After meeting with the company's owner to try and ascertain what is going wrong with the business, Sir Gerry sets up what is described on the voiceover as the 'ultimate sales test' for the company's Managing Director, John Woodruffe, to pitch the product to British department store House of Fraser. Visibly anxious before the pitch, Woodruffe expresses relief afterwards at how well it went. However, as he laughingly informs the crew that he is waiting for the cameras to stop filming so he can jump up and down, he suddenly wells up at the pressure of the situation and turns his back in an attempt to gather himself in private. This sequence occurs around halfway through the episode and demonstrates the very real stress Woodruffe is experiencing. Unfortunately, by the end of the programme, it is revealed that sales haven't picked up and that H J Berry & Sons have parted company with Woodruffe. With his Managing Director gone, all is not lost for the company's owner however as in the show's final 'reveal,' Sir Gerry announces that he still believes that the company has potential and, as such, he is willing to invest £1 million of his own money for a 60 percent share in the business, thus saving it from closure and, this time, bringing tears to the eye of its owner.

The £1 million deal struck in *Gerry's Big Decision* is by far the largest negotiated via a business television format but it nevertheless demonstrates what is at stake in such programming. By deciding to appear in the series, one man lost his job (and displayed his vulnerability onscreen) while another's company was provided a lifeline. With such high stakes, the audience is invited to experience the emotional journey along with the participants and this is possible due to the skilful way in which such programming can convey emotion through the use of close-ups and direct address. What is not shown however is that, like many of the deals struck on *Dragons' Den*, Robinson's offer did not come to fruition offscreen. It is perhaps more difficult to establish an emotional connection in the business gameshow however due to its links with reality television. This is because most forms of reality programming tend to be dependent on embarrassment and humiliation rather than establishing an emotional connection with the audience; except, it can be argued, in relation to the eventual winner. The risks posed in this instance are therefore related to the notion of reputation and the ability to prove oneself in terms of business skill. Yet, this can be difficult as many competitors are chosen more for their entertainment value than business ability.

Dominic Bird (interview with authors, 27 March 2009), executive producer of *Dragons' Den*, acknowledges that there can be a tension between entertainment values and documentary or journalistic integrity in such programming. Nonetheless, he maintains that far from placing people in the Den in order to produce embarrassment, the production team employs what he describes as a 'What if?' rule:

> There has to be something that you think, you know, they might not have all their figures, they might not be making profit – but the Dragon's just might go for this. What we wouldn't do is put someone in there just to humiliate them. Because actually. the Dragons don't find that funny, the Dragons would see through that and [the contestant] would be in and out in two minutes, and we probably wouldn't be able to use it.

Bird cites the success of Levi Roots (the creator of *Reggae Reggae Sauce* who entered the Den playing guitar and singing a jingle for his product) as one such example:

> He is a character; by rights, if you were just doing it on business plans alone, he should never have gone in the Den . But the feeling was he was just an amazing, inspirational person within the production who, you know, sort of deserved his moment in front of the Dragons.

With no real turnover and a poor grasp of figures, this was a risk that paid off for both the production team and Roots, who now has a thriving business.

It is, of course, less problematic to focus on the success stories while the 'losers' as it were are more likely to disappear from public view. There have, however, been a number of business show contestants that have objected to their treatment at the hands of both the production team, the wider media and, indeed the television viewing public, such as *The Apprentice* contestants Katie Hopkins and Lorraine Tighe. It is notable that for both of these women, their private lives and personal appearances were widely discussed in the tabloid press and indeed the issue of gender is something that we shall examine further in Chapter 6. In the meantime, we will turn our attention to the ways in which many of the ordinary people who take part in business entertainment formats often work to resist parts of the production process.

Resistance

The notion of resistance is integral to business entertainment formats. For example, both troubleshooter-based programming and business gameshows revolve around people being confronted by experts in their field who analyse and critique their business or their business skills before either informing them of what must be changed in order to succeed or simply firing them. In most instances, this invites some sort of struggle, as those who have built a business from scratch or who believe they have a proven track record in business find it hard to accept that an outside expert may know best. While this is understandable (and may well be correct in many instances), at its heart lies a contradiction, as the ordinary people who take part in business entertainment formats willingly put themselves forward knowing what the process will involve. Of course, this is not necessarily the case for those involved in the first series of an original format, but for those who follow a template has been set and therefore there is some sort of understanding of what will occur: 'Reality TV is eager to find "ordinary" people who embrace mediation, and who are only too willing to meet the camera's gaze head on' (Holmes 2010: 259–260). It is here that the 'casting' process becomes important, as much of the success of reality television depends on finding strong characters to take part and either pitting them against, or positioning them within a group of, other equally strong personalities.

As explained by Dovey (2008: 247), in a manner that echoes our argument throughout this chapter, lightly-constructed documentaries and highly-formatted reality gameshows might be best understood as 'simulations' (a definition derived from computer applications). Dovey (2008: 253) goes on to say how 'the majority of popular factual programmes are now based on events that have been set up and constructed by the producers themselves. On television the constructed documentary form has become dominant, its factual quality guaranteed only by the casting of non-actors in the producers' scenarios'. Although participants are cast to fill certain roles in the hope of creating drama and narrative then, an unknown element is nevertheless introduced to the process as characters act in unexpected ways when placed within the simulation. This is something that cannot be foreseen by all parties and indeed is where what we term 'resistance' often comes into play.

For example, as previously explained, the notion of resistance became a point of difference for the series *Property Ladder*, as participants regularly rejected Sarah Beeny's expert advice until the recession hit. While Beeny amiably accepted this with a slight roll of the eyes (and often reserved her sharper comments for the show's voiceover), the appeal of Gordon Ramsay as a troubleshooter, on the other hand, is based on his aggressive style of management and frequent use of expletives. *Ramsay's Kitchen Nightmares* is a much more confrontational programme therefore, with Ramsay consistently battling with the participants as they often try to resist his suggestions. In this sense, it can be argued that the series has much in common with perceived understandings of reality television (and therefore business gameshows) where the entertainment aspect of the show is insult-driven rather than based on offering constructive criticism. As such, the contestants have to be equally strong characters in order to withstand the troubleshooting process.

In the interviews and focus groups we conducted for this project however, *Ramsay's Kitchen Nightmares* was often singled out as being the business series that put forward the most practical advice, with Ramsay always offering simple solutions to make a restaurant more commercial (this does not mean that his suggestions do not face resistance however). As we discuss later in the book, these reactions to Ramsay by television executives and viewers can largely be attributed to his vocational status as a Michelin-starred chef and, until recently, successful restaurateur but it is significant that *Ramsay's Kitchen Nightmares* was not re-commissioned by Channel 4 in 2009, the same year that it was revealed that the chef's own business interests had run into financial difficulty.

The success of BBC2's *Mary Queen of Shops* is similarly based on Mary Portas's reputation as a retail and brand communications expert and in the first two series of the show she skilfully exhibited her extensive knowledge of fashion retail. The production team then sought to diversify the format however, first by taking on charity shops and then independent retailers. Much of the appeal of the subsequent *Mary Queen of Charity Shops* was seeing Portas out of her comfort zone. While still showcasing her knowledge of retail, Portas faced a different set of challenges as this time she was primarily dealing with elderly ladies volunteering their time for a good cause rather than people who had set up their own business due to a passion for the fashion industry. When the charity shop staff resisted her suggestions therefore, it wasn't their livelihoods at stake and she couldn't threaten them with impending closure or the sack. This generation and culture clash made for entertaining viewing with Portas's intervention eventually considered successful, albeit on a small scale.

Her next series, focusing on independent retailers, did not always reach a satisfying conclusion however. In one episode, in which Portas tried to turn around the fortunes of a struggling bakery, the owner rejected her suggestions before finally asking the cameras to stop filming and ejecting the crew from the premises. Angela Maher, the owner of the bakery, told Portas 'You don't know anything about this trade' before continually informing her that she herself had 36 years of experience in the bakery business. The struggle between the two women made for a tense episode that ended in the breakdown of the relationship and no hope of a makeover for the shop. Yet, Maher (Bakeryinfo 2010) has since stated that her shop was not in trouble and that her only reason for taking part in the series was because when approached by the production company, she was 'given the impression that [the] programme was to be a celebration of small businesses bucking the trend in the recession, while offering some advice and ideas for the future. There really was no mention of failing businesses or total reinvention'. This calls into question the assumption that people know what they are agreeing to take part in when they sign up for documentary or reality programming and, indeed, it demonstrates that in terms of production techniques, the troubleshooter format has much in common with its business gameshow counterpart. Essentially, this type of programming relies on the notion of being disciplined, with 'presenters, instructors, supervisors, wardens or the police using their powers to get the participants to do something that they otherwise wouldn't do' (Pinseler 2010: 140). But, as in the case of Maher, the simulated nature of the process nevertheless allows space for the 'unexpected' to occur (Dovey 2008).

Of course, in terms of resistance, participants can also use it to their own advantage. For example, many contestants in *Dragons' Den* turn down offers of investment, partly because the terms are not suitable but also because they understand the value of their appearance on the show as a public relations exercise. By generating interest in their products or existing businesses through the mass reach of a television series such as *Dragons' Den*, they can secure other deals offscreen rather than accepting those put forward by the Dragons (this often occurs even when the Dragons decide not to invest). Likewise, as we have already noted, part of the problem of a continuing business gameshow such as *The Apprentice* is that the annual success of the format works to attract people who simply want to appear on television, or develop a media career, rather than those who genuinely want a job with Lord Sugar. This results in contestants resisting the rules of the game in order to stand out from the crowd and be recognized primarily for their personality and performative skills rather than their business ability. Yet, it is not only those who are 'hired' on *The Apprentice* who can be considered 'winners', as many capitalize on the (positive or negative) publicity from the show to cultivate media careers for themselves. This includes, amongst others, Saira Khan (presenter of CBBC's *Beat the Boss*); James Max (LBC Radio presenter); Kate Walsh (presenter of Channel 5's *OK! TV*) and indeed Katie Hopkins (who went on to appear as a contestant on ITV's *I'm a Celebrity ... Get Me Out of Here!* in 2007).

Conclusion

In this part of the book we have been concerned with the textual nature of business entertainment formats and, as such, have examined narrative structure, the representations of entrepreneurs put forward and the key visual characteristics employed across a range of programming. We have also demonstrated how such programming occurs within a continuum that results in two strands of business entertainment formats dominating the television schedule in the United Kingdom. These are the troubleshooter format, which can be understood as lightly-constructed documentary, and the business gameshow, derived from emergence of more highly-formatted reality television. In each instance, although business forms the backdrop to such programming, we have shown that there is a focus on creating drama and narrative in an attempt to connect with audiences at an emotional level. This is achieved by situating business entertainment formats in recognizable sectors or within a competitive framework whilst also invoking concepts such as risk, relationships and resistance. In the following chapter, we turn our attention to the ways in which entrepreneurship is represented across a variety of media and how the narratives created by television shape discourses that are often utilized by entrepreneurs themselves.

Chapter 4

Enterprise, Society and Cultural Change

For the forty years up to 1980 the British had shown a lack of interest in money-making which puzzled foreign visitors ... The British disdain for money had long roots, going back to the first reactions against Victorian vulgarities, and reinforced by the imperial tradition of service and by two world wars which underlined military and moral values.

Anthony Sampson (1989: 23).

I want Britain to be a nation of entrepreneurs, a nation where talent and ability flourish.

Tony Blair, Prime Minister, House of Commons, 15 May 1997.

So far in the book we have examined the key role that changes in the television industry have played in shaping the range of representations around enterprise that dominate factual television entertainment. In this chapter we want to place the debate about television and its role in shaping cultural attitudes within a broader framework. We do this by switching our focus to the political and socio–economic position of entrepreneurship within the British experience. Starting with some historical context regarding the position of the entrepreneur within political discourse, we then examine some of the key narratives that have framed how entrepreneurs view themselves. We also investigate the ways in which a higher media profile, often driven by television, has altered the political profile and access to policy shapers and makers that these particular entrepreneurs have enjoyed as their celebrity status has increased. This specific aspect of the television entrepreneur is analyzed in more detail later in the book in Chapter 7.

This chapter will look at the central role that television and the media more generally play in shaping what we have come to understand by the terms entrepreneurship and the entrepreneur. We consider to what extent cultural attitudes to entrepreneurship are changing and whether these are reflected in economic activity while also questioning whether the term itself has become so ubiquitous in public discourse as to have lost its original meaning.

Historical Discourses of Entrepreneurship

There is a cliché that entrepreneurs are born, not made. If I think back on my experience, I know this is not entirely true. Yes, all entrepreneurs share certain personality traits, a high level of confidence and high levels of optimism, energy and determination. But the people who become entrepreneurs come in all ages, shapes and sizes, and their entrepreneurial skills vary considerably.

Sir Ronald Cohen (2008: 4).

As we noted in the opening chapter, there has been a range of attempts over the years to define the term entrepreneur and its attendant qualities. What we argue here is that rather that getting involved in what can prove to be a rather sterile debate around terminology, it is more insightful and instructive to examine how society defines the term at particular moments and what this process of defining tells us about the broader social and economic context and attitudes that exists to business. A related area of debate in entrepreneurial studies has been around the role of nature versus nurture in shaping and creating entrepreneurs. This is not of course a dichotomy specific to those concerned with how to create more entrepreneurs, but it does find itself mobilized in a number of cognate debates around whether there is such a thing as 'natural' talent or ways in which talent can be achieved through practice and training (Gladwell 2008).

Clearly, certain personality traits can enhance entrepreneurial development, as Cohen notes above, but the environment within which these traits get nurtured and honed seems to us to remain crucial. Entrepreneur, business angel and former *Dragons' Den* investor Doug Richard (interview with authors, 2 June 2009) lived and worked in the United Kingdom for almost a decade and feels that one of the key factors shaping entrepreneurial activity is the broader socio-cultural context:

> If I pick a 25-year-old entrepreneur, pluck him out of Glasgow, pluck him out of Cambridge and pluck him out of UCLA [University of California Los Angeles] – they are way more similar than they are different. And that's the bottom line. When it comes to entrepreneurs, they are precisely the same. The difference is the place.

The geographical location, Richard argues, means that the California-based 25-year-old will operate in a significantly more receptive environment that supports the entrepreneur than his British counterpart who, according to Richard, will find themselves dealing with more risk averse institutions.

Of course this does not negate the importance of personalilty traits in high achieving entrepreneurs. In his overview of the central role played by business in British society, BBC Business Editor Robert Peston (2008: 23) notes in relation to British entrepreneur Sir Philip Green how, 'the Philip Green story shows that natural flair accounts for the difference between an entrepreneur who makes a few bob and one who makes a few billion pounds. And indeed, some of that flair may be genetic – which is sobering'. Others, such as historian John F. Wilson (1995: 2–3) in his history of the evolution of business culture in Britain from 1720–1994, have argued that changing cultural attitudes towards business are absolutely crucial in shaping the broader 'business culture' of any society at any given moment. This point is echoed by Landes (1999) who suggests that the trajectory of economic development is intimately connected with the broader culture milieu that either encourages and normalizes development within particular societies or reproduces deeply rooted cultural barriers to entrepreneurial activity.

In his review of historical writing about business culture, Wilson (1995: 18) argues that two dominant ways of thinking about entrepreneurship have emerged; although he fully acknowledges that there remains considerable disagreement 'about exactly what constitutes an entrepreneur'. Key to the first discourse is the work of Schumpeter (1934) who helped define the entrepreneur as being central in the economic process, driving innovation in a manner to disrupt existing economic patterns and relationships. Schumpeter also viewed the entrepreneur as crucial in commercializing ideas and not necessarily being the inventor of an idea or product. Indeed one of the criticisms leveled at programmes such as *Dragons Den* is that many of the entrepreneurs pitching ideas on the show are inventors rather than exploiters of existing products, with the latter better representing reality. At its core, the notion of entrepreneurial innovation is a central part of what Schumpeter (1942) calls the creative destruction of capitalist economies.

The other discourse, articulated by Casson (2005), views the entrepreneur's intervention as less dramatic to the economic system. While it may be still innovatory, it is also more likely to be imitative of existing practice and thus implement only marginal changes and shifts in the development of a company. The Ewing Marion Kauffman Foundation, an entrepreneurial think tank, also fundamentally distinguishes between 'innovative' and 'replicative' entrepreneurship (*The Economist* 12 March 2009). Thus, across this scale, there are those entrepreneurs who make a significant impact in the broader economic system by driving innovation and major change (often creating large businesses in the process), through to those entrepreneurs whose innovation lies not in new inventions but in sustaining and growing businesses on a smaller more piecemeal manner. Across differing entrepreneurs we can see elements of the qualities outlined by Schumpeter (1934, 1942). However for the majority of entrepreneurs their work is more likely to be on the scale discussed by Casson (2005) and defined as 'replicative'.

For many contemporary entrepreneurs, there is also a sense that the increasingly ubiquitous nature of the term requires a certain simplicity when analyzing this area. For example, former *Dragons' Den* investor and technology entrepreneur Doug Richard (interview with authors, 2 June 2009) feels that 'entrepreneurship is a very long word for a very short activity. It is about somebody wanting to start a business. That's what it is, by formal definition, and we complicate it at our peril'.

Enterprise in UK PLC

In its major examination of entrepreneurship in 2009, *The Economist* (12 March 2009) argues that the last 30 years has seen a global (if uneven) sea-change in attitudes towards entrepreneurial activity and characterizes this as part of a wider shift from managerial capitalism to a more entrepreneurial model of capitalism.

At the core of this shift is a drive to innovate which has been facilitated by technological change, the mobility of communicative technology, the breaking of the social contract between business and the employer (or rather the notion of a job for life), generational shifts in attitude to entrepreneurship and the moving of this concept to the mainstream of economic thinking among policy makers and governments of all political persuasions. This is indicative of what we have noted in Chapter 1 as the hegemony of neoliberal thinking regarding economic development.

Structural and cultural context are however still crucial, and thus America remains a 'beacon of entrepreneurialism ... America has found the transition to a more entrepreneurial economy easier than its competitors because entrepreneurialism is so deeply rooted in its history' (*The Economist* 12 March 2009). This may well remain the case despite the worst economic crisis being experienced in the United States since the 1930s, although others such as economist Scott A. Shane (2008: 7) argue that 'America is becoming less entrepreneurial; a smaller proportion of the population starts businesses today than they did in 1910'. For Shane, part of the problem in the United States is that cultural myths (or illusions as he also calls them) around entrepreneurial activity have become so rooted in the country that they are blocking public policy thinking regarding the stimulation of the economy.

This point reinforces the key role played by cultural attitudes towards entrepreneurship that can be deeply ingrained and also embedded in broader legal and political structures. For historian Hywel Williams (2006: 93), a particular variant of what he views as the English (rather than British) entrepreneurial development is a discourse that still views the engineer or inventor as 'a figure of fun'; something he links to the particular infatuation with professional elites that exists in British political culture.[1] In his financial history of money, Niall Ferguson (2008) also examines how broader cultural and legal frameworks shape the role of money in society. For example, with regard to the issue of bankruptcy, Ferguson (2008: 60–61) notes how,

> The ability to walk away from unsustainable debts and start all over again is one of the distinctive quirks of American capitalism. There were no debtors' prisons in the United States in the early 1800s, at a time when English debtors could end up languishing in jail for years ... people in the United States appear to regard bankruptcy as an 'unalienable right' ... The theory is that American law exists to encourage entrepreneurship – to facilitate the creation of new businesses. And that means giving people a break when their plans go wrong, even for the second time, thereby allowing the natural-born risk-takers to learn through trial and error until they finally figure out how to make that million. After all, today's bankrupt might well be tomorrow's successful entrepreneur.

---

1   This discourse is regularly reproduced on television programmes such as *Dragons' Den* and was much in evidence around the 2011 winner of *The Apprentice*, Tom Pellereau, who described himself as an inventor.

While many parts of Europe remain more circumspect about the centrality of enterprise in social and economic development, cultural and political change has nevertheless occurred since the late 1980s, which has seen much European Commission political rhetoric embrace enterprise (through the Directorate General Enterprise and Industry) as a driver of the economy.

The Rise, Fall and Rise of the British Entrepreneur 1970–2011

In his 1996 work *Company Man,* Anthony Sampson explores the decline of the corporation and its attendant culture that shaped much of the industrial experience of both the United Kingdom and United States for a large part of the nineteenth and twentieth century. Sampson (1996: x) examines the 'social transformations behind industrial developments' and, in particular, the social and cultural impact that the collapse of corporate security has had on re-shaping the lives of people in the workplace. To this end, his study astutely captures a moment in the development of new business models and modes of work that became a seemingly routine part of workplace culture in the United Kingdom from the mid-1990s onwards. While the antecedents of this shift predated this period, Sampson is particularly interested in the emergence of what he understands as short-term, flexible, small scale businesses that view marketing themselves within an increasingly technologically connected global marketplace as a central part of their business. This shift from larger, more paternalistic organizations offering a designated career path to small scale, often short lived business entities perfectly captures some of the changes taking place within the television production sector in the United Kingdom during this decade. While Hang and Weezel (2005) argue that entrepreneurial skills have been central in the development of the media industries, Hoag and Seo (2005) go further and suggest that the role of entrepreneurship in the media industries has in fact been underestimated by economists in terms of the key function it plays in the culture of both for-profit and non-commercial media organizations. Indeed, in the United Kingdom, Born's (2005) study of the BBC documents the institutional struggles and challenges the public service corporation faced in attempts to reinvent itself in the face of political and economic change.

While Sampson does not directly address the television sector in his analysis, the parallels between broader structural changes in the economy and the industry are striking. At the core of Sampson's thesis is a concern with understanding the shifting perception of the role of entrepreneurship in shaping economic development and generating wealth along with the centrality of money as a driver of fundamental social change. He is fascinated by the manner in which particular forms of entrepreneurial activity come to define key economic and political moments and become part of broader narratives that both shape and are shaped by dominant political and economic thinking. Thus, the rise of corporate culture which shaped much of the twentieth century business landscape (and its subsequent decline and reinvention in the latter part of that century) are shaped by shifting ideas and values around the function and role of the entrepreneur in society.

For example, Sampson draws an historical analogy with the economic position of the railways in the United Kingdom and the role of those who shaped them in the nineteenth and late twentieth century. The nineteenth-century expansion embodied the function that entrepreneurial activity played at the core of an expanding economy. Yet, by way of contrast, Sampson argues (1996: ix):

> The most successful chairman and chief executives in Britain depict themselves as entrepreneurs and wealth-creators; but their achievements are too often in the opposite direction – cutting back and selling off the great structures their industrial forefathers built up. The history of the railways in Britain provides a kind of caricature of the changing role of entrepreneurship. [They] have made quick new fortunes, not by extending services or tracks, but by reducing staff, selling off rolling stock or 'rationalising' timetables.

Sampson makes two related points that are of interest. First he suggests that the 1990s saw many of these practices being justified by drawing on American economic parallels and second, he argues throughout the book that it is actually America in which a more innovative entrepreneurial culture has flourished, specifically around computers and telecommunications. Over ten years on, both these points remain pertinent when a special report into Entrepreneurship by *The Economist* (12 March 2009) states that 'since the Regan-Thatcher revolution of the 1980s, governments of almost every ideological stripe have embraced entrepreneurship' before going on to point out however that 'the world's greatest producers of entrepreneurs continues to be America' (*The Economist,* 12 March 2009). One issue that Sampson's book also highlights is the differing discourses and mediated narratives that emerged in the 1980s and 1990s around the position of the entrepreneur as an outsider or maverick, challenging the existing business infrastructure, and which is viewed more positively by the public for this often mythical anti-establishment status. The movement of a high profile media entrepreneur such as Richard Branson into the British rail network with Virgin Trains can be seen to encapsulate this shift during this time.

As noted in the quote from Sampson (1989) at the beginning of this chapter, by the 1970s in Britain, perceptions about entrepreneurship had long become disconnected from the heyday of Victorian entrepreneurial activity. The Victorian period was viewed as part of the industrial history of Britain, but with little to offer in terms of contemporary insight into the problems facing an economy that by the 1970s appeared to be lurching from one economic crisis to the next (see Sandbrook 2010). As we discuss below, the 1980s saw Victorian Britain being reimaged as part of a neoliberal political philosophy that established a political hegemony in thinking about the economy and wealth creation. In their biography of retail entrepreneur Sir Philip Green, Lansley and Forrester (2006: 21) note that when he first went about setting up a business in the 1970s, it was at a time when

'Britain had been short of entrepreneurs for as long as anyone could remember'. Indeed Sampson (2008: 208) recalls such a situation in Britain in the early 1980s and notes how, 'After years of commercial restrictions there were initially only a very few genuine entrepreneurs in Britain, most of them were foreign born'.

The 1980s were an important decade in changing British attitudes towards money and the creation of wealth. For Sampson (1989: 3) this was the decade that saw the rise of the financial and service sectors of the economy and in which money became detached from goods or trade. The return to supply-led economics, with its underlying philosophy of the trickle down impact of wealth, gained currency both in the United Kingdom and the United States. At the core of this was a celebration of wealth and while this has always been part of the entrepreneurial spirit of American capitalism it secured a new hegemony in popular culture and political discourse during this decade. In the United Kingdom the broad level of political consensus around wealth creation is quite striking if one considers that the top rate of income tax was 75 per cent under successive Conservative post war governments (rising to 83 per cent under the Labour governments of Harold Wilson and James Callaghan). Under the Thatcher government of 1979, this dropped to first 60 per cent and eventually 40 per cent and it was a Thatcherite free market philosophy which set the broader political agenda within which shifting public perceptions about the role and position of money in society took place.

The Discourse of Enterprise

Enterprise and debates about fostering a more entrepreneurial culture moved into the mainstream of political policy thinking during the 1980s. Lord Young (1990) recalls the various battles to introduce more business facing policies during his time at the Department of Trade and Industry, as well as efforts to promote enterprise through educational contacts and links. Young (1990: 261) was instrumental in creating the Enterprise Initiative in 1988 that aimed to get British business management prepared for the advent of the single European market in 1992. As part of this media campaign he enrolled the help of five entrepreneurs to appear in promotional material. These included Alan Sugar, Richard Branson and Sir John Harvey-Jones before they enjoyed any television profile of note (and before the former two were rewarded with knighthoods in 2000).

As Marr notes however (2008: 381), despite what Thatcherism came to represent, and its overall legacy was to place consumption at the centre of British cultural life, the original goals of Thatcher herself were really about re-connecting Britain with its Victorian values. The 1980s were to be the decade when images of the Victorian age would be mobilized extensively in both British political and economic discourse. For Marr (2008: 382), Margaret Thatcher, 'wanted to remoralize society, creating a nation whose Victorian values were expressed through secure marriages, self-reliance and savings, restraint, good neighbourliness, hard work ... Yet Thatcherism heralded an age of unparalleled consumption, credit, show-off wealth, quick bucks and sexual libertinism'. Ironically the Victorian age continues to be drawn upon as a period that still offers lessons for contemporary economic and social thinking. The new century, which has seen a growing interest around the ability of firms to achieve commercial success while displaying a level of social responsibility, has also seen 'enlightened entrepreneurs' from the Victorian age, such as Andrew Carnegie, Joseph Rowntree and George Cadbury being reexamined for the lessons they can offer contemporary business philosophy (Bradley 2007).

The explosion in financial services, in part facilitated by the City's deregulation in the late 1980s and the privatizing of nationalized sectors of the economy, meant that issues around private finance, pensions, stocks and shares all began to have greater prominence in public discourse. Marr (2008: 429) notes how privatization 'would become the major idea exported from Britain in modern times'. For Sampson, his 1989 book *The Midas Touch* was an attempt to capture this decade of change in which the financial and service sectors of the economy steamed ahead, while manufacturing was increasingly viewed as part of a dying old economy. In the United States, Sampson (1989: 16) charts the rise of conspicuous consumption, where people like Donald Trump became representative of the new rich who 'advertise their opinions and life-stories with an openness and individualism unlike their predecessors'. He also notes how, unlike previous American entrepreneurs, the new 1980s breed was keen to use the media to enhance their profile through the publication of memoirs and self-help books. As we examine later in this chapter, this pattern has been replicated in recent years in the United Kingdom, were the new generation of television entrepreneurs all have accompanying books deals which help to sustain their public profile.

By the end of the 1980s, Sampson (1989: 24) argues that 'The British now found fewer arguments against money-values, as socialism lost its appeal and the Churches became more interested in fund-raising and justifying their role in the market-place'. The media and newspapers in particular also played a key role in this process as they both reflected and reinforced the increasing interest in money and financial matters that existed among their readers. The print sector saw a massive increase in the space devoted to personal and professional finance (including shares, investments and consumer rights) and newspapers expanded their coverage of the money and business across both the tabloid and broadsheet sectors of the press.

If the 1980s marked the breakdown of the post-war political consensus and a higher public profile of the role of business and wealth creation in society, then even into the 1990s some entrepreneurs still felt that they suffered from a poor public image. For example, entrepreneur David Hall (1999: vii), whose research involves speaking and working with entrepreneurs from across the United Kingdom, argues that:

> We can trace it back to the elitist nature of British society a hundred or so years ago, when being in 'trade' was regarded as socially inferior to working in the professions or owning a country estate ... Although we've made great strides in

the UK over the past 10 years to make business attractive to the brightest and best, the stigma still regrettably sticks. Entrepreneurs in Britain are too often equated with racketeers and spivs, epitomized by the British TV character Arthur Daley. Arthur thrives in a world of dodgy deals and hoodwinked customers ... Stereotyping of this sort is regrettable and needs eradicating.

To what extent that this view remains valid today is more open to debate. Britain under the New Labour government elected in 1997, presided over an economic boom that would last for a decade and certainly both consolidated and then extended the rhetoric of enterprise across government departments, often tied into other neoliberal discourses around creativity, innovation and the knowledge economy. Fairclough (2000: 34) in his study of the language of New Labour notes how from early on Prime Minister Tony Blair was keen to 're-value' the term entrepreneur. In so doing he wanted to evoke positive associations with 'entrepreneur' and link it with being creative, innovative and initiative taking (Blair 2011: 116). Also, crucially Blair argued that these were deeply rooted British attributes that had lain dormant in some form and under New Labour would be rediscovered and upgraded for the new millennium. As such, he shifted the political lexicon to one that talked less of 'industry', 'business' or 'commerce' but rather the importance of 'enterprise' as a universal driver of the economy. In other ways this political shift in rhetoric connected with other discourses around a more modern and meritocratic Britain in which enterprise was be allowed to flourish.

During this time particular patterns of political attitudes to wealth creation and notions of financial equality became part of the new hegemony. In his analysis of the relationship between financial and political power during this period, Robert Peston (2008: 7) argues that:

> The really striking phenomenon under New Labour has been the triumph of the super-rich. To be clear, it is a worldwide phenomenon and not something unique to the UK. But the presence on British soil of a disproportionate number of immensely wealthy people, who are becoming wealthier by the minute, has been encouraged by Tony Blair and Gordon Brown.

For Peston, the New Labour government presided over a moment in British history that saw financial inequality in the United Kingdom grow again after a period under the previous Conservative administration in which that gap had narrowed.

These changes in attitude towards notions of wealth creation and the entrepreneurs so feted by governments was to an extent reflected in the shifting attitudes of key media outlets to the more general issue of the reporting of business and the financial world. Business journalist and broadcaster Jeff Randall started his journalism career in newspapers before becoming the BBC's first Business Editor in 2001. He was directly appointed by the new Director-General of the BBC Greg Dyke, who was keen to make sure that business issues were much more centrally addressed by the Corporation (Kelly and Boyle 2010: 5). Randall (interview with authors, 11 January 2007) argues that it was the print media rather than television that began to reflect these broader social, cultural and economic shifts that took root in the 1980s:

> There has been a cultural shift in attitudes to business and in many ways TV was slow to catch on to this shift. In the 1970s profit was a bad word. If you made a profit you exploited people. The representations were businessmen like Arthur Daley or Del Boy, or fat cats clipping boys around the ear as they were sent into the factory. There were no normal people in business. I think this was how the media classes wanted to see business. It changes in the 1980s, with the Thatcherite revolution [making] business acceptable and desirable and business moved from the business pages to the front pages. And I think newspapers were quicker to pick up on this than television. You see a growth in personal finance issues across the press; the *Sun* for example has had a business editor for years. Newspapers take business seriously.

> Why was TV so slow to react? It was part cultural, and also TV can be a clunky medium dictated to by pictures. It's hard work getting the pictures. People were interested, newspapers had worked this out. 9/11 had an impact. [Broadcasters] worked out that business news was popular. Philip Green and the takeover of Marks and Spencers, who couldn't be interested in that, it's better than a soap opera, it's for real. I tried to tell the story through the people, not the issues. If you make it dry, then you will get the audience you deserve.

For others the trajectory of the entrepreneur in Britain has been more circumspect and remains profoundly shaped by the broader historical contours of British economic and political development. Williams (2006: 92) argues that the particular power structure of British elites, and its ability to reproduce around professional elites, has meant that British entrepreneurship has shied away from 'the long and slow grind of building up industrial and manufacturing business within a world market.' Rather, he argues it tends to look for the short return and is keen to cut corners in this process. Williams (2006: 92) also argues that the mobilizing of rhetoric around the supposed entrepreneurial zeal of the Victorians that found political favour in the 1980s has now 'yielded to uncertain millennial platitudes about "technology", "innovation" and "creativity"'. Much of it, he (2006: 92) suggests is created by and given credence by a political professional class 'with little experience of such realities'.

This section has provided a brief outline of the broader political culture within which the entrepreneur in the United Kingdom both operates and is talked about within political discourse. The next section of this chapter examines the range of narratives that are constructed around the entrepreneur from the stories they tell about themselves, and also recognizes that since the mid-1990s one of the biggest changes has been the growing importance of the media industry itself in this broader process of promotion.

Narratives of the Entrepreneur: The Stories they Tell ...

The media has increasingly become the key way through which companies and individuals have built profile and brand identity among the public. Guthey, Clark and Jackson (2009: 8) argue that this is not a new process: 'Business figures are not newcomers to the game of celebrity ... they helped make up the rules of the game in the first place'. They cite John D. Rockefeller, Andrew Carnegie and J.P. Morgan as some of the groundbreakering businesspeople who helped shape the practice that would come to be called corporate public relations.

One of the most high profile entrepreneurs within the United Kingdom over the last 30 years has been Sir Richard Branson. Indeed many entrepreneurs regularly cite Branson as a role model, and in our own research he was universally identified across all focus groups as the person most closely associated with the term 'entrepreneur' (see Chapter 7). For serial entrepreneur Stelios Haji-loannou, Branson and the way he has built the Virgin brand over a number of decades provided key elements in the business model he adopted when creating and building the low cost EasyJet airline. In one interview, Branson (Davidson 2002) even indicates that he feels something of a father-son relationship with Stelios, who he has kept in regular contact with as his career has developed. At the core of this has been associating one key individual with the public facing image of the company. Branson (2008: 38) is clear that perceptions of the entrepreneur in British society have shifted over the last number of decades:

> In the 1970s, when we set up Virgin Records, no one in the UK used the word 'entrepreneur' anymore. Or if they did, they considered it something unsavory. A businessman running a number of firms was seen as a 'chancer' – the television comic stereotype was Del Boy, the wheeler-dealer on the outside of the law, in *Only Fools and Horses*, or *Minder's* Arthur Daley, the gin-drinking spiv played brilliantly by George Cole ... The UK media's view of business people has changed – but not nearly enough.

Branson himself is clear that his own definition of an entrepreneur and what entrepreneurship is about does not always chime with the popular perception of this activity. Indeed his definition is not one that you would expect to see in an academic textbook on the subject, but rather reflects the narratives he himself has helped to construct around the Virgin brand identity. For Branson (2008: 39) then,

> [entrepreneurship] is not about getting one over on the customer. It's not about working on your own. It's not about looking out for number one. It's not necessarily about making a lot of money. It is *absolutely* not about letting work take over your life. On the contrary, it's about turning what excites you in life into capital, so you can do more of it and move forward with it. I think entrepreneurship is our natural state – a big adult word that probably boils down to something much more obvious like 'playfulness' [original emphasis].

Of course Branson is acutely media aware, and indeed according to Guthey, Clark and Jackson (2009: 2) he sets aside 25 per cent of his time for public relations activities.

What has happened in the United Kingdom then since the beginning of the noughties has been a change in the mainstream media's willingness to engage with key business personalities often as a form of shorthand in making sense of complex business issues. This is part of a wider process of personalizing complex news issues that is not unique to business related news. But also on the back of the programmes discussed in Chapter 2, it creates a platform for a generation of entrepreneurs to gain media traction through their supposedly expert comment. In addition, a 24-7, always-on media culture thrives on comment and opinion, while an interconnected media infrastructure both promotes celebrity as well as commodifies it through books and other media types of content. In this way the United Kingdom echoes what Sampson (1989) identified in the late 1980s in the United States, where through books (self-help and autobiographies) and television appearances, the business guru enjoyed a high media and political profile.

With the exception of Sir Richard Branson and also Lord Sugar, who has long satisfied Guthey, Clark and Jackson's (2009) description of a 'business celebrity' (due to a high media profile gained through public relations campaigns surrounding his Amstrad business in the 1980s and his time spent throughout the 1990s as Chairman of British football club Tottenham Hotspur), television programming has served as an entry point for each of these entrepreneurs into the media landscape and thus the broader public consciousness. While they have undoubtedly achieved a certain level of success within their own sectors, it is not the case that they have been feted by their peers for their exceptional skillset and knowledge or have reached the upper echelons of the international business world. Indeed, there is an argument that suggests if these individuals were at the top of their game business-wise then their time and energy would be devoted to their offscreen projects rather than television programming. As Chris Gorman (interview with authors, 31 March 2010), the serial entrepreneur and founder of DX Communications who has also appeared as a mentor in the business entertainment format *Make Me a Million* for Channel 4, suggests:

> I think the more successful entrepreneurs don't have a TV profile. You won't find that many of the really successful ones ... I mean Alan Sugar is probably the highest, the most successful of the ones with a TV profile, but he hasn't actually grown anything since he started the TV stuff – that was all done beforehand. If anything, some of his business has gone backwards since then. I can't think of a sector where somebody who has got a media profile is doing much better than those without.

Instead, what television entrepreneurs demonstrate is the potential to cultivate first a successful televisual image and then wider media profile that can be exploited by cultural intermediaries into an individual brand, selling the aforementioned television programmes along with business books, biographies, public speaking engagements and even political ideas. This then feeds into their own business interests at the same time as establishing them as a celebrity in which their public and private personas are increasingly blurred.

Brand Building and Myth Making

As Guthey, Clark and Jackson (2009) convincingly argue, public relations (PR) is integral in understanding the narrative of corporate culture more generally and also in explaining what Wernick (1991) has called the age of 'promotional culture'. Certainly the rise of the celebrity entrepreneur has been underpinned by the centrality of public relations and media management agencies in shaping media discourses and developing the individual as a 'brand identity'. Again, it is worth noting that this isn't a new process. Miller and Dinan (2008) document the rise of business and corporate PR influence on both media and public policy from its professional origins in the United States, Britain and Germany at the beginning of the twentieth century. They also note how in the last few decades, the United Kingdom has seen an explosion in PR and lobbying agencies all shaping public, political and media agendas during a period of massive extension in media provision and outlets. They, along with others (Davies 2008, Hargreaves 2003), are critical of the extent to which journalism has generally become symbiotically meshed with public relations and wider media management strategy. It is this combination of expanded 24-7 media and public relations influence that has facilitated and helped sustain the celebrity industry that has evolved in recent years.

Using the media to help create a brand identity or promote business interests has a long history across British popular culture. As we have explained, Sir Richard Branson has assiduously used media influence and public relations to establish his myriad businesses and in so doing has himself become synonymous with the Virgin brand. At one level, Branson's (Branson 2008: 63) strategy has been clear: 'Publicity is absolutely critical ... You have to be willing to use yourself, as well as your advertising budget, to get your brand on the map. A good PR story is infinitely more effective than a full-page ad, and a damn sight cheaper.' For others such as Bower (2008), the Virgin publicity machine has also worked hard throughout Branson's career to avoid or deflect difficult questions regarding some of his business activities and as a result his public profile and popularity remains high. The political and public policy dimension to the rise of the British celebrity entrepreneur is examined in more detail in Chapter 7, where we examine the access to political networks that media profile helps to cultivate.

There also remains a strong element of media mythology around the 'rags-to-riches' motif of many of the narratives closely associated with the modern day entrepreneur. Some of these discourses come from television's engagement with real life material or in the tales entrepreneurs tell about themselves through the media. From Sahar and Bobby Hashemi's (2002) account of the building of the

Coffee Republic brand to Duncan Bannatyne's (2006) story of building a business portfolio, the 'anyone can do it' discourse is paramount (the title of both books). For others such as Scott A. Shane (2008: 160) the problem with such broader cultural myths is that they bedevil the policy discussion of the role of entrepreneurs in society: 'We need to change the way we think about entrepreneurship. Our collective belief that the typical entrepreneur is a hero with special powers that lead him to builds a great company, which innovates, creates jobs, makes markets more competitive, and enhances economic growth, is a myth'. From a different perspective, others such as Robert Kelsey (2010) argue that the image of the entrepreneur, often self-cultivated by those who use the media to promote their own image and brand, is simply not indicative of the vast majority of people engaged in entrepreneurship.

For Kelsey (2010), this stereotype of the risk taking, confident, charismatic, ambitious entrepreneur does not reflect that most are ordinary people starting small businesses because they want to work for themselves. As such, they never scale up in size and indeed this image is, he argues, likely to put people off attempts to work for themselves. While Kelsey is concerned about the negative impact of these stereotypes, for Shane (2008: 62), who also notes that 'the typical entrepreneur looks a lot like your next door neighbour', this raises issues about the value of supporting all types of entrepreneurial development. In other words, he argues that only a small number of businesses or enterprises will really significantly change the economy and the policy challenge is to find and focus on these and not the plethora of small enterprises dotted across the economy.

Conclusion

What we have argued in this chapter is that broader social, political and cultural shifts have meant concerns over the role of enterprise and the 'entrepreneur' have shifted and changed over time and television has often lagged behind in capturing these changes and bringing them to the screen.

We also suggest that the broader political shifts in the centrality of enterprise and entrepreneurship (which were given increased emphasis with the New Labour government from 1997), while not new, do provide a backdrop against which perceptions around the role of the entrepreneur in society are changing. Television representations of risk, business and a more individual lifestyle achievable through one's own enterprise fit with this discourse (that runs across all the main political parties in the United Kingdom) and also with the self-image of the independent television sector itself during the late 1990s and the first decade of the new century.

Television never operates in isolation from broader cultural and political shifts; it both amplifies cultural trends as well as reacts to an ever changing segment of the audience. We argue that an increasingly commercially orientated independent television sector, producing material for both the BBC and Channel 4, is populated by people more in tune with the changing nature of attitudes to work and risk. As journalist Andrew Davidson (interview with authors, 20 April 2009) suggests:

> If you are running an independent company and you are out of work as much as you are in work, and you are constantly having to live on your wits and are only as good as your last project … you are much more likely to be sympathetic in understanding with what is going on in a commercial world than, say 30 years ago when it was mainly state funded broadcasting,. And the sort of people who ran broadcasters, who came from maybe a privately educated Oxford background, would have no idea of commerce, and may even have a sort of out of date, slightly snooty idea that trade was something that wasn't very interesting.

Against the backdrop of an economic boom and a growing consumerist culture, television reproduced in part its own cultural milieu. With its strong London based roots, its heated economy and relatively affluent media environment, it's unsurprising that television and enterprise in all its forms felt comfortable with each other for most of the noughties.

Thus we find that representations of the entrepreneur and entrepreneurship on television, while much expanded from previous decades, are still constrained by the institutional codes, conventions and forms of television production. At the same time broader cultural attitudes towards the role of enterprise in both social and policy circles mean that particular ideas have become much more mainstream and to some extent 'normalized' and 'naturalized' about the entrepreneur in society, even if they are largely constructed and not necessarily particularly accurate. The next part of the book examines in more detail how audiences make sense of these range of representations and how this feeds into a wider understanding of the role and position of the entrepreneur in contemporary society.

PART II
Audiences, Television and the Entrepreneur

Chapter 5
Understanding the Audience: Engaging with Television

The Apprentice is a true TV phenomenon. Since its 2005 debut, it has steadily grown in stature, getting promoted from BBC Two to BBC One and pulling in ratings nudging nine million. It's won Baftas, spawned Junior and Celebrity spin-offs, and seen Lord Sugar's 'You're fired!' catchphrase enter common pub parlance. but does it serve a wider purpose beyond watercooler entertainment? Is the Beeb behemoth good for British business?

Michael Hogan, *Shortlist*, 5 May 2011, 41.

Thus far our research has looked at the historical development of business entertainment programming on British television and analyzed the two main strands that have developed over the years in the form of the 'troubleshooter' format and the 'business gameshow'. We have also considered the ways in which business and entrepreneurship are represented across a variety of media with both television and entrepreneurs themselves shaping discourses and narratives around these activities. In this part of the book, we move our focus away from examining television institutions and media texts to look at the ways in which the wider viewing public engages with both business entertainment formats and the concept of entrepreneurship more generally in society. Essentially, the remainder of our study seeks to 'ask the audience' through semi-structured focus groups about their levels of engagement with business on television, their knowledge and understanding of business and the term entrepreneur and the relationship between television representations of entrepreneurship and the role and function of the entrepreneur in cultural and economic life.

In Chapter 5 we look specifically at how members of the audience engage with a range of business entertainment formats *as* television and consider issues relating to the representations of business and entrepreneurship that television constructs. We are interested in which formats are regularly viewed by respondents and why, how they categorize and value the different types of formats and representations on offer and the levels of importance placed on factual and entertainment modes of address. In essence, we seek to examine how members of the audience may respond to and make meanings from what they see on screen and how this impacts on their knowledge and understanding of the worlds of business and entrepreneurship. In so doing, this discussion considers some of the complexities surrounding the issues of authenticity, ethics, identification and realism that occur in relation to the pleasures involved in watching factual entertainment programming.

In Chapters 6 and 7 we focus specifically on audience engagement with the entrepreneur on television. In particular we explore how the range of representations offered on television connects with the experiences that viewers may bring to these programmes. Of interest here are the ways in which the term entrepreneur is understood by members of the audience, the characteristics associated with entrepreneurialism and the connection between televisual discourses of entrepreneurship and those that circulate amongst audiences. We are also keen to identify differing patterns of understanding along demographic lines, particularly in relation to gender, as well as investigate the debate about the importance of role models in shaping patterns of behaviour among audiences in relation to entrepreneurship. Finally, we consider the rise of the 'celebrity' entrepreneur and examine some of the connections between media and business elites.

There are a number of challenges related to focus group research and some of the problems we experienced relate to the focus group setting and the position of the researcher in particular (see Skeggs, Thumim and Wood's fascinating 2008 article on the various methods of researching audiences and reality television and the associated challenges). For instance, the motivations of respondents for taking part in this study cannot fully be determined while an academic researcher asking questions within a specific group setting can sometimes lead to respondents answering in ways they think they should rather than offering more genuine thoughts. This differs depending on the construction of each group. For example, the division of gender or differences in age, background and occupation produce different group dynamics. Respondents are essentially being asked to present their thoughts and opinions within a public forum for the purposes of academic research thus there are also issues of performance to consider (both in terms of asserting opinion within the group and intellectually). We indicate these issues were appropriate throughout the following chapters and attempt to deal with them accordingly. Further information on the design of the focus groups is included in the Appendix.

Watching Business on Television

> I am surprised at the amount of business programmes on TV ... I don't know what
> that says about what we are looking for in terms of entertainment or factual-based
> programmes or whatever but there are masses of them (39-year-old male operations
> shift manager, Glasgow).

Respondents who took part in our focus group study were asked to be familiar with at least one example of a business entertainment format on television. This requirement was set in advance so as to enable each person to draw on their personal experiences of viewing such programming and participate in discussions about their various attitudes and responses. Their level of engagement was left unspecified however, so it was not the case that they had to be 'fans' of a particular show or have watched a wide range of the formats available. For the most part, respondents were familiar with more than one example because they appeared to enjoy this type of programme. A very small minority however claimed 'I don't watch any of them', despite being aware of the set requirements of the research. While people's motives for taking part in the study or for watching business on television were not explicitly addressed, it is the case that when engaged in conversation, these particular respondents were aware of the range of business entertainment programmes on offer, discussed many of the characteristics of the format and, indeed, referred to examples from specific episodes.

Comparing the statement 'I don't watch any of them' with extracts from the ensuing discussions highlights some of the complexities of this type of research. For example, it draws attention to what it means to actually *watch* television? The television set in modern households is often simply on in the background while people do others things or a programme may attract the full attention of one member of the household while another glances at it intermittently. Indeed, it is also the nature of television that many formats, such as daytime magazine shows, panel shows, chat shows and clip shows are filled with excerpts from other programmes, allowing viewers to see segments without actually having to watch a programme in its entirety. Moreover, television programming is covered extensively in other media, such as newspapers and magazines for example, and therefore information about specific episodes, storylines or characters can be encountered at a distance. With this mind, what emerged from the focus group discussions was not that this small group of respondents had never watched business entertainment programmes but rather they did not watch them *regularly* or consider themselves *fans* of the format. As such, they were still familiar with examples of this type of programming and indeed held some strong opinions relating to a number of the issues raised.

One such respondent explained that she didn't own a television set, as 'I don't have the time for that'. However she felt the need to watch *The Apprentice* online because,

> you hear people talk about it and I just wanted to know what they were talking about because I do like to be involved [in conversations]. And I realized *The Apprentice* is a big chunk of people's discussions, so I did watch it and I learned a lot. But I must admit I was drifting in and out (51-year-old female artist, Glasgow).

These comments are notable as they not only demonstrate that television programmes no longer have to be viewed on an actual television set according to the broadcasting schedules (while at the same time reinforcing the belief that watching television itself is somehow less worthy of our time than other pursuits), but they also show that although viewers are not always fully immersed in programmes, television does still play an important role in people's lives by providing a shared experience that forms the basis for discussion, gossip and analysis around particular issues and topics. This highlights our earlier acknowledgement that television does not exist in isolation but rather is part of a wider media and social context that can lead to programmes such as *The Apprentice* becoming part of an everyday discourse that helps shape meanings around business and entrepreneurship, regardless of whether or not people actually tune in to watch.[1]

In contrast to the examples given above, there was also a small minority of respondents who displayed a keen knowledge of the various business entertainment programmes under discussion, as evidenced in the following extracts from one Glasgow-based group:

> [*Gerry's Big Decision*] was the only one [of the visual prompts] I hadn't seen, but I was aware of it and I have been looking for it, because I watch all these programmes, so I would watch it if I knew [when] it was on (53-year-old female marketing consultant, Glasgow).

> Well, you see, I tend to watch an eclectic range of them. So, for example, there is one that we've not mentioned and I can't remember the guy's name, it might even have been Gerry somebody, who went into the NHS [referring to *Can Gerry Robinson Fix the NHS*] (54-year-old female IT consultant, Glasgow).

These were amongst some of the few respondents who explicitly professed to being attracted to business entertainment formats and therefore enthusiastically sought them out within the viewing schedule. It was these viewers who were most likely to reference programmes that were not used as visual prompts within the course of the focus groups, thus displaying their wide knowledge of the format and fostering discussion about its' lineage. This included early business formats *Troubleshooter* and *Back to the Floor*, one-off series or programmes with a short broadcast run such as *Can Gerry Robinson Fix the NHS?*, *All Over the Shop* (BBC2, 2008), *Million Dollar Traders*, *I'm Running Sainsbury's* and *Big Chef Takes On Little Chef* and returning hits *The Hotel Inspector*, *The Restaurant*, *Undercover Boss* and *Benefit Busters* (Channel 4, 2009–).

Some respondents also professed an interest in seeking out what they saw as being special interest programming for a minority audience only for a series to lose its appeal once it gained success and thus could be considered 'mainstream'. While this trajectory is evident in the transition of *The Apprentice* from BBC2 to BBC1, it was *Dragons' Den* that tended to dominate discussions of this type with many feeling that the show's 'unique concept' had become 'a bit dated now'. Indeed, one respondent mistakenly thought *Dragons' Den* had made the same transition as *The Apprentice* due to what he regarded as its now wide popularity:

---

1   The finale of the seventh series of *The Apprentice* (BBC1, 17 July 2011) attracted a record 10.7 million viewers at its peak, with an average of 9.1 million watching throughout the two-hour episode.

I didn't know [*Dragons' Den*] existed [until] somebody told me there was a
programme on Channel 2 that was really good and it felt as though it was a kind
of geeky programme … and then it went to BBC1 and it became cool and I think
a lot of the business programmes we are talking about tonight have become cool.
(39-year-old male operations shift manager, Glasgow).

These statements tell us something about the cultural status of television
programmes and how certain types of viewers consider themselves 'risk-takers'
through their viewing choices, preferring a 'unique' or 'geeky' series rather than
programming that has become 'cool' or part of the mainstream. The absence of
any explicit mention of *The Apprentice* from this discussion also highlights the
importance of scheduling and brand identity to broadcast channels. For example,
having nurtured the show on BBC2 for its first two series, which controller Roly
Keating (Day 2006) describes as helping to 'build *The Apprentice* into one of the
most talked-about and successful series of recent years', it was then promoted to
BBC1 where, as Hogan (2011) notes, it found a larger audience and made even
more headlines (see epigraph above). This successful transition and the lack of
discussion about it in our focus groups suggest that the series fits with the BBC1
brand identity in a way that *Dragons' Den* may not.

The self-confessed 'non-watchers' of business programmes and their
'enthusiast' and 'special interest' counterparts made up only a small number
of participants in the focus groups however. For the most part, respondents
understood business entertainment programmes as relating to four recent
examples of the format, namely *The Apprentice, Dragons' Den, Ramsay's
Kitchen Nightmares* and *Mary Queen of Shops*, with the former two in particular
dominating discussion across each group. Notably, as we have demonstrated
in Chapter 4, these programmes can be divided into two groups, the 'business
gameshow' (*The Apprentice* and *Dragons' Den*) and the 'troubleshooter' format
(*Ramsay's Kitchen Nightmares* and *Mary Queen of Shops*). As we will go on
to consider, this was something that respondents were aware of, even though
they were unlikely to use these specific terms. In contrast, Channel 4's *Property
Ladder* and *Secret Millionaire,* two other programmes that were used as visual
prompts within the groups, generated more debate over whether or not they could
be understood as business programmes. With the former considered to have
links to lifestyle programming and interior design and the latter seen as focusing
on philanthropy and 'the emotional side of business', the hybrid nature of the
formats proved problematic for viewers in assessing their relation to business
and entrepreneurship. Other formats used as visual prompts, such as Channel 4's
Gerry's Big Decision and BBC3's *The Last Millionaire* were less well-known,
raising questions about scheduling, promotion and target demographics. With
all of this in mind, we will now go on to consider some of the main findings that
emerged from the research.

Positioning Business TV Programmes within Factual Entertainment

> You can understand why they are grouped together because they do have a business
> theme running through the middle, but they do have different sections as well
> (25-year-old female receptionist, London).

One of the main points to arise across all of the focus groups in our research was the acute awareness respondents had of the different types of business programmes available on television and how these relate to other existing factual entertainment formats. As demonstrated by the above quote, the viewers we spoke to understood that while they were gathered to discuss 'business entertainment programmes' in general, this term does not sufficiently describe the two main approaches to business and entrepreneurship adopted across the range of programmes examined. Neither does it draw attention to the characteristics or qualities these programmes share with other formats, such as documentary, lifestyle programming and reality TV. Although respondents did not always refer to the categories of 'business gameshow' and 'troubleshooter' in the ways we have outlined, they clearly differentiated between the two and also positioned them differently in relation to other examples of factual entertainment. This finding is similar to that of Hill (2008), whose work on audiences and factual television demonstrates how viewers are aware of the many changes that have taken place in factuality in recent years and indeed respond to the various styles within one programme in multiple ways.

In the first instance, respondents in each of the Glasgow and London focus groups categorized many business programmes as an example of reality TV. In a similar manner to our discussion in Chapter 3, this occurred within a continuum. Troubleshooter formats such as *Ramsay's Kitchen Nightmares* were only occasionally referenced in relation to reality television while *Dragon's Den* was discussed in this context more frequently. In both cases this occurred typically in discussions around the 'tough' personalities of Ramsay and the Dragons, their ability to 'play God' and the potential to 'humiliate' the people taking part. The majority of respondents however saw *The Apprentice* as a classic example of the format, with the series regularly compared to both *Big Brother* and *The X Factor* (ITV, 2004–) due to its group challenge dynamic and presence of a judging panel. Many comments revealed a nuanced understanding of the relationship between these programmes in terms of the importance of characters, the role of the expert and the ways in which the skills of the contestants (or lack thereof) are represented within a range of shows. This is in addition to acknowledging the status of reality TV in wider society as an example of television's 'dumbing down' and suggesting that business entertainment programmes offer something more 'intelligent' due to the subject matter involved. Here are some extended extracts from across the focus groups that highlight the above issues:

> I don't know if everyone will agree, but I almost see *The Apprentice* [as] being
> a more intelligent *Big Brother* because it's the dynamic of watching people

working together and I think *Big Brother* is past its heyday, so then maybe people are switching to something like *The Apprentice* instead. (27-year-old female personal assistant, Glasgow).

It's the one reality show that people are not ashamed of saying they watch is *The Apprentice* (25-year-old self-employed trainer, London).

It's also like *Big Brother* where the big characters stay in and the people that might not be as crazy or as loud or as obnoxious don't. Not because of their talent or their business sort of potential. It's because it's like a reality show and you kind of see these other people voted off who could be amazing business people. (33-year-old female human resources manager, London).

You could trace it all the way back to *X Factor* . you know, the kind of reality TV thing I guess. *Dragons' Den* is almost like a panel [of judges] and Gordon Ramsay is like Simon Cowell [in terms of his onscreen 'nasty' persona] (37-year-old male general manager, Glasgow).

That was going to be my point, because it goes back to people, I think, failing on television. You know it's like *The X Factor* thing. [The auditions are] one of the best things about it, [although] I don't enjoy it . people enjoy seeing people fail, you know, is this a British thing? Because we like complaining, I don't know? (28-year-old male planning consultant, Glasgow)

There's also something I think that goes through all of [these programmes] which is almost like the *X Factor* theme, which is something about exposing people's lack of skills. (34-year-old guidance teacher, Glasgow).

The final two comments above begin to raise questions about what types of pleasures viewers experience from watching these shows and this is something we will go on to consider in the next section of the chapter.

The most frequent comparison made between troubleshooter programmes and other types of factual entertainment was that of the makeover format, with the term 'makeover' being explicitly used along with other phrases and words such as 'turning something around', 'change', 'reveal' and 'before and after':

I think a lot of the other programmes, like *Mary Queen of Shops* and Gordon Ramsay's *Kitchen Nightmares*, are kind of like makeover shows almost. Do you know? It's a bit like turning something around and there's always some kind of change in it, so it's more of a kind of reveal, like a makeover show. And I think that's kind of how it differs from things like *Dragons' Den* which is kind of purely about, you know, is more about business . [A troubleshooter programme] always has to have a makeover at the end of it. It's always just like we have done the business bit and then we go away for three days and you get [your business] totally done up, new mirrors, new seats, whatever and it just becomes like a home makeover show by the end of it (24-year-old female facilities administrator, Glasgow).

[Gordon Ramsay] changes around the food, he does a makeover and he spends a lot of money. It is a regular format that you can see in each episode coming again and again (40-year-old male security services supervisor, London).

I like watching the before and after. So you see before, when everybody's struggling, and that gentleman [seen in a clip from *Mary Queen of Shops*] wasn't even getting any money. And you see afterwards where their business is booming or, not even let's say boom, but making some money and you go, 'Ah haven't they done well for themselves?' And you do, you go hot. You feel really warm about it, you go, 'They've done really well, I'm really pleased.' It's like you know them but you don't (25-year-old female receptionist, London).

In relation to both the transformation element of the makeover and the comments made by the last respondent about the pleasures experienced by the viewer on seeing someone do well is the notion of the 'journey' or some sort of business or personal 'progression':

Journey's a part of it as well, I think, [in] a lot of them. Like the ones I most enjoy are the progression of a business, and that's why I think Ramsay's [programme] appeals to a lot of people, because it's a start, a middle and an end. Whereas maybe the more cold financial ones like the *Dragon's Den* are not. [They are] kind of more short term (27-year-old male charity outreach worker, Glasgow).

Drawing on these comments, there appears to be a sense amongst respondents that troubleshooter programmes are more emotionally engaging, making viewers feel 'hot' or 'warm', while the gameshow elements exhibited in *Dragons' Den*, for instance, are more 'cold'. This is due to a variety of reasons and indeed the division between 'troubleshooter' formats and 'business gameshows' becomes more complex in discussions around *The Apprentice* due to the cumulative nature of the series. It is also not as simple to suggest that emotionally engaging with a programme makes it more pleasurable as the following section will now examine.

The Pleasures and Problems of Business on Television

Emotional Engagement

Emotions are something everyone can relate to. Not everyone is going to be interested in a business programme but everyone is interested in human emotion (44-year-old female self-employed partner, Glasgow).

It wouldn't be prime time television if [the programme-makers] weren't exploring the emotions. If it was just a dry business programme, you know, 'this is the business' [then] it would be a documentary (33-year-old corporate events manager, Glasgow).

These observations by two Glasgow-based viewers recall comments made by a number of industry professionals about television's ability to communicate emotion effectively and how this is one of the key features of successful business entertainment programming:

These days television isn't a very good place for getting your facts, because you can get facts anyway [via the internet, for example]. Television is a medium that is primarily good at communication emotion, and what's interesting is to link emotion to ideas. My favourite programmes on BBC2 are always [about] emotion with ideas (Jane Root, former Controller of BBC2, 1999–2004; cited in Kirk 2004)

Viewers do not care if a business is making money but if you can get them rooting for someone in the first five minutes, if you can make them feel that this person is human, like you in some way, [then] that makes the viewer want to watch. [To] get them hooked on caring about the person there has to be something at stake; if this deal doesn't happen, four hundred people lose their jobs or whatever (Michele Kurland, formerly of the BBC's Business Unit and Executive Producer of *The Apprentice* from 2007 onwards, interview with authors, 11 January 2007).

The above statements highlight the way in which business entertainment formats tend to use business as a backdrop through which to explore human emotions and relationships. In order to attract viewers and make them 'care', the 'cold' financial aspects of business are often suppressed at the expense of the 'warmness' of emotional story arcs in which real people are shown taking risks. The discussions that occurred between respondents in our focus groups suggest that this manifests itself differently in the two strands of programming on offer.

For example, by focusing on one or two businesses over the course of an hour, troubleshooter programmes provide some sort of context that respondents suggest make it 'easier to understand' particular industry sectors (such as retail, restaurants and hotels) and 'empathize' with the individuals involved. Viewers get to see 'behind the scenes' in these programmes and observe the types of 'struggles' faced by the people running small to medium enterprises (SME's), thus gaining an understanding to some extent as to 'what is at stake' in terms of the attempts made by the troubleshooting experts to turn the businesses around. Significantly, one of the pleasures of the format was the fact that the onscreen troubleshooting process always appeared to be successful and that this success was achieved by applying the 'same basic principles' week in, week out. For many, the result was 'a bit like a fairytale' with the perception being that there's never any 'failure' in these programmes. As such, the viewers we spoke to often experienced the shows as 'emotional rollercoasters', with the participants 'upset' at the beginning before being 'so happy later on' following the end of the process.

This perceived happy ending is bound up with the 'makeover' or 'reveal' aspect of the most recent wave of troubleshooter formats and becomes more complicated outside the confines of the episode. For example, with the narrative of each episode tending to culminate in a service-based business being relaunched on the advice of the troubleshooter, the question of whether the business will remain solvent in the real world is not the main objective (although it is addressed in 'Revisited' segments that are added to certain troubleshooter formats following their initial broadcast). As such, there are only a few instances in which the onscreen troubleshooting process is actually seen to fail due to resistance on the part of the participant.[2]

Conversely, it was felt that business gameshows are constructed in a way that distances the viewer emotionally from events. For instance, the short, edited pitches presented on *Dragons' Den* appeal to some respondents precisely because it does not allow them to become emotionally engaged in the contestant's situation. The 'varied' nature of the show was welcomed as respondents had 'no idea who's going to come in with what idea' and enjoyed the fact that it was 'completely different each week'. Due to the lack of context given about the participants and their products however (apart from in occasional follow-up programmes), many also felt that *Dragons' Den* was too 'general' and 'abrupt', describing it as 'a numbers game' and emphasizing how it is 'more about the money side' rather than the satisfaction or enjoyment gained by running your own business:

> A lot of it is about the money [but] people get into businesses because they enjoy it . yet [many of these programmes] focus on the money and with *Dragons' Den*, if someone's doing something they really enjoy and it's not going to make a lot of money then [the Dragons] rubbish them and say, you know, 'you need to do something else' or 'this is not a business investment' . [But] it could be. They just might not get rich from it (35-year-old female self-employed trainer, London).

This last point is important as it demonstrates Michele Kurland's argument that viewer's do not necessarily care if a business is capable of making money but rather are seeking to engage with the people involved and care about their situation.

Dragons' Den can be limiting in this sense because, as one London-based respondent pointed out: 'In terms of the viewer there is only really two outcomes

---

2   For example, as we discussed in Chapter 3, the opening episode of the third series of *Mary Queen of Shops* (BBC2, 7 June 2010) saw Mary Portas being asked to leave the premises of Angela Maher's bakery after the pair disagreed over Portas's makeover suggestions for the business.

which is either they invest or they don't invest. When they do invest I kind of want to know now what is going to happen? I want to know what the next stage is' (21-year-old male student, London). In this sense, audiences cannot follow the 'journey' of the participants from beginning to end but instead are simply provided a snapshot of the pitching process (although they are able to follow the journey of the product if it subsequently makes it to market). However, this in itself can be a dramatic and emotional process and indeed many respondents explained how they were able to emotionally engage with the show by relating to the pressurized situation the budding entrepreneurs find themselves on entering the Den. Furthermore, respondents admired the participants for taking risks that they themselves may not be willing to do: 'I wouldn't give up my job and take that risk and that is probably why I watch [*Dragons' Den*] . I have thought about it but, in a way, they are doing it on my behalf and I can see all the pitfalls and learn from those mistakes' (25-year-old female sports manager, London). This was something that occurred across all focus groups in relation to the many types of programmes available; that in order to be able to empathize with the participants on screen, many respondents appear to adopt a reflexive viewing position by asking themselves 'what would I do?' or 'how would I react?' if placed in a similar situation.

Unlike other business entertainment formats, *The Apprentice* was the one series explicitly referred to across a number of groups as a 'gameshow'. This is largely due to the constructed nature of the tasks but also the way in which contestants compete with one another not necessarily in terms of business acumen but with regards to personality. As Holmes (2008: 14) explains, in a reality gameshow 'a competitor's progress through the game is based on some sort of popularity contest' and this is echoed in the following statements:

> The people are like gameshow contestants really because they are fairly hapless. Although they make these grand claims about being the top seller in England or what have you, they're all pretty naive and have not really got any [business credentials] (59-year-old male company director, London).

> I would say *The Apprentice* is much more purely entertainment because [the contestants] are not talking about real businesses; it is a gameshow to all intents and purposes. So out of all of them, as much as I love it, I would say that it is even less business oriented than Gordon Ramsay because he is dealing with a real business [and] these guys are on a sort of quiz show basically, aren't they? (38-year-old male property developer, London).

Despite the distancing effect of the gameshow device however, the serial nature of the competition and the personalities of the characters work to slowly engage viewers emotionally over a number of weeks:

> *The Apprentice* is more addictive and you do feel yourself getting more involved … getting sucked in and having to watch it the next week so you are finding out what happens next and that's all about the characters, I guess, and the fact that they are the constant throughout the programmes (28-year-old female office manager, Glasgow).

This statement once again echoes Kurland's argument about the key feature of successful business entertainment formats being the ability to get the audience 'rooting' for someone and 'hooked' on caring about a person because they have something at stake rather than assessing their business potential per se.

In contrast to *The Apprentice*, where respondents found themselves being 'sucked in' on an emotional level despite its obviously constructed nature, the programme that was found to be most explicit in its attempts to emotionally engage the audience was Channel 4's *The Secret Millionaire*. 'I always cry at *Secret Millionaire*' was a common response across all groups, although opinion was divided on whether this was a good thing in terms of it being a pleasurable experience. On the one hand, a number of respondents explained how they enjoyed the series due to the way it 'touches the soul' and 'tugs on the heart strings' by focusing on successful entrepreneurs 'putting something back into the community'. This approach was seen by some as a welcome contrast from the harsh business worlds depicted in *The Apprentice* and *Dragons' Den* as it challenges the idea that 'emotion and business have to be two sort-of entities' while also taking the 'hard-nosed edge off entrepreneurs'. However, many respondents also voiced concern about what they saw as the programme makers actively setting out to manipulate the emotions of viewers:

> I sometimes get frustrated by the emotion side. because it's almost as if, you know, on cue this is the time you should start greeting [crying]. You know, this is the emotional side and you have this rollercoaster of emotions that is almost fed into you, it's almost as if you don't have a choice. This is what the programme is making you feel and wanted to make you feel (29-year-old male sound engineer, Glasgow).

This reaction is bound up with the structure of the format, as the 'staged' nature of the process becomes increasingly evident to viewers with the broadcast of each series and thus impacts on the ability of some to emotionally engage with or take pleasure in the seemingly altruistic acts played out on screen:

> Have they not cottoned on yet? Someone turns up and says 'I am doing volunteering and have brought this camera crew with me' and [the people in the community] are like, 'okay' (27-year-old female personal assistant, Glasgow).

> Can we have our million [pounds] now? (24-year-old female corporate communications assistant, Glasgow)

This exchange within one Glasgow group not only drew laughs from the respondents but also highlights the importance of authenticity within these types of programmes along with the issue of ethics as the motives of the various people involved were questioned; the eponymous millionaires, the programme makers and indeed the deserving recipients with their supposed *spontaneous* reactions to receiving a cheque from someone they thought to be a kind-hearted *volunteer*. The issue of authenticity and motivation across all business formats is something we will now go on to discuss further followed by some of the ethical considerations involved in such programming and the issue of social class in relation to aspirational desires and audience enjoyment.

Authenticity and Motivation

In order for audiences to emotionally engage with business entertainment formats over a period of time, we found that perceived authenticity, with regards to the motivations of the entrepreneurs, judges and troubleshooting experts featured, was a crucial factor. The viewers we spoke to had a complex relationship with the business entertainment programmes discussed, as they were constantly negotiating between what they saw as genuine altruistic intentions or 'passion' for a particular industry sector and more cynical motivations with regards to providing a performance and furthering a personal agenda. Although recognizing the commercial potential of such programming and the gains to be made by appearing on a successful business series, respondents felt overall that television entrepreneurs and experts should be doing it for 'the right reasons'; with the offscreen activities of those deemed to do so often cited. This echoes Bonner's (2011: 24) argument that the key aspects of authenticity and sincerity are 'the degree of consistency between the performance, the persona and such features as the individual's private life as are public knowledge'.

While an onscreen bullying persona may be entertaining for some, as we shall discuss in the following section, it must be perceived to be fuelled by altruistic notions if it is to emotionally engage certain sections of the audience:

> Gordon Ramsay can be seen as a bit of a bully but underneath his [onscreen] persona, he does have quite a kind heart. He does care about the businesses he is trying to help and you feel he does actually care about the people [involved]. I think that's also true of [Mary] *Queen of Shops* etc. These individuals are trying to help (52-year-old female retired local government officer, Glasgow).

> [The Dragons] are doing it for the right reasons. Okay, it makes a lot of money for the telly companies too but it is from the heart and I think all the Dragons, because they know how hard it is, are in some ways doing these people a favour [even though] it seems really cruel (54-year-old female marketing consultant, Glasgow).

> There's a serious side to *The Apprentice* because Alan Sugar is [working in the Department of Business, Innovation and Skills] at the moment ... and the first thing he has done is set up an apprentice scheme in government ... and he is promoting that in businesses. So there is some element of good in it. I mean, it's good to see the humorous side of the TV [programme] but, you know, to see him as an individual and what he is doing, it's [also] good (43-year-old female personal assistant, London).

These statements draw attention to the ways in which some viewers may well consider what they are watching to be 'entertainment with a purpose', the phrase used by Andrew Mackenzie, then Head of Factual Entertainment at Channel 4, to describe successful factual entertainment formats (The Factual Commissioning Forum, 11 March 2009) and which is exemplified by Lord Sugar's involvement with the former Labour government's apprenticeship scheme. However, it is also the case that viewers may use descriptions such as 'trying to help' and 'from the heart' as an attempt to justify the more cruel or ethically questionable aspects of the format, such as bullying behaviour, the potential for humiliation or the commercial and personal gains to be achieved. Either way, there is often an element of disavowal at work, which, as Quimby (2005: 717) usefully explains, 'might be understood by the phrase "I know. but all the same"'.

For example, as we have previously touched on, many respondents noted that there never seems to be any 'failure' in troubleshooter-based programmes, with the process always concluding with a 'happy ending'. This was particular notable in the American version of *Ramsay's Kitchen Nightmares* in which a heavy reliance on drama and transformation was highlighted by those respondents familiar with the series. Often describing the show as something of a 'guilty pleasure', the viewers we spoke to explained how the American version 'feels more staged' in comparison to the British original and 'doesn't ring as authentic' or have any 'value'. Visually, the US series was seen as being 'glossy' while in the United Kingdom everything is a 'bit dull and grey'. Although the two versions undoubtedly share similar traits, there appears to be an implicit understanding that British business entertainment programming is underpinned by public service ideals that make it a more worthwhile or valuable viewing experience rather than something to be a guilty of; although this did not necessarily make it more enjoyable for all respondents. Yet, despite the seemingly more authentic or worthy motivations of the British examples, a number of respondents were nevertheless aware that the perceived successes displayed onscreen were still only confined to the duration of the episode (in the form of the relaunch), with many reporting that they had since read about businesses that had appeared within such programming going bankrupt at a later date. This, again, did not always affect enjoyment of the format and suggests that on some level many viewers engage in the aforementioned psychic mechanism of disavowal. Although aware that the troubleshooting process that unfolds onscreen may not be entirely successful or work as a long-term solution for the participants involved, our focus groups suggest that viewers nevertheless often submit to the pleasure of an emotional story arc that depicts the business as being saved by the episode's end.

This tends to occur when a series is in its infancy however. For those programmes that have experienced success over a number of years, such as the aforementioned *Ramsay's Kitchen Nightmares*, and are thus no longer considered particularly 'novel' or 'unique', it was felt that the limitations of the format were more likely to be exposed with the motivations of the expert and the role of the production team queried. This position is demonstrated in the following statement:

> I used to watch *Ramsay's Kitchen Nightmares* but I went off it after a while ... At the very start of the series you really believed that he was really wanting to go in and help take these businesses forward and then, obviously, you see him leave at the end and he says 'oh, we will keep in touch' but does he ever, and do we really know that? Actually there was something in the media, last week I think it was, [Ramsay] helped a woman called Momma Cherri in Brighton I think, and there was a whole big story about her moving to bigger premises and everything and then, last week, she has been made bankrupt and she says he never helped at all basically. So I think once it's all finished, it's finished. But there was [a statement] from the production company saying he's a busy man, you know, so I sort of realized that in my own mind. I just never really watch it anymore (28-year-old male planning consultant, Glasgow).[3]

There is a sense then that when formats are first launched, they have seemingly fresh and original qualities that lead viewers to suspend disbelief and emotionally engage with the process unfolding onscreen. As audiences become more familiar with an ongoing format however and the outcomes become increasingly predictable, the contrived nature of the process becomes apparent thus leading some viewers to begin questioning what they see. This is particularly true of *The Secret Millionaire*, in which the authenticity and motivation on the part of the philanthropic entrepreneurs was questioned along with the ethics of the programme-makers and issues around social class.

Ethical Considerations and Social Class

In discussions of Channel 4's *The Secret Millionaire*, respondents noted how the series takes as its focus a section of society not usually visible in more aspirational examples of business-related content. While many appreciated the fact that the series visited 'deprived and down and out areas' and understood it to be a significant departure for this type of programming (and also, one could argue, for

---

3   In 2009, Momma Cherri's Big House restaurant went into administration, having appeared on Series 2 of *Ramsay's Kitchen Nightmares* in 2005 and relocating to bigger premises in 2007. Momma Cherri has since appeared on programmes such as *This Morning* as a TV chef and published a cookbook.

the majority of entertainment-based television), there was nevertheless concern about the motives of the entrepreneurs taking part and the 'onscreen' journeys constructed by the programme makers:

> Although [the millionaire entrepreneurs] are doing good things for [a particular] community or business or whatever, they are pushing their own agenda so that they can become more famous themselves ... the people on *The Secret Millionaire* aren't completely selfless, they are on it for a reason too ... You know, if they wanted to actually do it for selfless reasons they would just do it without being filmed, without a film crew around them. They are obviously wanting something out of it, whether it be more fame or just showing people what a nice person they are (24-year-old female corporate communications assistant, Glasgow)

> You know, everybody thinks [*The Secret Millionaire*] is about helping the people [from deprived communities]. But actually the biggest journey [the programme makers] chart is the change in the millionaires; however edited it is (33-year-old female corporate events manager).

These statements raise a number of ethical considerations related to the power relations inherent in the series. Rather than give a voice to an underrepresented section of society, the 'journey' that viewers are asked to identify with is that of the millionaire philanthropists and their sudden appreciation for the comfortable lifestyle they lead as the cameras follow them on their return home (see Kelly 2008). This is something that respondents were aware of and indeed uncomfortable with, particularly as the millionaire businesspeople were seen to have something to gain by using their television profile to boost both their commercial interests and sense of personal achievement. This is an aspect that we shall consider further in the following chapters, specifically in relation to converting media and cultural capital into political influence.

As one of the less well-known programmes amongst our respondents, *Gerry's Big Decision* was often confused with *The Secret Millionaire* due to the emphasis on Sir Gerry Robinson investing up to a million pounds of his own money in an attempt to turn around failing businesses that he feels have potential. For one respondent familiar with the series however, similar concerns were again raised about the actual implementation of what tends to be represented as a generous and charitable donation: 'With *Gerry's Big Decision*, it was like 'Go on Gerry' [because] he's giving away a million pounds. But then, it's like, "I'm taking 63 percent of your business [so] in five months you will be making my tea"' (37-year-old male general manager, Glasgow). With no follow-up programme that sees the deals through to completion, there is little understanding of how the investment (or lack of) may impact on the businesspeople involved. Instead, the process is again perceived to conclude with a happy ending, despite the fact that the million pound deal referred to in the above statement never came to fruition after filming had completed and the family-run business thus went into administration. While the London groups touched on some of these ethical issues, a more considered debate took place about motivation, power relations and the aspirational nature of business entertainment formats in general amongst the Glasgow respondents. This was partly due to the presence of social class in the Glasgow discussions both indirectly (as we have highlighted in relation to *The Secret Millionaire*) and directly (with regards to *Property Ladder*).

The importance of social class to this type of programming is evident in the different reactions north and south of the border to *Property Ladder*, which was the one show that did not generate any discussion across both locations regarding emotional engagement with the participants onscreen. In London, the focus was instead on the aspirational nature of the series and how to turn property into 'something that's potentially going to give you lots of return'. A number of respondents also described themselves as property developers and highlighted the responsibility television had to depict the true nature of the property business, especially in the current economic crisis: 'I mean I'm in that business so I know how hard it is. You can't take the chances that I used to take. I just have to be careful and I think the [rebranded *Property Snakes and Ladders*] is showing that' (60-year-old male property developer, London). Overall, the London viewers we spoke to seemed more indicative of the type of aspirational audience Channel 4 actively sought with its blend of 'transformative lifestyle programming' discussed in Chapter 3.

The response to *Property Ladder* was however slightly different in Glasgow where, rather than place themselves in the position of the aspiring developers and consider how to make money from property, many respondents actively distanced themselves from this sort of thinking and showed slight disdain for the programme:

> I always just think it's about really smug middle class people. I can't bear to watch it because they are so obvious [in their aspirational desires] (32-year-old female office and finance coordinator, London).

> I think stuff like *Property Ladder* ... the question, is that a business programme? I think it kinds of masquerades as one but it's basically selling demand for a lifestyle and for a certain kind of class-based thing (29-year-old male sound engineer, London).

These are some examples of the issue of class in these programmes being explicitly addressed in the Glasgow groups, something we found absent in London. This was not an area that we set out to look at in detail however, and indeed our respondents were not representative of the wider viewing public, therefore further work has to be done to be able to fully consider these differences (see the 2008 article by Skeggs, Thumim and Wood for a more detailed class-based audience research around reality television). What we will look at now is another complex issue that divided respondents, namely the notion of passing judgement within these programmes and whether watching people fail is regarded as a source of pleasure.

Passing Judgement

> UK reality TV, then, offers a culture of judgement: judgements meted out on particular bodies in front of large, unseen audiences. (Couldry 2010: 80).

In comparing business entertainment programmes to talent show formats like *The X Factor*, respondents continually drew attention to the ways in which successful entrepreneurs and experts were asked to pass judgement on either failing businesses in troubleshooter-based programmes or budding entrepreneurs in the business gameshow. As highlighted in relation to our discussion of authenticity and motivation, and in keeping with the talent show format and reality TV, such assessments were regarded as being 'frank' and 'harsh' with an element of 'cruelty' also being present. While we have explained how a number of viewers we spoke to saw this as something of a necessity, or rather a 'cruel to be kind' approach in which the successful entrepreneurs and experts were doing it for 'the right reasons', there were other responses that tended to be divided according to age.

On the one hand, there was a small group of respondents across all groups who felt that the judges and experts featured in business entertainment shows were often 'rude' and 'nasty' and reported their dislike of behaviour that resulted in people being 'embarrassed, laughed at, humiliated or bullied' for the purposes of a television programme: 'The girl in tears, I mean who wants to see that? I don't. TV, when it's showing news programmes or documentaries, tears and misery, we know it exists [so] why do it [on entertainment programming too]?' (54-year-old male self-employed marketing consultant, Glasgow). There are two points to note about this group. First, despite proclaiming that they did not enjoy this approach to factual entertainment, these particular respondents were nevertheless familiar with this type of programming. Thus, in a similar manner to the self-confessed 'non-watchers' of business entertainment formats (and indeed some of these respondents belonged to both groups), it seems that they were either encountering such programming passively rather than actively tuning in, or they were able to enjoy other aspects of each series that offset the more rude and nasty elements on display. It is also the case that they may have agreed to take part in the focus groups in order to actively express their dislike for such programming but this does not account for their knowledge of the range of formats discussed. Second, this group of viewers tended to be over 25 years old, with many of them being in their fifties, the upper age range for our focus group respondents. While some suggested that they had developed this opinion over time, others seemed more circumspect about discussing the possible pleasures of this approach within a public forum, explaining how the auditions in *The X Factor*, for example, are 'one of the best things about [the show]' before clarifying, of course, that they themselves 'don't enjoy' this aspect.

In contrast, for those respondents aged between 18- and 25-years old, there was little mention of feeling uncomfortable with the more unforgiving processes exhibited in these programmes but rather a direct acknowledgement that their enjoyment is largely bound up with being able to judge other people and indeed the drama of watching contestants fighting and competing amongst themselves to avoid failure:

> I think that's my main part of the enjoyment of programmes like this, is actually judging people and ... saying do you really deserve that, do you deserve that prize, do you deserve to get that money? (18-year-old female student, Glasgow)

> [The viewers I know] don't actually talk about the business ideas or the strategies [the candidates] use. For instance, the Margate [task in Series 5 of *The Apprentice*], no-one was talking about the ideas ... they were talking about the fights between [contestants] and what's going to happen in the boardroom rather than the businesses. (18-year-old male student, London).

With reality TV and reality gameshows in particular being somewhat normalized for the 18- and 19-year-old respondents in our groups (having grown up with it on their television screens), there is a sense that they were not only unapologetic about enjoying such programmes and the pleasures they felt at the expense of others' discomfort but they were also unconcerned about how this would reflect on their character. Moreover, they did not feel the need to discuss the 'value' of business entertainment formats in terms of providing them with information, something that we will consider further in the final section of this chapter.

It is the case however that these findings can also be related to the various ways in which demographic groups identify with the people and situations depicted in business entertainment formats. For instance, to return to former Dragon Doug Richard's (interview with authors, 2 June 2009) argument highlighted in Chapter 3 for a moment, he suggests that adult viewers understand the show differently from their younger counterparts and thus experience different pleasures:

> To my mind what you are actually seeing is a difference of focus. The adult is emotionally tied to the entrepreneur's failure while the kid looks at the entrepreneur and thinks 'I could do a better job. I am empowered by it'. The adult looks at it and says 'oh my God, it is so embarrassing that somebody like me is failing in public'. The kid is saying 'somebody like them is failing, but I can do better'. And so it is hugely aspirational and empowering for these teenagers: 'Well it ain't that hard, I am going to go and do it'.

While the younger viewers we spoke to did not appear to be especially entrepreneurial and preferred the entertainment rather than aspirational aspect of the programmes, there was a sense that they did not recognize themselves in the people failing onscreen and therefore felt no embarrassment at their actions or predicaments.

This lack of recognition is a point that was highlighted by one of the more mature respondents taking part in the focus groups:

> Generally, we never recognize ourselves in something we watch on television, particularly reality shows. You know if we're really truthful to ourselves, you watch *The Apprentice* [and] I see myself in various characters I've seen ... much younger than me of course, and like, I was young once ... so I remember what I was like and some of the outrageous things I said [and] did (60-year-old male property developer, London).

This suggests that while older viewers may be more likely to identify or empathize with the budding or failing entrepreneurs and thus experience discomfort when viewing such programmes, younger viewers are able to place themselves in the position of the successful entrepreneurs and experts thus allowing them to pass judgment on the performance of the contestants with more ease. While our older focus group respondents continuously asked themselves how they would act or react if placed in a similar situation, the younger members of the group were more concerned with considering who truly deserves a helping hand or who should secure the coveted job or investment on offer. Thus, as Richard argues, there is a difference of focus across different age groups.

In the final section of this chapter we will now move on to consider how respondents discussed these programmes in relation to offering realistic representations of the worlds of business and entrepreneurship and the use of an entertainment mode of address.

Realism and Entertainment within the Business Entertainment Format

> To me it's just business with a small 'b' ... It's not really about business at all. To me it's 100 percent about entertainment. I don't think business with a capital 'B' lends itself to television. How do you do that? How do you start with the idea? How do you deal with the hard work and the graft and, you know finding a site and hiring staff? I mean, it's just not sexy. It [does] not lend itself to editing and people going 'Ooh, ah, he's now looking for new premises, ooh!'
>
> (39-year-old regional pharmaceuticals manager, London).

Across all groups, discussions of whether business entertainment formats are realistic or true to life in their representation of the worlds of business and entrepreneurship were complex as respondents displayed an acute awareness of the impact that production methods, the limits of television formatting and the commercial nature of the medium has on notions of realism. Moreover, there was an understanding of how the presence of television cameras has an effect on the actions and performances of the people involved with an overall sense that the tasks and situations featured were constructed for the purposes of television entertainment rather than to reflect realistic business practices in contemporary Britain.

Production Methods

In the first instance, a number of respondents discussed the production methods used in business gameshows and highlighted some of the discrepancies between what is presented on screen and the filming and editing process. With regards to *The Apprentice*, this centred on the combination of studio and location filming in the series with no distinction made between the two. While the viewers we spoke to in Glasgow focused on the use of a studio for the boardroom showdown, many London respondents were more specific, drawing attention to the fact that the programme makers 'keep showing Canary Wharf' even though Lord Sugar's company and the job on offer is 'based in Brentwood'. This appeared to highlight a disconnect between the extended onscreen interview and the actual job offered to the winning contestant, with little information provided about the latter.[4] Some felt that the end job was not particularly important however as many of the contestants were simply 'seeking celebrity status'. This differentiated the show from *Dragons' Den*, as there was a sense that although people may enter the Den for publicity reasons, 'they are still serious about their businesses'.

Despite the notion that the contestants on *Dragons' Den* are somehow more 'genuine', there was nevertheless an acknowledgement that the filming and editing process may impact on their presentation skills. While some noted how the Dragons 'can interview people for about two hours and you only see the bits edited for television', others pointed out how difficult it is to effectively present your business without access to the relevant paperwork or figures:

> [The producers] say … you're not allowed to bring any notes or papers in and that just adds to the, I suppose, entertainment. Because sitting here, I might know my figures [and] what my business can do but, in front of TV cameras, I would probably forget it all. But it could be very easy to say you are allowed to take one piece of paper in with you with whatever information you want on it, but then that kind of takes away the entertainment of watching them sweat (36-year-old male property manager, London).

This divided respondents as to whether or not the process could be considered 'realistic'. For those with experience of business, a small number of respondents suggested that 'there is nothing threatening about it to go to your bank manager' or

---

4   The use of a studio as the boardroom in *The Apprentice* and the fact that contestants shoot their exit in a taxi on the first day of filming are increasingly being referred to however in articles such as 'Revealed: Secrets of *The Apprentice*' (*Radio Times*, 16–22 July 2011).

asking for investment, a view that appeared to conflict with the harsher environment represented on television. Others, on the other hand, described the situation as a much-needed 'reality check' for potential entrepreneurs. In a similar manner to *The Apprentice* however, there was a sense that whatever happens onscreen (regardless of realism) is only part of the process: 'I find myself wondering when I watch *Dragons' Den* . at what stage does the real bank manager or accountant come in and sit down with the people that [have] agreed to give up [a] 20 percent [stake in their business]' (27-year-old male IT consultant, Glasgow).

There was little sympathy however for the participants of such programming, with respondents across all groups generally agreeing with the suggestion that 'all the people who go on TV, choose to go on TV', therefore 'they know exactly what might happen to them'. Yet, a small number raised concerns with regards to the production process and the level of agency (if any) afforded to the participants:

> I think there is a grey area [because] basically the process of producing a show like that is kind of inauthentic and it is writing a narrative. I think you could argue that those people are actors in a devised piece of theatre which people are watching, whether they are complicit in it or not. Obviously they are real people with a real relationship with each other, but they are responding to situations which are kind of charged for entertainment value (29-year-old sound engineer, Glasgow).

This statement followed a discussion in which members of one Glasgow group acknowledged that participants are often cast to fill a particular role by producers before being presented in such a way that audiences are encouraged to 'pick your hero or your villain' and make 'moral judgements' which are based on things that aren't particularly to do with the task in hand or the suitability for the job. This therefore highlights the performative and narrative aspects of business entertainment formats rather than the more realistic representations of everyday life that viewers may expect to find in factual programming.

The Contemporary Business Landscape

Across all business entertainment formats, there was also an agreement that many of the processes depicted onscreen are far removed from actual business practices. Thus, just as entrepreneurs have access to relevant facts and figures when pitching in front of real-life Angel Investment initiatives, the tasks issued in *The Apprentice* do not necessarily correspond to most people's idea of the contemporary business landscape, as highlighted in the following exchange that took place in one Glasgow group:

> It doesn't really fit with what business is nowadays, because how many people actually go out and spend £100 and buy a van and buy some veg[etables] and start their own business? I mean … all the tasks they are doing are not really

relevant to what modern business is. Most people who are on the show have worked in sales and telesales and stuff like that, call centres and stuff, so the tasks they are set … it's just to see who wins and who loses (27-year-old female personal assistant, Glasgow).

You know, [the contestants] have probably made their money in graphic design or. software development. They have not made their money selling fruit and veg on a street corner (29-year-old female marketing manager, Glasgow).

These statements are not so much about the business potential of selling fruit and vegetables but rather the notion that *The Apprentice* has seemingly failed to find ways to visually represent Britain's development into a primarily service economy or indeed the rise of the internet and digital media. This means that tasks involving selling fruit and veg to passersby or, indeed, troubleshooter formats that take viewers behind-the-scenes of shops, restaurants and hotels, have become something of a default setting for television programme-makers who have increasingly limited their representation of business to certain sectors and tasks that they believe are recognizable to the audience and visually interesting to shoot.

There are valid reasons for this concentration however, as producer Michele Kurland (interview with authors, 11 January 2007) explained to us in relation to the rise of female-run internet businesses:

One thing I would love to do on entrepreneurship is women and eBay and how women have used this in a business context, borrowing on credit cards because the banks will not lend to them and so on. But it always ends with a woman taking parcels to the Post Office, so it doesn't really work on television.

It must be noted however that some of these difficulties are being slowly overcome as producers try to find ways of connecting with other areas of business. For example, in Series 7 of *The Apprentice* (which was broadcast in May 2011 after our focus group research took place), there was a change of emphasis as contestants no longer competed for a position with one of Lord Sugar's companies but rather for £250,000 worth of investment to start their own company. While this is something we shall discuss further in the next chapter in relation to the problematic relationship *The Apprentice* has traditionally had with the notion of entrepreneurship, the tasks featured in this series also began to engage with more relevant areas of the contemporary business landscape, such as designing a mobile phone application and creating and publishing a free magazine.

Conclusion

This development within *The Apprentice* is interesting as although the above statements raise questions about how these programmes relate to actual business practices, our focus groups suggest that the concentration on specific areas and types of tasks in the business entertainment format do not necessarily impact on people's enjoyment of the shows discussed. Instead, there was an overwhelming recognition that television 'is a business' and, as such, television companies 'have to sell ad space and to do that they need to appeal'. Thus, we found that across all of the groups, respondents were largely knowledgeable about television as a medium and aware of the many complexities involved in the production of factual entertainment programming of this type. Due to the formatted nature of the shows and their prime-time position on public service terrestrial channels, there was an agreement that although primarily entertainment-based, the use of weekly, repeatable narratives nevertheless allowed such programming to put forward certain basic principles about business and how to succeed in certain sectors in ways that are accessible to a wide audience. This ability to inform or instruct audiences on business and entrepreneurship is something that we will examine further in the following chapter, specifically in relation to issues of representation and the use of role models.

Chapter 6

The Television Entrepreneur:
Representations and Role Models

I always feel a bit of an idiot saying 'I am an entrepreneur', because I'm not. Normally I say I am a businesswoman, because anyone can be an entrepreneur, can't they?

> Claire Young, runner-up on Series 4 of *The Apprentice* (interview with authors, 29 September 2009).

I think perceptions of who is an entrepreneur and what you mean by [the term] entrepreneur have been challenged and developed over the years. [For instance] things like social entrepreneurship seem to be more acceptable these days, more part of the mainstream agenda ... Ten years ago or so, it would have been quite easy to summarize an entrepreneur as an amateur Richard Branson type character. I think it's a bit more challenging these days and you are seeing more diverse people.

> Peter Grigg, Head of Policy and Research, Enterprise UK (interview with authors, 12 February 2010).

A number of key themes emerged in our focus group discussions regarding the value of business entertainment formats in offering a range of meanings and representations around entrepreneurship to a mass audience. In this chapter, we begin with an examination of how respondents make sense of the term entrepreneur and its associated characteristics before looking at the relationships between understandings of televisual discourses, the position of entrepreneurship in the everyday lives of our focus group members and entrepreneurial narratives. We then move on to investigate debates around the importance of role models in shaping patterns of behaviour amongst audiences before considering this in relation to representations of gender in business entertainment formats.

Who Wants to Be an Entrepreneur?

Definitions and Perceptions of Entrepreneurship

As noted by Steve Parks (2006: 1 – see the epigraph that opens this volume), most people have preconceived ideas about what constitutes an entrepreneur and we wanted to explore this further by asking respondents what types of images, ideas or characteristics they associate with the word. In the first instance, we found that the contestation evident in academic debate around the definition of 'entrepreneur', as highlighted in Chapter 4, was also prevalent amongst the viewers we spoke to. Although some understood the term as simply meaning a business owner (and thus referred to shopkeepers, for example), most viewed it as being indicative of something more than this, involving attributes such as the following: 'risk-taking, creativity, working in different environments, courage, drive, youth, being single-minded, having spirit and being visionary'. Indeed, the range of attributes cited by respondents was relatively consistent across all groups with common factors including 'being self-taught rather than academically educated, dedicated and focused, having charisma and often displaying contempt for authority', with the latter positioning the entrepreneur in opposition to corporate employees.

Despite the positive associations evoked by many of these qualities, most focus group members did not recognize or place themselves within this frame of reference, including one respondent who had won awards for enterprise but who preferred the more generic term 'businesswoman':

> Well yes, you know, I have won the odd award or whatever but I just find it amazing that folk say, 'oh, that's the most enterprising business in Glasgow' and, you know, who are they looking at? Because I don't think of that as enterprise, I just think well I have got a set of skills and I apply that (54-year-old female IT Consultant, Glasgow).

This lack of identification between our respondents and the entrepreneurs depicted on television is something we identified in Chapter 5 but indeed it must be noted that, within a British context, describing oneself in a public forum using loaded terms such as those listed above may be considered too uncomfortable for some. With this in mind, it is perhaps significant that of the small number willing to define themselves in such a way, many were currently in the employ of someone else and thus had difficulties articulating their exact use of the term: 'Even, like, on my Facebook I describe myself as an entrepreneur as opposed to a businessperson. It's funny, I have to think about why I've chosen that word, so yes, let me come back to you on that one' (34-year-old male estate agent, London). While possible explanations for the use of the term include potential plans to set up a business or recognizing in their character some of the entrepreneurial qualities listed above, it is clear that respondents had various problems both with defining the term and discussing it within a public forum.

Another reason for this emerges when we consider the negative ways in which the word 'entrepreneur' was generally viewed with regards to its value and everyday use. Again, across the groups, there was a consistent use of terms such as 'pretentious, a gambler, arrogant and money-grabbing' as well as direct references to some of the television stereotypes we discussed at the beginning of the book, such as Arthur Daley and Del Boy the wheeler-dealer characters of *Minder* and *Only Fools and Horses* respectively: 'I'm looking at everybody's age here, Arthur Daley, *Minder*, you know that [character] was the lovable rogue and I think he called himself an entrepreneur' (39-year-old male operations shift manager, Glasgow). While these references were evident amongst those respondents aged 30 years and over, they were not so resonant with younger viewers whose television experiences were less likely to feature these specific characters and who also tended to be less harsh in their assessment of the characteristics surrounding entrepreneurship. There was an emerging consensus across all groups however that that the word 'entrepreneur' had become something of a 'TV term that makes [business] sound more interesting [than it is]' and that its increasing association with reality television and indeed the concept of celebrity was 'helping to cheapen' it, something we will consider further in Chapter 7.

Representations of entrepreneurship within factual entertainment programming also led to an overwhelming perception amongst respondents that entrepreneurs were 'young, rich and successful':

> [The term 'entrepreneur' has] got quite a young kind of feel to it, I mean you don't hear about somebody that's just become an entrepreneur at an [older] age … It's just when I hear that word I think young, dynamic, quite motivated, driven (26-year-old self-employed female, Glasgow).

> I think for me, the younger you are in terms of commitment the more encouraged you are in those kind of shows because you aren't jeopardizing things like, you know, your house of your family … The only people I notice on *Dragons' Den* who are of an age, sort of 50 plus, have always retired or already [have] security and then they are just bored in their shed and create something (25-year-old female estate agent, London).

These statements are notable for two reasons. First, they highlight how young people are more likely to both take part in and engage with reality-based programming on television. As noted in the previous chapter, 'entertainment' was recognized as a key element in the appeal of many of the programmes discussed, particularly in attracting and speaking to younger audiences (with the latter appealing to both producers and broadcasters). For many of those we spoke with already running businesses, it was felt that business entertainment formats did not entirely translate or fully capture the real-life experience of an older demographic active in starting and developing businesses.

Second, the above statements demonstrate how such representations of entrepreneurship on television can impact on audience understandings of what types of people are more likely to be entrepreneurs in the real world. For example, the perception amongst respondents that entrepreneurs are young is contradictory to statistics which reveal that 'the average age of the founders of technology companies in the United States is a surprisingly high 39 – with twice as many over age 50 as under age 25' (Stangler 2009: 4). The economic contribution of 'high growth "third age" entrepreneurs' (those over age 50 who set up innovative start-ups that create significant employment) is something that has also been documented in the United Kingdom (Botham and Graves 2009: 2). We would argue that this perception is not solely caused by television but rather wider media narratives that circulate certain myths about entrepreneurship. Moreover, the fact that respondents also perceive entrepreneurs to be 'successful' not only raises questions about how they subsequently understand those who are deemed as having 'failed' within the troubleshooter and business gameshow framework but also alludes to wider British attitudes to failure; something which, as we highlighted in Chapter 4, is regarded in other cultures as being an integral part of entrepreneurship. These complexities were explicitly addressed by only a small number of respondents across all groups however, such as one London-based viewer who interrupted discussion to state that 'everyone has sort of equated entrepreneurialism to success which I think is a mistake' (23-year-old male business development manager, London).

These varying responses suggest that although attitudes towards entrepreneurial activity and traits in general were viewed as positive by the members of the audience we spoke to, some stigma still remains with regards to the term itself and indeed its televisual representations. While this could be considered a hangover from previous decades when entrepreneurs were cast as villains within the media and attracted suspicion within the corporate world, it is also the case that there is still scepticism around its definition and practical everyday use: 'If somebody said to me, "I am an entrepreneur", I would be like, "what does that *mean*?"' [original emphasis] (18-year-old female student, Glasgow). It is perhaps unsurprising then that, apart from a small number of respondents who, on the whole, had aspirations of running their own businesses, the majority of our focus group members were uncomfortable defining themselves as such.

The slippery nature or ambiguity of the term, as it were, is something that is echoed in many business entertainment formats and the discourses surrounding them. For example, Lord Sugar (*Management Today*, 1 May 2001) of *The Apprentice* has himself questioned the use of the term, stating that 'people shouldn't be allowed to use the word entrepreneur. It's used too frequently, it should be illegal. I can't call myself a lawyer or a doctor, because I don't have the qualifications'. In his autobiography, Sugar (2010: 12–13) also suggests that,

> it's certainly not something you call yourself. It should be a term used by a
> person when describing another's abilities. I refer to my entrepreneurial spirit as
> I have been branded an entrepreneur so many times by so many people that I feel
> I've earned the right, and I can see what it takes to be labelled as such.

While Sugar occasionally praises the contestants on *The Apprentice* for their entrepreneurial skill, respondents in the focus groups questioned those who described themselves as entrepreneurs by asking why, if they saw themselves as 'self-starters' and 'go-getters', they had not already set up their own businesses and were instead applying for a position to work for someone else: '[*The Apprentice* contestants] have that safety net, they're employed working for large organizations

... If you're an entrepreneur then ... the main difference is you're taking the risk and hang the consequences' (59-year-old male property developer, London). To respondents, the contestants on *The Apprentice* contradict many of their previous definitions and understandings of the term; contradictions that we have described as often being present within the format itself. However, with the seventh series of the BBC version of the show (broadcast in May 2011), this issue was directly addressed with a change in format that offered £250,000 investment from Lord Sugar for the winner to start a new business.

While this change occurred after our focus groups had been conducted, it is notable that the seventh series was won by self-confessed 'inventor' Tom Pellereau. With the final task involving the pitching of a business plan, this led many media commentators to highlight the similarities with its BBC stablemate *Dragons' Den* and indeed a number of our respondents felt that *Dragons' Den* itself often confused the term 'entrepreneur' with being an 'inventor' or developing a new product or service. This is despite the fact that many of the businesspeople involved in the focus groups made the point that they themselves had achieved success largely by doing something that already existed but in a better or more cost effective manner. Indeed this point echoes that made by Duncan Bannatyne (2006), one of the Dragons on the BBC show, who argues that his own career has never seen him invent anything but rather his ability lies in identifying gaps in often already well developed markets.

These examples highlight some of the complexities surrounding the term entrepreneur in relation to negative discourses and lack of concrete definition in particular, and perhaps begin to explain why many respondents were reluctant to describe themselves in such a way. As we will now go on to consider however, our focus group findings also reveal how respondents' attitudes to business entertainment formats and their appreciation of entrepreneurship was largely dependent on their own position within what can be described as the entrepreneurial cycle.

The Entrepreneurial Cycle

While it is not the specific aim of our study to determine whether business entertainment formats on television encourage actual entrepreneurial activity amongst viewers, what does emerge from this research is that the personal background of respondents in terms of their relationship to entrepreneurship contributes significantly to their understanding and evaluation of these types of programmes. Although it is by no means only businesspeople that are attracted to such programming, we found that what stage respondents are at in the entrepreneurial cycle or indeed whether they have any experience of or desire to be involved in entrepreneurial activity impacted on the various ways in which they engaged with the formats. Essentially, respondents can be divided into three categories. First are those who describe themselves as employees or unemployed with no experience of running their own business or desire to do so. Second are those at the beginning of the entrepreneurial cycle, who have aspirations of running their own business or are in the early stages of making this happen (although for the purposes of our study they may have described themselves as an employee). Third, are those further on in the entrepreneurial cycle who define themselves as business owner, entrepreneur or self-employed and thus possess some sort of experience of running their own business or working for themselves.

As we have discussed in Chapter 5, the majority of respondents across all focus groups reported quite complex viewing experiences in terms of entertainment and informative modes of address within the business entertainment format and felt that most of the programmes discussed were able to successfully convey both when evaluated on their own terms, or rather as factual entertainment formats broadcast in prime time to a general (rather than specialist) audience. For example, due to their formatted nature, respondents noted how the same basic principles about business and how to succeed in certain sectors are continually put forward and that the use of a repeatable narrative makes it possible for a wide audience to comprehend:

> It's the same message every time and see, once you have watched six episodes, it eventually drips in and it's there forever … 'it's a good idea but is it a business?' [an example of a question repeatedly posed on *Dragons' Den*] (39-year-old male operations shift manager, Glasgow).

> It's [always] the same form isn't it; small menus, home-made rustic food. Every bloody restaurant [visited on *Ramsay's Kitchen Nightmares*] and that's what it is (28-year-old radio producer, Glasgow).

> Just like children, you don't sit them down and teach them maths, 1,2,3, but you tell a story as a way of communicating. If Gordon Ramsay says [to a restaurant owner] 'Okay, your message is not too clear because you are selling this and that and the other and you have three [different] menus', you understand they have to be [more] focused (40-year-old male security provider, London).

These statements demonstrate how certain business principles resonate with a large number of respondents regardless of any direct use or intentions to act on them in their working lives.

For some operating more at the margins of our focus groups however, there was disagreement around these issues. Of those who described themselves as having established a business and were thus further on in the entrepreneurial cycle, a small number tended to dismiss any informative or instructional element of such programming because it did not replicate their own experience of business:

> I think they are just totally unrealistic, especially *The Apprentice* for example. About two years ago I think it was, [the contestants] each had an appointment set up with Harrods, with a buyer. Now for anybody in business, trying to get into Harrods to see a buyer, you would be waiting months and months and

months if you get there at all, and these guys had it, you know in the palm of their hand. So it's just so unrealistic and it doesn't actually represent, in my opinion, the problems a small business has in the start-up phase, just to get an appointment with a buyer, that's my experience ... these programmes should be more responsible and give a truer picture of the reality of what it's like out there. (54-year-old male self-employed marketing consultant, Glasgow).

This statement was countered by another member of the group with the question 'I don't think that's the premise of *The Apprentice* though, is it?', a viewpoint that was similarly voiced by other respondents across both locations:

There are many other channels which, if I wasn't doing anything more interesting on a Sunday morning, I will watch that are far more business-oriented. If you want to know about business or the economy or markets, it's there for you. What they show you on prime time television channels is, I think, different. It's not supposed to be there to give you business advice. It *highlights* business issues but it's certainly not there to *educate* you in business issues and I think that's the difference [our emphasis] (43-year-old female personal assistant, London).

It can be argued therefore that by expecting this type of programming to replicate their own experiences of business, this small group of respondents overlook the primary objectives of the programme makers, which is to make an entertaining factual series aimed at a general audience.

This was in stark contrast to the more positive terms used by many of those in the early stages of the entrepreneurial cycle. These respondents found the range of shows on offer informative in terms of conveying business skills and appreciated this more than any entertainment value offered. Discussing *Property Ladder*, one London-based viewer we spoke to who was seeking to enter the construction industry explained 'I sometimes sit there writing things down to be honest. You know, certain things Sarah Beeny says' (29-year-old female administrator). With regards to the experts and successful entrepreneurs such as Beeny who appear on these television shows, terms such as 'inspirational' and 'role models' were used, with many respondents going on to seek out biographies or business books they had published in order to find out more information: 'I love *Dragons' Den*, Theo [Paphitis] is my favourite; in fact I have read his autobiography. I am in the middle of reading Duncan Bannatyne's and in the next couple of years I hope to open my own business, so that's why I find it inspirational to me' (24-year-old male sales rep, Glasgow).

Despite this enthusiasm for the entrepreneurs featured, business entertainment formats were also considered to be cautionary in many ways, bringing home some of the risks involved in pursuing an entrepreneurial direction in real life: 'I'm planning to set things up next year and it's really scary because there are so many things you need to do. And when you watch people on *Dragons' Den* and they're just not prepared or they haven't got the figures, they haven't done their research, it's quite sad' (34-year-old female recruitment consultant, London). Significantly, this cautionary aspect was something that also chimed with our final category of respondents; those with no experience of running their own business or desire to pursue any kind of entrepreneurial activity.

For this group, the depiction of some of the difficulties involved in the day-to-day running of a business and particularly the impact shown on lifestyle offers confirmation that they are better suited as an employee: 'I wouldn't want the stress of my own business and not sleeping at night. I want to have a payslip at the end of the day and that's it. You know, everyone is different, it's different personalities' (33-year-old female corporate events manager, Glasgow). However, many felt that the task-based structure and emphasis on communication and presentation skills within these programmes resulted in tips and advice that they could apply in their working lives regardless of what sector or position they occupied. What we would argue then is that although a small number of respondents believe that television producers and broadcasters have a responsibility to present audiences with (what they themselves consider to be) more 'realistic' representations of business and entrepreneurship, there was an understanding amongst the majority that business entertainment formats on television can only ever offer a partial view of such activities. As such, while certain information and types of instruction are present, the overall emphasis is on providing entertainment, something that we will now go on to examine in relation to the types of narratives around entrepreneurship that feature in business entertainment formats.

Entrepreneurial Narratives   The need for content to be exciting within business entertainment programming was identified across all focus groups along with the importance of the format in shaping the narratives on offer. In the first instance, there was an awareness amongst respondents that businesses on television appear more exciting than the reality because 'boring businesses such as play parks aren't represented onscreen' (a view that echoes Michele Kurland's point, highlighted in Chapter 5, about female-run internet businesses not being suitably 'visual' for television). Likewise, many felt that the range of entrepreneurs on television remain limited, as they 'all seem to be millionaires':

> I would say being an entrepreneur is definitely a lifestyle choice. You know, I think you see the sexy front end of it [on television] but what you don't see is probably a lot of personal sacrifice, a lot of 18 hour days and that's [suitable] for some people but not for a lot to be honest (37-year-old male General Manager, Glasgow).

With this in mind, there was also an understanding that the demands of formatted television help shape the ways in which entrepreneurship is characterized onscreen. For example, due to the competitive framework of business gameshows and the role of the expert in the troubleshooter format, entrepreneurial activity is often characterized as being particularly aggressive. There is an alternative to this however, in the form of 'social enterprise', which was highlighted in focus group discussions by those with personal experience of the sector.

Social enterprises were defined by respondents as having a different agenda in business because they are 'not all about the balance sheet' and instead harness entrepreneurial skills for social ends. While across the focus groups most people were indifferent to the term and unaware of this strand of enterprise, a small number with direct experience of the sector were very clear about its usage and how it differs to traditional forms of entrepreneurship:

> I have met some social entrepreneurs as well who have ran social enterprises and
> ... who have had that self belief and that drive and been dynamic but not been
> purely balance sheet motivated. [They] have been more about sustainability,
> social capital and all those other ideas and they have been the people who have
> made the biggest impact on me, personally, just because they seem to have had
> a broader appreciation of things maybe rather than someone who has sold hard
> and fast (27-year-old male charity outreach worker, Glasgow).

On discussing some of the meanings surrounding social enterprise, there was a feeling that television had begun to touch on this largely neglected area through series such *Jamie's Kitchen, Jamie's Chef* and *The Secret Millionaire*, programmes that engage with community projects in some way and challenge 'the idea that all entrepreneurs have to be hard-nosed'. However there remains a distinct lack of public awareness of how these enterprises operate and how, for example, they are distinctive from say the charity sector. It is significant that respondents with no direct experience of social enterprise nevertheless recognized Jamie's Oliver's *Fifteen* restaurant as an example of a different type of business.

This highlights the reach and influence of prime-time television programming as the creation of Fifteen was documented in *Jamie's Kitchen* and, although not specifically referred to in this way throughout the series, is now described on Social Enterprise UK's website (Accessed 1 September 2011) as 'one of the country's most famous social enterprises'. Raising public awareness of this area through television coverage may be increased however with both the BBC and the BIG Lottery Fund UK joining forces for the production of *Village SOS* (BBC1 2011–), which follows ten community businesses across various rural locations in the United Kingdom that, with lottery funding of up to £400,000 and the allocation of a business mentor, attempt to help regenerate small villages (although notably, like *Jamie's Kitchen*, the show does not explicitly use the term 'social enterprise' but rather 'community business').

It is perhaps not surprising that the idea of the social entrepreneur remains slightly intangible to the viewing public because, as explained by Johansson (2004), the stories that television tells often conform to broader myths about entrepreneurship. For example, the 'rags to riches' motif is one that is both well established and easily recognized by the viewers we spoke to:

> I think the traditional idea of an entrepreneur is, for me, is the sort of 'rags to riches' story; started with nothing [then] going into something else (25-year-old male banker, London).

> I think it is more entertaining to watch probably the 'rags to riches' [narrative] than someone who is born into money and they have been given the money to start off a business; because obviously that is too easy. Better to see, you know, real people (25-year-old female estate agent, London).

Alan Sugar and Duncan Bannatyne were most frequently cited as examples of this supposed 'traditional' path to entrepreneurship and indeed many of the media discourses (Davidson 2001, Barber 2007, Caesar 2009) surrounding both men work to emphasize how a low income, working class background and lack of academic qualifications is no barrier to becoming a successful entrepreneur but instead can instil a commitment and desire to become financially self-sufficient. Indeed it could be argued that, as demonstrated in the above quote, 'real people' or a 'real entrepreneur' appears to equate to those from a 'working class' background.

This is something that is similarly reinforced in an episode of *The Apprentice* in which Lord Sugar (or Sir Alan, as he was at the time), meets contestants outside the housing estate in which he grew up in order to demonstrate his meteoric rise within the business world. Slater's (2007: 8) research into divisions in attitude between what he describes as the 'Enterprise Culture entrepreneur', rooted in the late 1980s and early 1990s, and the 'New Economy entrepreneur', emerging from the dot com boom of the late 1990s, expresses 'the contrast between older and newer entrepreneurial styles as a face-off between Alan Sugar and Richard Branson'.

The differences between these two types of entrepreneurs are echoed by one viewer who compared the 'rags to riches' experience with that of Branson: 'Duncan Bannatyne and Alan Sugar come from very, very similar backgrounds and [have] a desire to make money, so that obviously drives them. Richard Branson ... he came from a very, very wealthy background, private school and all the rest, so his desire was something else that drove him' (44-year-old female self-employed partner, Glasgow). Moreover, it was also recognized that Branson likewise did not go to university and struggled with dyslexia, leading one viewer to question the relatively simplistic 'rags to riches' motif and suggest that the drive required to be a successful entrepreneur may have more to do with 'overcoming adversity': 'Do you think it's always from 'rags to riches' though? I mean Richard Branson didn't come from a very poor family, he came from quite a wealthy family, but he had really bad dyslexia and it's sort of overcoming an adversity which I sort of identify with' (28-year-old male planning consultant, Glasgow). On the whole, it was agreed that there was something that characterized those with entrepreneurial drive from an early age: 'You know whether it's a disability like dyslexia or whether it be poverty; you know there's something there that actually pushes them forward' (40-year-old male health and safety consultant, London), while Branson in particular was referred to as having a maverick personality: 'Richard Branson is probably the only person I know who embodies that. He is like, oh yes, let's go to space' (18-year-old male student, Glasgow).

Another theme that runs strongly through the stories television tells us about the world of business is that of the entrepreneur as 'business guru', helping to save those who are struggling while also encouraging us all to be more enterprising. Again, within our focus groups, certain television personalities were more likely to be cited as exemplifying this type of behaviour, with the experts who act as 'troubleshooters' occurring most frequently, such as Sarah Beeny, Gordon Ramsay, Sir Gerry Robinson and Mary Portas. In contrast, other entrepreneurs who appear on business entertainment formats were regarded as using television to publicize their own businesses and enhance their media profile.

Peter Jones of *Dragons' Den* was predominantly viewed in this way, largely due to recent appearances advertising the price comparison website MoneySupermarket.com:

> Peter Jones [advertising the] MoneySupermarket brand ... he made money out of that, he's making money for himself (28-year-old male planning consultant, Glasgow).

> It's like every advert, they're just all over it. So it's like they virtually use that as their own selling point again to improve their own businesses. Like MoneySupermarket has got Peter Jones everywhere, all over it (25-year-old male graphic designer, London).

Alan Sugar tended to divide opinion, with viewers recognizing that his appearances on television had allowed him to gain more media capital and political influence, particularly with regards to his then government appointment under the Labour administration (something we discuss in the following chapter). Nevertheless there was a widespread feeling that his own background still contributed to him possessing a genuine passion for encouraging business, entrepreneurship and the need for more apprenticeships:

> He seems to be involved at all levels doesn't he? I think he uses television not for his ego or for his own purposes or for his own businesses, but to further what he wants to give back to the type of people from the background that he came from. I mean he came from a community 50, 60 years ago who had nothing and now there are communities here with the same. He's trying to instil that through apprenticeships, not just the Apprenticeship programme, the television programme, but through things that you don't hear or see in the general run of things. (50-year-old male jeweller, London).

This statement is indicative of an apparent wider awareness of Sugar's longstanding involvement with the government's apprenticeship scheme and the way in which his television profile works to enhance this. With this in mind, we will go on to examine some of the debates that arose with regards to business entertainment formats and the issue of role models.

Television and Business Role Models

> The UK has more and more role models of entrepreneurs that have done extremely well and it all seems very accessible and this is where television comes in. If you are confronted with role models of people who look and sound like ordinary people you might know they don't seem so far away from what you might be able to achieve
>
> (Julie Meyer, CEO and Founder of Ariadne Capital and Dragon in the Online Den, interview with authors, 2 September 2009).

Before its demise in 2011 as part of wider governmental fiscal belt-tightening, the charity Enterprise UK was specifically tasked by both business agencies and the Department of Business, Innovation and Skills (BIS) with encouraging entrepreneurship among young people across the UK. Its then Head of Policy and Research, Peter Grigg, was well placed to see the impact that television representations have on this section of the population. For him, programmes such as *Dragons' Den* have raised the profile of particular types of enterprise among younger audiences; although he also notes that differing parts of the audience have differing attitudes and behavioural patterns towards entrepreneurship (interview with authors, 12 February, 2010).

The research findings of Enterprise UK (2009) into attitudes towards entrepreneurship echoes aspects of our own work. For example, their study identifies 'self-starters' as those who are heavily influenced by some of the media role models, but only because they are already highly motivated about starting their own business. At the other end of the scale are those who are not particularly interested in becoming involved in entrepreneurial activity and, again, this view is likely to be reinforced through engagement with television coverage. Between these two groups, the research identified what was described as 'Creative Team Players' and 'Independent Seekers', with the former more likely to be interested in social enterprise activities, and the latter driven by a desire to work for themselves. In many ways these two groups are likely to see aspects of themselves in differing elements of the range of representations that television offers around entrepreneurship.

What is interesting about this work is that while an organization such as Enterprise UK recognizes that television programmes can inspire and provide role models, it is also acutely aware that the audience is in fact complex and multi-layered even when focusing on only the youngest segments. Indeed a key point that emerges from our own research is the extent to which many of these programmes succeed in connecting with younger audiences in ways that traditional broadcasting around business did not:

My 12-year-old daughter will sit down and watch any one of those. She would not sit down and watch *Newsnight*. (44-year-old female self-employed partner, Glasgow)

I think these programmes in the last four or five years have inspired young people into business ... maybe at the beginning, they weren't so much for young people, [but] now young people watch them [and] are inspired (21-year-old male student, London)

One of my sons absolutely loves [business entertainment formats]. He's 14 [and they] fascinate him. (60-year-old male property developer, London)

Of course, while our focus groups did not include under-18s, many of those aged 18 to 21 who took part were themselves at school when programmes such as *The Apprentice* and *Dragons' Den* were first broadcast. Moreover, business entertainment formats appear to be suitable for a range of age groups within the family, hence the anecdotal statements above.

As noted by Down (2010: 185–186), these programmes also regularly act as an 'etiquette guide' for sections of the audience and we found that in this sense, television tends to have a greater impact on those people with less experience of business:

The reason why I think these programmes are more popular with a younger audience is that experience counts for a lot, and I think people who have been in business for a number of years and have had a lot of trial and error find these programmes of less relevance [to them], as opposed to somebody who has maybe just come out of university and is quite interested in making that progression into the real world and gaining that hands on experience. (28-year-old male property administrator, London)

Focus group respondents often noted how the narratives in these programmes often highlighted 'what not to do' as well as 'how to conduct yourself in various business related situations'. Thus, the transmission of 'soft skills' becomes an important way through which sections of the audience engage with such formats because, as we have previously noted, these can be applied in a variety of situations. Business entertainment formats often reinforce important messages around presentation skills, the challenges of working as part of a team and the techniques required for successful team building and leadership.

A recurrent theme in public discussions about programmes such as *The Apprentice* is the issue of role models and the messages that this type of programming sends out regarding 'business role models' in particular. Across the groups this promoted considerable debate and discussion. In the first instance, there was a perception that young people are attracted to wealth and fame and, as such, the successful entrepreneurs featured in *Dragons' Den* have become inspirational figures because of their millionaire and celebrity status. Older members of the focus groups (aged 30 years and over) also felt that by growing up with these programmes, the possibilities of starting a business may appear more tangible for young people than it did for many of their generation. Thus television was regarded as being one part of the wider configuration of influences through which younger viewers may make decisions about the possibility of starting businesses.

The fact that programmes and formats like *Dragons' Den* are used across schools as a vehicle for encouraging younger people to begin thinking about business was again understood to be related to the personality-led aspect of this process. Television entrepreneurs were perceived to sit alongside musicians, actors, sports stars and celebrities in a media landscape that offered possible avenues of social mobility for younger people:

> I think these programmes make everything much more easier to accept for young people, they are kind of being born into it, you know, like some people have been born into the computer age or the mobile phone age .. so they take everything much more for granted and for them to start a business I mean, or start anything, it's so much easier [while] for a lot of people maybe of a certain age it's like so daring, you know. So I think these television programmes make everything much more acceptable for this generation (51-year-old female artist, Glasgow).

Of course the possible impact that certain individuals may have on audiences was not restricted to the younger segment of that audience, as even amongst older respondents there was a consensus that one of the pleasures involved in such programming was the ability to also see aspects of yourself among the various business people featured:

> I think its role models for any age to be quite honest, I think we can all learn from something and I am quite sure we have all, whether it's an interview or a meeting or whatever, I think we have all taken wee tweaks of what we have learnt from *The Apprentice* and applied that to our own lives. So yes, I think you can have a role model whatever age you are (44-year-old female self-employed partner).

Indeed many of the high profile entrepreneurs from television often split opinion among the groups.

Amongst respondents across all focus groups, the most discussed personalities were Gordon Ramsay, Alan Sugar, Sarah Beeny, Mary Portas and Jamie Oliver. For many of the Glasgow-based respondents, there was a feeling that Ramsay had become a bit of a Scottish stereotype and thus a television caricature of himself in *Ramsay's Kitchen Nightmares*. However, this view was tempered across the groups by a consensus that, as explained in Chapter 5, he possessed a 'passion' for business and acted in the best interests of the restaurants he visited. Some respondents pointed to the Dragons as offering more positive role models than Lord Sugar of *The Apprentice*, in part because they are seen as being currently successful and perhaps less abrasive in their manner. However, perhaps unsurprisingly given his London origins, among the London groups Sugar tended to play more strongly with respondents, with many of them also admiring his offscreen commitment to apprenticeship schemes and his efforts to encourage business development more generally.

Significantly, Jamie Oliver was regularly cited by respondents across all groups as a positive role model, despite the fact that no excerpts from his shows were used as visual prompts. He was seen however as having produced a range of programming about businesses that have at their core a 'social conscience' and again his authentic 'passion' for the causes he is involved with (such as campaigns for better school meals and improved diet as well as offering employment opportunities to disaffected youths) was widely admired: 'There's nothing wrong with still getting something personal out of it whether it's monetary or satisfaction or whatever, but it's the knock on effect for how it helps so many other people and opens doors and opportunities and stuff' (33-year-old human resources manager, London). Again, the audience clearly differentiated between the range of business formats on offer and, more specifically, the people appearing on business gameshows and troubleshooter-based programmes. For many in the groups, the latter format meant that, as a viewer, they were more likely to empathize with the struggles depicted but, as the people involved were unsuccessful in their business ventures, they were unlikely to be perceived as role models. The 'troubleshooters' themselves however, such as Sir Gerry Robinson, Sarah Beeny and Mary Portas, were highly valued often for their ability to both listen to the various participants and be passionate about helping the 'real' people they were dealing with.

By way of contrast, respondents were largely interested in the various ways in which contestants on *The Apprentice* relate to one another and 'treat their peers' as it was felt that their 'true' personalities were revealed through this process. Indeed there was an awareness that while 'nasty people' on shows such as *The Apprentice* may be good for entertainment, this was not the only way to behave in business with a number of respondents noting that, significantly, it is often some of the 'nicer people' that usually win through at the end. It was also recognized that many of these programmes offer positive representations of ethnic minorities, with the BBC singled out as being particularly strong on this. Among Asian members of the audience groups this profile was welcomed although their own family role models and networks were identified as the key shapers of their business aspirations. Nevertheless, these programmes were praised for offering a presence to ethnic minorities that is often lacking in other areas of television output and this was deemed as a broadly positive aspect of business-related television content. Running through much of the discussion about role models across the groups was also the issue of gender and the manner in which these programmes represented women in business.

The Gender Divide

> There seems to be an abundance of men on television but there aren't really that
> many incredibly successful women, certainly not ones who want to go on the telly.
> So does that mean that they are all incredibly clever and don't want to go on the
> telly because they know it's going to make them look like an idiot?
>
> (28-year-old female research scientist, Glasgow)

The issue of gender representations on business related programmes raised some contrasting views across the focus groups. The male groups, while offering some comment, broadly did not view the lack of women entrepreneurs on television as a significant absence; a view that was in marked contrast to the attitudes of female viewers. Amongst this group it was agreed that those women that did appear as television presenters and experts brought something distinctive in their approach. For example Ruth Watson and Alex Polizzi from Channel 5's *The Hotel Inspector* were viewed as indicative of this contrast:

> Take the *Hotel Inspector*, I think the women are more constructive and less
> destructive and maybe it's a coincidence, but I wouldn't be surprised if that's a
> female way of dealing with problems, rather than full on attack. You know the
> Gordon Ramsay type approach. It would be a much more sympathetic approach
> I would think (54-year-old female marketing consultant, Glasgow).

While recognizing that women needed to be strong in a business environment, there was a perception that, for example, neither Sarah Beeny nor Mary Portas suffered by being less abrasive in their manner.

The element of television producing and constructing both characters and indeed caricatures is also important in this process. Certainly Sarah Beeny was herself aware (having worked in a male dominated building industry before coming into television) of some of the tensions that may exist between onscreen and offscreen personas. While Beeny (interview with authors, 4 March 2010) explained to us that her own personal style was one that preferred to shy away from confrontation rather than seek it out, this aspect of her personality was not initially what television producers wanted for her onscreen identity:

> I think being a woman there are clever ways to get what you want. To be honest,
> dare I say it, you don't have to go in with the old size tens and kick ass to be taken
> seriously. I sometimes think less is more and you can still be just as successful.
> Gordon Ramsay, Alan Sugar and so forth are all produced [for television] don't
> forget as well. I mean, if I went as far as my producers wanted me to, I would be
> a bitch .. it's an endless argument [and] I don't really want to [have to] say, you
> know, these people [the participants] are twats.

Beeny is also acutely aware of the distinctions between offscreen and onscreen personas, and how the importance of performance on television can be crucial in shaping a programme's identity:

> Alan Sugar and Gordon Ramsay probably aren't in any way as tough to deal with as they appear on television, I am sure they are probably charming. I mean, actually, I have met Gordon Ramsay and he is very charming .. I sort of think he maybe should have said [to his producer], actually I don't really want to be so macho, I am sure it was much more this shade of him that they produced .. and you can end up with a bit of a caricature.

Across the respondents from all groups there was a perception that television expects certain roles to be played through particular television formats and that expectations exist about how men and women should react in particular circumstances. There was also an awareness of the importance of the editing process in shaping perceptions and the expectations that differing formatted television environments produce:

> I think with *The Apprentice* the women come across as completely wrong, 'Oh I am business savvy and I am cut throat'. But when you get real women putting in pitches on *Dragons' Den* they are just normal people who happen to be women who have got a business idea (28-year-old male property administrator, London).

For many, the centrality of the television format was viewed as crucial in defining gender roles, with business gameshows in particular focusing on conflict and aggression. It was argued that *The Apprentice* for example, 'reinforces the stereotype that women have to pretend to be like men to get anywhere in business' (and indeed it is notable that in the opening episode of each series the teams are split according to gender to allow their different ways of working [if any] to be compared).

Yet for all the macho posturing, alternative spaces did exist within the formats and groups noted how this was often reflected in the eventual winner of the series:

> But there are still different types of ways of doing business and, even as a male, you don't necessarily have to be testosterone filled and a hardcore sales person [or] go-getter. That is why I liked the first series of *The Apprentice* because you had someone like Tim, who was very reserved, but his style of business was very effective and how he comes across to people. I think they need to focus more on that. (38-year-old male security supervisor, London).

Indeed all respondents tended to equate a set of masculine terms with business activity, for example 'strong, aggressive, dynamic and arrogant'. As such, these terms were not viewed positively when applied to women. It was often suggested that different rules for men and women applied and that to be successful in business you have to be determined and self-centred, but 'when women do this they are labelled as being a bit of a bitch' or 'it just looks nasty and horrible when [women in business entertainment formats] sound like a man'. It was recognized that while these attitudes may still exist in differing environments, there was also a failure of television to reflect the broader cultural changes taking place in workplaces as many businesses have tried to 'move away from the man-eat-man world where people feel uncomfortable working under a woman'.

As noted at the start of this chapter, the lack of business people who associate with the term 'entrepreneur' was even more acute among women, reflecting broader perceptions from work carried out by Enterprise UK. Peter Grigg (interview with authors, 12 February 2010), then Head of Policy and Research, explains how 'we have found, over the years, that perhaps women, to a larger extent than men, would dislike the term entrepreneur because of the associations with quite masculine power'. This also brings us back to the debate around role models and the importance of media profile in relation to female entrepreneurs. Among the audience members we spoke to there was a strong assumption that there were fewer women in top business positions and that in part television reflected and indeed helped reproduce this imbalance.

It is also interesting to note that those women who appeared on television as the sole 'expert' or 'business guru' were much better received than say someone like Deborah Meaden, one of the Dragons on *Dragons' Den* who was unfavourably compared with the male Dragons by both male and female respondents. Typical of the responses across the groups to Meaden were comments such as: 'She is just so stern, I wouldn't look at her to be my role model'; 'feminine is not a word I would associate with her'; 'she's really aggressive I think. I find her scary'; 'She's not what I would call a role model for women who are supposed to be getting mentoring in that kind of environment'. Meaden (2009: xii) herself has described being on *Dragons' Den* as being in a highly competitive environment that 'resembles an endless fencing match'. She notes how she often had to be assertive with the other Dragons as she established her place in the programme and attempted to make her voice heard (she joined in Series 3 in 2006). Offscreen, however, a number of business writers and commentators consistently indicate she is far from the grumpy, unsmiling persona constructed in the programme.

For example, journalist Deborah Ross (*Daily Mail*, 18 June 2009) found her completely unlike her television image, describing her as someone who 'laughs a lot', while a profile on Meaden in *Women and Home* magazine (Virr and Young 2009) quotes her sister as saying how 'Deborah's TV persona is very different to her real-life one. Viewers see her as curt and abrupt, but she's much softer in reality'. Andrew Davidson (5 April 2009), one of Britain's most experienced business journalists, similarly noted in his interview with Meaden for *The Sunday Times* that:

> Meaden, 50, is a complete surprise – tough on the outside, so funny underneath; able to flick from steeliness to chumminess in the time it would take you to

switch channels. Perhaps the producers of *Dragons' Den*, about to shoot series seven, are missing a trick. She says they edit her nasty. They should try editing her nice. 'But I guess it's not what I am there for,' she shrugs.

There is a tendency of formatted television to turn people into caricatures of themselves then, something clearly recognized by Meaden herself and indeed members of the audience. What is interesting is that while the viewers we spoke to were often aware of this process of construction, they appeared more likely to believe that male businessmen on television may have another side to their 'TV' personality than their female counterparts.

In all the discussions around gender and representation on television, there was clear recognition across respondents that all of these programmes exist within a broader media landscape and culture. While television may offer one of the defining sets of narratives around those women who feature in business entertainment formats, it is print and online media that appear to flesh out these stories and provide specific context and depth to particular television narratives, as noted in the following exchange in one Glasgow group:

> I don't notice any difference in the genders [of participants and experts] until I read the papers the next day (27-year-old male IT consultant, Glasgow).

> Women are still expected to act in a certain way. Aggression or anger is seen as negative [so] they can't be as bold as the men as it becomes a character flaw. That's what's picked up in the press (42-year-old female writer, Glasgow).

Of course appearing on television also presents life-changing challenges for the participants in these programmes and for *female* participants this can be particularly acute. For example, Claire Young (interview with authors, 29 September 2009), the runner up on *The Apprentice* in 2008, explained to us the impact on her life after the series she appeared in began broadcasting on the BBC:

> I was nicknamed 'the Rottweiler' in the press, and they *liked* me. But it is absolutely bananas, like you get followed everywhere. You can hardly get home, you have got people going through your bins, you have people somehow accessing your friends email addresses and getting hold of them, you know, 'sell your story on Claire'. Everywhere you go, somebody wants to talk to you about *The Apprentice* – doctor's surgery, dentist, everywhere, it's ridiculous [original emphasis].

What is interesting is that while the majority of these programmes are broadcast by public service channels, in the form of the BBC and Channel 4, much of the framing of the broader public discussion around them takes place across other media, which more often than not is commercially orientated. To this end, for example, newspapers are happy to mobilize whatever caricature or story line they think will gain them profile and add commercial value to their organization.[1] In this context the debates and struggles regarding representations of women in the media more generally find themselves getting played out within the specific context of the 'business entertainment format'.

Conclusion

What is crucial in understanding any impact such programmes may have on audiences is being aware that what people bring to their viewing experience remains central to how these programmes are engaged with. Those with less experience of, or who are seeking to enter the environments television represents are more likely to be influenced by its construction of the world. What television also clearly does is help shape the broader climate within which these meanings and representations around issues of value and legitimacy get constructed and, in the case of the 'entrepreneur', help also to set an agenda for how that term is understood by the general public. The relatively narrow frame, for example, that suggests entrepreneurs are all millionaires, or that they tend to work in retail or services, does help set the parameters within which large sections of the public understand or make sense of particular concepts such as 'entrepreneur'.

What emerges from this chapter is that business entertainment formats do offer role models but not in some universal one size fits all mode. The broader social context within which audiences engage with these programmes helps shape what they take away from them. Our research certainly found echoes in some of the work being done into regional shapers of entrepreneurial activity across the United Kingdom (Enterprise UK 2009). The London groups, for example, were marginally more likely to recognize themselves in the television representations of business and entrepreneurship than those watching in Glasgow. As Peter Grigg (interview with authors, 12 February 2010), then Head of Policy and Research at Enterprise UK notes, this reflects the complex picture of entrepreneurial activity across the country:

> There are regional differences and what you find is a slight difference between, for instance, self starters who are in greater supply in London .. we noticed in the northeast and northwest there seemed to be lower start up rates but that the percentage of women self starters in those regions was higher. So actually perhaps there is something going on, quite interesting, that we have some quite strong female entrepreneurs in the northeast and northwest. Regionally,

---

1   For example, when Hilary Devey joined Meadon on the *Dragons' Den* panel in 2011, numerous press articles and reviews were primarily concerned with her personal appearance, with one in particular describing her as 'like Cruella de Vil with shoulder pads' (Wollaston 2011).

a fear of failure is one factor in explaining regional differences. Again fear of failure is sometimes a perception thing rather than a real fear, and for a lot of entrepreneurs, probably fear of failure is what keeps them going and keeps them lively. But there seems to be some regional discrepancy about attitudes to risk and things that might put you off starting up. There seems to be fewer problems with risk in London and the southeast than in other parts of the UK.

It is also important to note that entertainment remains a central element in the audience engagement process, however much this is viewed by business people as creating a distorted image of business and entrepreneurship. We return to this argument in our final chapter but, in the context of what we have discussed so far in this part of the book, it is worth reflecting on the experience of some of the participants of *The Apprentice* who have forged a business career and public profile through their appearance on the business gameshow.

Claire Young (interview with authors, 29 September 2009) for instance notes how, in her experience, television and its use of entertainment-led formats has made a significant impact among younger audiences in terms of encouraging them to engage with business:

> I do a lot of work with young people and the cut through which *The Apprentice* has .. they might be in a classroom, not interested in academia, not listening to their parents, not listening to the teachers, and it is a form of communication for them which they feel quite comfortable listening to because it is entertaining, it is reality TV. But they are picking up information from it and, you know, I have had the naughtiest teenagers in the country come up to me and say 'yes, I want to be like you when I get older'.

Thus as we argue throughout the book, differing programmes clearly offer different levels of intensity and engagement and a business gameshow such as *The Apprentice* has the ability to attract various segments of the television audience with each group taking something from it.

When respondents were asked to name who people thought was the single most high profile and successful entrepreneur in the United Kingdom however, every group across all demographics highlighted Sir Richard Branson. While Branson did enjoy a brief television profile with his *Rebel Millionaire* reality show which ran for one season on the Fox Network in America in 2004–2005, it is testimony to both his business acumen and formidable PR skills that he remains so rooted in the broader popular imagination. It is also perhaps indicative that until relatively recently Branson did not appear to have much competition in terms of other high profile British entrepreneurs. We argue, along with Peter Grigg in the opening quote in this chapter, that this is clearly changing as a range of business related formats are increasingly broadcast and perhaps, just as importantly, these programmes and the 'celebrities' they help construct go on to enjoy a media and public profile significantly enhanced by a content hungry digital media ecology. It is to the rise of the celebrity entrepreneur in the contemporary television age and the wider implication of this process for both the public and political culture that we turn our attention in the following chapter.

Chapter 7

Television Business in the Age of Celebrity

Gordon Brown will make his most audacious bid to show himself as the unbeatable 'Prime Minister in waiting' this week with a remarkable series of meetings with foreign leaders and the launch of a groundbreaking aid initiative backed by the Pope. In what one aide described as an effort to 'show what a Brown premiership will look like', the Chancellor told *The Observer* yesterday of his vision for an 'X-Factor' Britain. He said the reality TV music programme, as well as shows like *Dragons' Den* and *The Apprentice,* promoted 'aspiration, how anyone can achieve things' – key to the agenda he hoped to bring to Number 10.

> Neil Temko, Brown outlines his vision for an 'X Factor' Britain, *The Observer,* 5 November 2006.

The Government has tasked retail specialist Mary Portas, star of the TV show *Mary Queen of Shops*, with turning around Britain's ailing high streets. The TV presenter, has been asked by Prime Minister David Cameron to carry out an independent review into the future of the high street.

> Rosie Baker, Mary Portas asked to revive high street, *Marketing Week*, 17 May 2011.

As Temko (2006) and Baker (2011) note above, politicians of all political persuasions have been keen to associate themselves with the television entrepreneurs. Throughout the book we have referred to the 'celebrity' status of a number of television entrepreneurs and in this chapter we will consider this in more detail by examining some of the connections between the media and business elites. It is important to recognize that this is not a new phenomenon however. For example, in their analysis of the relationship between business celebrity and the celebrity business, Guthey, Clark and Jackson (2009: 5–6) argue that rather than being another area of society that has become influenced by celebrity culture, business celebrity has actually been integral to its rise. This is because the development of the American commercial public relations industry (that supports, constructs and helps maintain the celebrity industries), initially grew out of the concerns of big business regarding adverse media coverage administered to key business figures such as John D. Rockefeller in the early part of the twentieth century. Explaining the central role played by what they term 'business culture intermediaries' in 'the manufactured co-production of business celebrities', Guthey, Clark and Jackson (2009: 4) suggest that this is crucial in understanding the position of business figures in contemporary public and media discourse. The 'business culture intermediaries' cited in their work include public relations agencies, journalists, editors and photographers, a list to which we would also add television companies, executives and broadcasters.

In their subsequent typology of business celebrities, Guthey, Clark and Jackson (2009: 13) identify the categories of celebrity entrepreneurs, celebrity business leaders/Chief Executives and celebrity management gurus, with their research focusing on the latter of these two. They also concentrate primarily on the media and cultural industries in the United States, while at the same time recognizing the global nature of the circuits of communication that help sustain these celebrity cultures. Our focus in this chapter is on the celebrity entrepreneur and the television and media industries in the United Kingdom. In particular, this chapter develops themes identified earlier in the book and is interested in understanding both the role played by key business celebrities in converting their media capital into various forms of political capital, as well as analyzing the perceptions that exist of the celebrity entrepreneur among viewers of business entertainment programmes.

We have examined the relationship between political, business and media elites elsewhere (Boyle and Kelly 2010) and the first part of this chapter draws on some of this work. What we wish to argue here is that the rise of the 'business entertainment format' in the United Kingdom from the 1990s onwards has helped propel a new generation of British entrepreneurs into public life. As we argued in Chapter 4, for many decades British entrepreneurs had little public profile beyond the narrow confines of the business press, with the notable exception of Sir Richard Branson. The increased profile of business across television output has brought a new wave of entrepreneurs to public prominence in the last decade or so. Many of these people have successfully harnessed the media capital they have generated to enhance their own businesses, as well as enjoy increased influence and access to political and policy elites.

Business Advisors and Policy Networks

In their research into the relationship between the media and politics, Davis and Seymour (2010: 739) argue that,

> As societies become more 'mediated' so the elevation of public figures is increasingly linked to their ability to generate a positive public profile through the mass media. Politicians, artists, film stars, authors and others each gain professional status, in part according to how consumer-citizens actively respond to media representations of them.

To this list we would add businesspeople and entrepreneurs who, as we have noted throughout the book, build on initial television exposure to accumulate various forms of media capital that brings them to the attention of policy makers and politicians.

By this we mean the ways in which politicians attempt to mobilize the public profile of certain business celebrities and pull them into the policy arena, either as consultants and policy shapers, or as advocates for governmental policy often in the field of enterprise and business. As Littler (2007: 239) argues for example, 'we can not only think how the celebrity CEO Alan Sugar becomes a brand through the interrelationship between a wide variety of media formats. we can also consider how this is connected to a broader and specifically neoliberal cultural-economic discourse of meritocracy'. Underpinning this symbiotic relationship is the assumption (which may or may not have actual merit) that politicians appear to believe that these individuals will both raise the media profile of their initiatives and influence the public and various stakeholders in society in a manner which politicians appear incapable of doing themselves.

Of course as we outlined in Chapter 4, the role of business people advising government or being pulled into the rarefied networks of policy formation is not new. However, traditionally these advisory positions have been held by very senior executives, such as the involvement with the Conservative government of Lord Hanson (The Hanson Group) and Lord King (British Airways) during the 1980s. While these senior executives still form part of the advisory network of government through bodies such as the Business Council of Britain, in addition to this group there is another crop of business people operating within the orbit of government and policy circles that have in common a high media profile, largely created through television. James Harding (interview with authors, 15 March 2007), then City Editor and now editor of *The Times*, told us that, 'None of the people who appear on television are significant business people. Some are great ambassadors for business and some are lousy, but most of them are TV personalities, and hats off to them, that is a difficult thing to do. But they are not running British Airways'. In other words while their access to the political elite has in part been secured by their business background, it has been significantly enhanced by their television and associated media profile.

When Sir Alan Sugar became a Labour peer in the House of Lords and an (unpaid) advisor to Lord Mandelson at the Department of Business Innovation and Skills (BIS) in 2009, it was at a time when it was widely acknowledged that his business profile had been in relative decline for a number of years but his public profile, through the BBC version of *The Apprentice*, had never been higher. Indeed, Daisy Goodwin (interview with authors, 13 March 2009), former executive producer of *The Apprentice* for Talkback Thames, notes that:

> Interestingly [Sugar] is the man who has gone from being a business figure now to a TV star. Business wise he is not really a player any more but TV wise he is a star. So it is quite interesting how, as TV people become more business-like, businessmen have become sort of divas.

In many ways this political fixation with high media profile business 'stars' reflects a broader cultural shift around the mediation of politics and the function of aspects of celebrity. In his autobiography, Lord Sugar (2010: 565–582) documents in some detail the media and political firestorm that erupted over his appointment.

It was driven by criticism of his appointment from the Conservative Party and the *Daily Mail* newspaper, but picked up on by other media outlets as the story gained momentum, and centred on what these critics saw as a conflict between Lord Sugar working as advisor to government, taking the Labour whip in the Lords and fronting *The Apprentice* on BBC television as a general election loomed.

In the end the BBC held firm, just, and re-scheduled a 'junior' version of *The Apprentice* featuring 16 and 17-year-olds to run after the general election in 2010. Our own research indicates that none of our focus group respondents saw any conflict in the roles occupied by Lord Sugar however, as all viewed the show as being apolitical in terms of party politics. Indeed a number noted that ultimately it was a pro-business programme that, while ideological in this sense, played to no political party. What these events demonstrate however is the *perceived* importance that political elites place on having celebrity business endorsement and the *perceived* impact they believe this may have on the public. The campaign against Sugar led by the then shadow culture minister Jeremy Hunt was also informed by an anti-BBC ideology and an individual personal antagonism towards the Labour supporting Lord Sugar that stretched across the Conservative Party and the *Daily Mail.*

Against a backdrop of a political culture often fixated with the importance of image and the usage of public relations and media management in broader political communication, what politicians are buying into is the mediated image of the 'television entrepreneur'. Doug Richard was one of the original Dragons to feature on the BBC2 series in 2005. His background as an angel investor long predates his involvement in the show, but he is clear about the impact that having a television profile has in allowing access to political elites. Commenting on the ability of fellow Dragon Peter Jones to gain direct government backing from then Prime Minister Gordon Brown for his National Enterprise Academy launched in 2009, despite having no experience of the education sector, Richard (interview with authors, 2 June 2009) is scathing:

> Why would a Peter Jones [type] be there? He is not qualified on any level. So what [kind of] Peter Jones is it that is putatively qualified? It is a fictional one, it is a persona that was created by the BBC. The thing that is really sad is not that Peter Jones has fallen for the persona that has been painted of him, but that Gordon Brown has. And some people would say he is just using him – no way, because he is actually using his proposals – not just using him as a figure. So we now actually have government turning to fictional persona to drive policy. People who should know better, and should be actually looking to real accomplishments and be able to discern what is real from what is fiction, have fallen for the fiction. That is an astonishing indictment of our current situation.

This particular government decision was also controversial because Jones appeared to be given Whitehall backing at the expense of an academy focusing on engineering that was championed by the inventor and entrepreneur Sir James Dyson.

For Richard, this change of focus can in part be attributed to Gordon Brown believing that due to his higher media profile, Jones would garner more plaudits and associated media headlines than Dyson. Richard argues that 'the reason Gordon Brown pick[ed] him is because Peter is still on *Dragons' Den* and James Dyson has never been, so one [persona] is real and one is fictional'. Indeed the media coverage became a Dyson versus Jones story in which various allegations about why one proposed project (around nurturing engineering and under discussion for a number of years) was dropped in favour of the lower cost National Enterprise Academy (fostering and teaching entrepreneurial skills) championed by Jones. We would argue that while there were clearly a range of issues associated with each project, the media profile of Jones (with no experience in the educational field), his ability to network and understand the policy machine of Whitehall and his strategy of dealing directly with the Gordon Brown, were important factors in the successful endorsement of the scheme.

Richard (interview with authors, 2 June 2009) himself acknowledges that his invitation to chair the Conservative Party's Taskforce on Small Business in part came from his own media profile: 'Would I have been asked had I not been on *Dragons' Den*? No I would not have'. Indeed his connections with the Coalition government continued after this and included him travelling with Prime Minister Cameron as part of a United Kingdom trade mission to South Africa in 2011. Although he has 25 years' experience of working both in the United States and United Kingdom with government programmes to encourage small business development, again the media capital he has accrued through television helped facilitate political access.

The Dyson connection does not end there however. Sir James, who through his innovative Dyson range of products has also cultivated a media profile (although not, it must be noted, a television profile like that of Jones), was asked in 2009 by David Cameron's Conservative Party to write a report looking at how best to develop Britain as a high technology exporter within Europe and beyond. Entitled 'Ingenious Britain', the Dyson report (2010) appeared a year later and examined the cultural, educational and economic shifts in emphasis required to re-focus Britain as a high technology, engineering and design economy. It was warmly endorsed by the Conservative Party with Ken Clarke, then Shadow Business Secretary, indicating that any Conservative government would broadly follow the report's agenda and recommendations.

The Political Business Class

We would argue that the growing use of celebrity business endorsement is indicative of a recognition that most senior ministers in the United Kingdom are professional politicians with little or no 'real life' business experience; part of what Oborne (2008: 6) has called the 'political class' who often lack credibility with the business community and public more generally: 'Members of the Political Class make government their exclusive study. This means they tend not to have significant experience of industry, commerce, or civil society'. Thus, for politicians lacking a business 'hinterland' these 'business experts' lend, in the eyes of politicians at least, credence and credibility to their political interventions in these areas of policy formation. In this way the relationship is different from other forms of celebrity endorsement that politicians have traditionally mobilized as they associate themselves with leading stars from the world of sport and the entertainment industries.

In other respects these 'television entrepreneurs' are also benefiting from an increasingly symbiotic relationship between political and media elites. Again this is not new, but there has been a step change in the level of integration between political and media networks of power (Oborne 2008: 257–8, Davis 2007, Stanyer 2007) since the 1990s. The intensification, since the election of New Labour in 1997, of a London-centric social networking circuit that brings together the political, media and business classes is well illustrated in the memoirs of former *Daily Mirror* newspaper editor Piers Morgan (2005) where he recounts the numerous occasions he was invited to Downing Street by Tony Blair or would meet senior government ministers on the social circuit. Likewise, Duncan Bannatyne had been making donations to the Labour Party since 1997 and was a well-known businessman in his North East base. Yet, following his appearance on *Mind of a Millionaire* (BBC 2003) and as one of the original Dragons on *Dragons' Den* his profile changed dramatically as he found himself being invited to speak with Gordon Brown in Downing Street and play a role in shaping government schools policy around encouraging entrepreneurship (Bannatyne 2006: 275). This is in addition to the media and television career he has subsequently developed.

The extent to which the News International phone hacking scandal which finally gained significant public profile in 2011 will alter the networks of power between media, political and business elites in the United Kingdom remains to be seen. Unquestionably it has weakened and severely damaged the position and influence of the media mogul who has dominated British media politics for decades, Rupert Murdoch. However the nature of elite networks of influence, enhanced by celebrity, social and geographical ties will not simply disappear, but rather get re-calibrated in ways that remain difficult to predict.

In the case of the television entrepreneurs it appears therefore that just as the vocational skills possessed by these entrepreneurs bring them to the attention of television producers in the first instance, their televisual skills and ability to cultivate a wider media profile then allows them access to the political elite, enabling them to air their opinions, contribute to policy and even establish national education centres (as in the case of Peter Jones) with the backing of the British government. While in a similar manner to traditional celebrity networks this is partly about a common currency of media profile. For the new generation of 'television entrepreneurs' it also reveals, as we have noted, a perception among the political class that these business celebrities are more likely to reach out and connect with the public on business issues than politicians are. Indeed this process is taking place against a wider global shift in the rise of what, rather uncritically, Bishop and Green (2008) have called 'the age of philanthrocapitalism' where 'celanthropists' or celebrity givers such as Bill Gates, Bill Clinton, George Soros, Bono and Sir Tom Hunter form networks of influence between government, foundations, think-tanks, the super-rich and celebrity culture to shape and influence global change in policy areas such as the environment. Again, while the issue of using celebrity to advance particular political narratives is not new, these new types of networks do operate on a global level like never before.

The Television Entrepreneur

As we have argued throughout the book, in the United Kingdom the rise in popularity of programmes such as *Dragons' Den* has also offered another vehicle through which to establish a media profile. For instance, while each of the Dragons to contribute to the series over the years have had previous business careers (as without this they lack the credibility that is vital to their image on the show), none had any particular public or political profile. This quickly changed following their involvement in the BBC series, although this is in part dependent on their own individual interests in developing this aspect of their business identity

Rachel Elnaugh was the first female entrepreneur to appear on *Dragons' Den*, a situation that afforded her a certain cachet within the public's consciousness. However, during filming of the second series her business Red Letter Days ran into serious financial trouble and was eventually sold to her fellow Dragons Theo Paphitis and Peter Jones. Following her appearance on the BBC programme and demise of her company, she subsequently wrote a book (Elnaugh 2009) in which she interviewed entrepreneurs about the role that failure has played in their business careers. She also recognized the key role that appearing on television has played in her ongoing career. For example, in a similar manner to the original troubleshooter Sir John Harvey-Jones (1990), Elnaugh was deluged from the moment the show was broadcast with emails from people wanting her opinion, advice and time with regard to business issues. She thus found herself becoming a 'celebrity entrepreneur' and, even with the collapse of her company, this profile allowed her to develop a career through mentoring, public speaking and endorsements that without her television status would simply not have evolved.

Certainly the ability to build a media career has been one of the advantages for many of the entrepreneurs who have appeared on business television programming. From *Dragons' Den* alone this includes Duncan Bannatyne's various TV appearances (*Fortune: Million Pound Giveaway* ITV, 2007; *Beat the Bank* BBC2, 2008; *Bannatyne Takes on Tobacco* BBC2, 2008; *Out of the Frying Pan* BBC2, 2010 and *Duncan Bannatyne's Seaside Rescue* Virgin 1, 2010) through to Peter Jones creating his own eponymously named television company and appearing in a range of television advertising campaigns for companies such as British Telecom and MoneySupermarket.com.

For Dominic Bird (interview with authors, 27 March 2009), Executive Producer of *Dragons' Den*, the combination of compelling content, the right format and a sprinkling of celebrity culture is what enables the show to connect with its younger audience:

> There is now a sense that there is a younger generation who see being a Dragon or being a business person as a cool thing to do ... I am sure this is related to being on TV, the same way that often people aspire to the celebrity side of life. Thus the glamour of it being on TV has made it accessible to those people, and you can't argue that celebrity isn't massively powerful ... I mean, in the same way, why would ad agencies spend so much money on having celebrities front their campaigns? It's a powerful thing. But celebrities haven't driven *Dragon's Den*, the format is bigger than the individuals.

When James Caan, head of private equity firm Hamilton Bradshaw, joined the programme in 2007 he was unprepared for the impact his appearance would have on his personal and professional profile. Initially contacted through a talent scout who recruits for television companies, Caan (2009: 356) has seen his television profile pull him into media and political circles with lightning speed:

> Appearing on *Dragons' Den* has had an impact on my business as well as my personal life. I now get more invitations to many more events, parties and charity fundraisers, as well as requests to offer my opinion on things like *Newsnight*, *Sky News* and *Bloomberg*. I am asked to talk about the economy or comment on changes to the trading environment, but sometimes I get asked my opinion on whatever is in the headlines. During one interview I was even asked what impact the Indonesian elections would have on the economy. I had to stop myself saying live on air: *What Indonesian elections?* [original emphasis]

Caan had also developed good contacts with the then Labour government and Gordon Brown in particular on the back of his increased media profile. In 2009, he was invited by Lord Mandelson to become Co-Chair of the Department of Business, Innovation and Skills' (BIS) Ethnic Minority Task Force, part of whose remit it is to ensure that black and minority ethnic entrepreneurs have access to appropriate business support and as we note below this relationship with government has continued under the Coalition government since 2010.

Of course, along with the development of a television profile and burgeoning political influence, each of the Dragons have also been pursued by a publishing industry keen for them to produce the almost obligatory biography or 'how to succeed in business' book documenting their rise to dominance within the business world. It is here again that the 'rags to riches' narrative is reiterated and celebrity entrepreneurs are positioned as viable role models for the wider public.

PR Management and Social Media

For most of the Dragons, their media profile is controlled by key public relations agencies. For Duncan Bannatyne it is Phil Hall Associates (PHA) run by the eponymous former editor of the *News of the World*. PHA specializes in reputation management and celebrity PR and includes other celebrity entrepreneurs such as Gordon Ramsay among its clients. Peter Jones retains Max Clifford Associates (MCA), one of the most high profile celebrity PR agencies in the United Kingdom. MCA also work with television entrepreneurs such as Simon Cowell (*The X Factor*; *Britain's Got Talent* ITV, 2007–) who co-produced *American Inventor* (through his company SyCo Ltd) with Peter Jones Television for ABC in 2006. Indeed Jones (2007: 231) recalls how when he had the idea for the programme it was to Clifford he brought the proposal to allow him to pass it to Cowell.

Lord Sugar of *The Apprentice* uses Frank PR to assist in his image management, a leading company in the United Kingdom that seeks to work with both household-names and small entrepreneurial start-ups (an ethos in keeping with Sugar's own commitment to fostering enterprise and encouraging apprenticeships). A core element in this circuit of promotion is the ability to gain profile across a range of media platforms and outlets. For previous winners and contestants of *The Apprentice*, many of whom have since set up their own businesses, building a public persona through business-to-business media has been important. A number, including the winner of the first series Tim Campbell, use the agency Taylor Herring Public Relations who work with Talkback Thames and the BBC on the programme and have a Celebrity PR division. As a result, television entrepreneurs are regularly featured in *Business Sense*, the largest circulation business magazine in the United Kingdom, with Campbell appearing on the cover of the Spring 2010 edition as the British government's new social enterprise ambassador. In short, by appearing on television and through careful public relations management, these entrepreneurs now have a public platform that was denied them previously no matter how successful and wealthy they may have been.

While PR companies act as cultural intermediaries that seek to extend the media profile and individual brands of their various clients at the same time as remaining largely invisible from public view, there has also been a new development in what Marshall (2010) terms the 'promotion and presentation of the self' through the use of social media. As a number of scholars have sought to explain (Horton and Wohl 1956, Tolson 2001, Drake and Miah 2010), the relationships established by celebrities and their audiences using 'old' media such as television has tended to be based on what is best described as 'para-social engagement'.

This involves the recognition of the difficulties involved in celebrities communicating individually with members of the mass audience and thus instead focuses primarily on a one-way flow of communication in which viewers are encouraged to develop 'real but imagined relationships' with celebrities in the public sphere (Tolson 2001: 451). However, this has begun to change recently in two ways. First, the development of reality television has created feedback mechanisms through voting systems for example, which Drake and Miah (2010: 62) describe as 'a popular reflexive device allowing audiences to play and interact within the boundaries of the format'. Second, the emergence of social networking websites has allowed celebrities to begin to interact more directly with their audience (although it is often the case that Facebook and Twitter sites are also administered by public relations companies as part of a wider management strategy).

For those celebrities who do assume control of their online profile however, social media allows them to present a 'public private self' (Marshall 2010: 44) that provides further exposure and access to their individual lives. Moreover, Marshall (2010: 45) also explains that 'the currency of Twitter is that it is much more connected to mobile delivery and thus gives the sensation of immediacy'. Establishing a sense of immediacy is something that television has previously sought to do through the use of direct address to camera that we discussed in Chapter 3. But social networking provides added interactive and instantaneous elements by allowing other users to comment and post messages and by revealing the location of the celebrity or the types of activities they are engaged in at any given time. This helps create 'new forms of mediated intimacy between celebrity performers and their publics' (Drake and Miah 2010: 62) that can either work to circumvent or enhance more traditional public relations routes.

It is the case that each of the television entrepreneurs discussed above all have a Twitter profile, and indeed it is here that they often identify themselves as entrepreneurs and television personalities rather than as business people per se. While the value of this type of social networking in terms of extending business brands and garnering influence and power is yet to be determined, it can be argued that online profiles do add to the celebrification process and bestow further cultural capital on those who take part.[1]

The fusion of politics, celebrity and the role of business gurus continues apace in the United Kingdom despite a change of government. Sir Philip Green (initial choice to be the face the British version of *The Apprentice*, but too busy for television) was invited in 2010 by the new Prime Minister, David Cameron, to 'carry out an efficiency review of Government spending, focusing on commodity procurement, property and major contracts' (Lansley and Forrester 2010). This was followed, in early 2011, by Mary Portas, the retail consultant and television business guru, being asked by the Department for Business, Innovation and Skills (BIS) to carry out a review into the future of the retail sector in Britain's high streets.

---

1   In 2011, James Caan became the first celebrity entrepreneur to launch a 'Business Secrets' Smartphone application providing advice for aspiring entrepreneurs.

The Celebrity Entrepreneur and Public Perception

This fusion of celebrity, political and business culture, while hidden to some extent from wider public scrutiny, does not go unrecognized by the broader viewing public of business programmes. As one viewer noted:

> I think entrepreneurs have become more and more associated with celebrity in recent years because I think a lot of celebrities now have got a lot of money behind them. Whether you're an artist, musical artist or acting, you have got the money, you have got the image, you have got the ability to sell products. David Beckham is an entrepreneur, he is a footballer, but he is [also] an entrepreneur … I think a lot of entrepreneurs now want that celebrity status because they have got the money, they have got everything, but they want the fame and they want the recognition. That is why I think you get a lot of entrepreneurs going on these TV programmes now, because it is a way of them getting into other markets. (39-year-old male procurement executive, London).

Across all of the focus groups there existed a strong perception that many of the participants that appeared on a range of business related programmes viewed their involvement as an entry point into a media related career. Indeed, as particular formats become more established it was argued that this process becomes more pronounced. For some viewers, this resulted in a loss of interest in the format as participants appeared more media aware and simply intent on attaining fame. Of course, this was more prevalent in reality type formats which were contrasted with, for example, the three part BBC and Open University series *Can Gerry Robinson Fix the NHS?*, in which Sir Gerry Robinson investigates the problems associated with reducing waiting lists in a mainstream National Health Service hospital. Here the participants were nurses, NHS managers and clinicians, none of whom were seeking to enhance their media profile by appearing on such a programme.

As noted in Chapter 3, many former contestants of *The Apprentice* in particular have been successful in developing media careers following the exposure they secured by being on television. Even for participants on *Dragons' Den* however, who are generally perceived to be more interested in furthering their business (rather than media) profiles, the exposure that new product ideas and start-up companies can achieve often outweighs some of the downsides of appearing on the programme. Ralf Klinnert, the Scottish based Managing Director of Funky Moves Ltd had a two hour grilling in the Den (edited to around ten minutes for the television broadcast) and despite initial negative feedback eventually secured funding from two of the Dragons, Theo Paphitis and Peter Jones, for his interactive fitness game for children. However, after over a year's 'due diligence' the investment from the Dragons fell through. Klinnert (Resource Newsletter 2011) was surprised by how often this happens and suggests that as very few investments from the Dragons are followed through the programme is primarily 'about entertaining the public, not about business investment'. Yet, despite this, the publicity has been good for his business, as one of the hardest things any new start-up enterprise faces is being able to gain market and public profile.

Among our audience respondents there was widespread recognition that the new generation of television entrepreneurs, such as Lord Sugar or Peter Jones, all benefited in their own business lives from increased television exposure. Typical responses as to why these business gurus should wish to appear on television from across the respondents included the following:

> They can invest their money in other businesses and don't need a camera in front of them but [the Dragons] have thought, 'I quite fancy that'. It's maybe another challenge to them, they become very successful in the field of making money and they want to go into something different and be successful (39-year-old male operations shift manager, Glasgow).
>
> I think that's a kind of career progression, kind of career change as well ... I will do what I am very good at on telly and then I will maybe go on and do something else (35-year-old male museum manager, Glasgow).

The importance of the influence that media exposure confers was also identified along with the business benefits that entrepreneurs enjoyed from increasing their media profile:

> I think a lot of these people do it for two reasons. One of the reasons [is] just to advance the business ... but on the other hand, I think the people that do have some kind of financial satisfaction, want something else than just business and success. So being on television, it can be quite fun and kids even look at you differently and say 'wow, I want [to be like] that on TV'. If [they] can work and influence other people's lives through television, what could be better than that? (51-year-old female artist, Glasgow).
>
> [There was that] marvellous moment in *Dragon's Den* when one of the people coming in says to Duncan or Peter, 'but you have got such influence, you can pick up the phone and get through to the head of Marks and Spencer's', and you can feel Duncan or whoever go, 'yes I can, yes, I have that influence' (55-year-old male copy editor, Glasgow).

Thus the ways in which capital acquired through media exposure is then translated into other fields of influence, as discussed earlier in this chapter, was widely recognized amongst respondents. Most did not have a major issue with this process as they often supplemented this view with a positive perception regarding the offscreen good work many of the television entrepreneurs did for British businesses or charity work. They also felt that for all the limitations of the range of role models offered by celebrity businesspeople, particularly to a younger audience, in many aspects this version of celebrity was more valid or useful than the lure of celebrity culture offered through programmes such as *The X Factor* or *Big Brother.*

As mentioned throughout the book the role played by the wider media culture was crucial in helping to build a broader profile for many the entrepreneurs. While television was their original source of fame for many, with notable exceptions such as Lord Sugar, whose previous involvement as Chairman of Tottenham Hotspur Football Club meant he had long been the subject of media coverage, it was the wider infrastructure of the media, from print to online, that both supplemented and helped construct the public identity of the entrepreneurs. Thus for some such as Duncan Bannatyne his access to political powerbrokers and politicians like Gordon Brown was only one part of the benefits that accrued from his media exposure. As noted above, Bannatyne also fronted and appeared in a number of other television programmes as well as documentaries:

> People like Duncan Bannatyne are making documentaries on things that have nothing to do with business like doing a documentary on smoking in Mauritius and South Africa and places like that. So I think they have got the money but now they want to diversify into that celebrity status so I think entrepreneur has become, maybe to the younger generation more affiliated with celebrities (28-year-old male property administrator, London).

> Alan Sugar loves being on telly, you can tell. He doesn't need the money, he loves it, I love the way he says 'I have laid this on', he's not paying for any of it, the BBC are. I have laid on this penthouse apartment and he's not paying for it, but he just loves it doesn't he, being on telly? They all do (38-year-old male property developer, London).

As has been the case throughout this study, the positive or negative impact such representations have divides opinion.

For example, the *Daily Telegraph's* technology correspondent Milo Yiannopoulos (2011) covers start-ups in the technology sector and views the rise of the celebrity entrepreneur as having a potentially negative impact on new entrepreneurs who appear to view aggressive promotion as an integral part of getting ahead in business:

> We live in an age of aggressive, vacuous self-promotion, for which reality television – including shows ostensibly dedicated to business, like *The Apprentice* and *Dragons' Den* – must bear some responsibility. But is it too much to ask of the wealth creators that they keep it real? There appears to be a pernicious cult emerging, especially within the technology industry, of 'famous for being famous' entrepreneurs, who swank around with D-list celebrities at awards ceremonies when they ought to be in the office, building their businesses and creating jobs.

Yet as Guthey, Clark and Jackson (2009) demonstrate, self-promotion has been an aspect of business life since the early days of mass media development in the nineteenth century. The social media environment may allow this to take place to a greater degree in the digital age but technology companies in particular, and those involved with them, have always been at the forefront of self-promotion.

Indeed even among those perhaps sceptical of the business content in many of these programmes, the research around the impact of these representations does also indicate that they are re-reshaping the views audiences have about entrepreneurship. For example, Levie, Hart and Karim's 2010 report, entitled 'Impact of Media on Entrepreneurial Intentions and Actions', indicated that of the non-entrepreneurs surveyed, 58 percent viewed entrepreneurship more positively because of the television coverage. Furthermore, although two thirds of non-entrepreneurs did not think their most watched business format offered a realistic depiction of what it is like to run or start a business, around 12 percent of *new* entrepreneurs nevertheless said that this type of television actually had an effect on their start-up decision.

Conclusion

As we have noted, the term entrepreneurship has become increasingly popular in both popular and policy discourse in the United Kingdom since the election of New Labour in 1997. Moreover, with the help of television programmes such as the BBC's *The Apprentice* and *Dragon's Den*, certain entrepreneurs enjoy a mainstream media profile and political influence significantly different to that which existed even a decade ago. The change of government in 2010 has not significantly altered this trend. The Department of Business, Innovation and Skills (BIS) under Vince Cable has set up an Entrepreneurs Forum, which aims to offer informal advice on enterprise policy. The 17 strong panel includes former Dragon James Caan, Tim Campbell, winner of the first series of *The Apprentice*, and the two online Dragons, Julie Meyer and Shaf Rasul. Thus, the media capital accrued through television has often been converted into a political currency allowing high profile entrepreneurs to be used by government and other public and private organizations to promote entrepreneurial activity. The most obvious example of this, as we discussed above, being the appointment by then Prime Minister Gordon Brown in 2009 of Sir Alan Sugar, star of the BBC's version of *The Apprentice*, as his new 'Enterprise Czar' with a specific remit to help small and medium sized enterprises throughout the United Kingdom. Sir Alan – who became Lord Sugar in the process – has become one of Britain's most high profile entrepreneurs at a time when his business activities have been scaling back, but his media profile has never been higher.

One of the successes of the business entertainment format on television then has been its ability to utilize key individuals as a way of humanizing and demystifying the often clandestine world of business and this approach appears to have since been transferred to the political arena with politicians similarly using business celebrity endorsements to simplify the complex and byzantine field of policy formation. Securing such high profile individuals plays into a wider media agenda in which personalizing complex processes has become a key characteristic of news journalism. Thus, political ideology is increasingly reduced to the personalities of the various party leaders while specific 'villains' were singled out as being responsible for the global banking crisis at the end of the noughties. In essence, the mediation of 'celebrity' in all its forms has become a fixation with politicians keen to connect with the voting public, despite the fact that the perceived influence of such an approach on media audiences has yet to be proved.

Indeed we would agree with Couldry and Markham (2008: 418) who caution against making general assumptions about the role of celebrity culture as part of any political programme to re-connect with voters. Our own research has indicated that where viewers are in terms of their own business background will shape how they engage with broader television representations of entrepreneurship (Boyle and Kelly 2011). However, what is of interest here is the extent that the notion of celebrity endorsement through its 'false intimacy' with the public has become embedded in perceptions about the role these 'television entrepreneurs' can and should play in the broader arena of policy formation.

It seems to us that understanding the continuing key role played by networks and their relationship with power in all its forms remains crucial in understanding celebrity. Particular forms of media capital appear to allow access to particular circuits of communication, but exploring the barriers of entry to networks also remains important. Celebrity networks are often about a shared common currency of media profile, however for the new generation of 'television entrepreneurs' it is also representative of a perception among the political class that this group are more likely to reach out and connect with the public on business related issues than politicians are.

Conclusion
Knowledge, Television and Understanding Business

I think we need to be careful, not everybody is meant to be an entrepreneur.
Julie Meyer, CEO and Founder of Ariadne Capital and Dragon in the Online Den
(interview with authors, 2 September 2009).

As an entrepreneur the whole concept of 'you're fired' [in *The Apprentice*] is so far from reality and is just not the way one would run a business. But in terms of engaging the public it is fantastic.
Lord Bilimoria, Co-founder of Cobra Beer, *The Independent on Sunday*, 1 May 2011.

Throughout the book we have been concerned with understanding both the changing nature of the television industry and the role played by business entertainment formats in framing how audiences engage with representations of business and entrepreneurship. What has also been evident during the researching of this book, is that a broader public debate has also been ongoing that has focused on the impact of programmes such as *The Apprentice* and *Dragons' Den* on the image of business and the messages transmitted about business culture.

There has been no shortage of media surveys (some academic, most commercially orientated) into the usefulness of 'television entrepreneurs' as role models for people in, or thinking about entering, the world of business. Survey work conducted by Nottingham University Business School (Binks 2009) for example concludes that small businesses are not well represented on television and that business entertainment formats distort public perceptions of business. In the same year, the Institute of Leadership and Management found that of the business managers it surveyed, 31 percent chose Lord Sugar from *The Apprentice* as the worst possible career coach (*Management Today*, 9 May 2011). Indeed the supposed impact of a programme such as *The Apprentice* may extend even further, as the Journal of the Royal Society for the Promotion of Health (2008: 52) reported that reality television apparently helped encourage bullying in the workplace: 'A recent Samaritans survey said over 80 percent of British people feel they have been bullied at work and work-elated stress experts says (sic) programmes like the BBC's *The Apprentice* might be making things worse'.

Other initiatives however, which are often centred around young people, have viewed these programmes more positively. Examples include the Make Your Mark campaign (2009–), which is supported by the National Endowment for Science, Technology and the Arts (NESTA), schools across England and the television Dragon Peter Jones and aims to encourage teen entrepreneurs to think about the possibilities business may offer them as a career. Peter Grigg (interview with authors, 12 February 2010), then Head of Research at Enterprise UK, notes the difficulties of executing a behavioural and cultural campaign such as Make Your Mark and how business entertainment formats can feed into this:

> [For a] behavioural and cultural change campaign to demonstrate the impact it is having over the years is notoriously difficult. But there are ways to do it and you have to take a bit of a leap of faith at times and trust in it, you know, in a sort of logic model ... by influencing attitudes, building the skills and confidence of young people so that if they do have an entrepreneurial desire, they will do it better and maybe quicker in future. So television is great, the media is great, but you also need that on the ground support that is out there for those who want to start up.

At times, however, the criticism of television entrepreneurs, which mostly comes from other sectors of the business community, has become personal.

For example, in a piece for the *Daily Mail* newspaper in 2011, Luke Johnson, former Chairman of Channel 4 and serial entrepreneur, launched a scathing attack on *The Apprentice*, dismissing it as 'loathsome show' with a 'panto villain host' and an 'insult to business'. He noted how the programme had become a caricature of itself as entertainment values had usurped any innate business content it may once have had. His attack was also aimed at the BBC who he viewed as being hostile to business culture, despite once producing a show he admired, the original *Troubleshooter* with Sir John Harvey-Jones.

We would argue however that what those who criticize business programmes are really doing is making value judgements about television as a medium and the different types of factual programming on offer. Thus, Luke Johnson attacks the *The Apprentice* (which takes the forms of a business gameshow derived from reality television), for what he sees as an overemphasis on entertainment, but gives his approval to troubleshooter programmes in the observational documentary tradition, like the aforementioned *Troubleshooter* and indeed Channel 4's *Undercover Boss* which he describes in the same article as a 'much more enlightening show'.

Our research shows that audiences, on the other hand, and young audiences in particular, are more likely to acknowledge the key role that entertainment plays in attracting and retaining television viewers. Furthermore, they also recognize that in addition to offering entertainment through a competitive structure and the performative skills displayed by contestants, business gameshows can provide information on a range of 'soft skills', including the importance of preparation and presentation, the challenges of working as part of a team and the techniques required for successful team building and leadership. In addition, audiences also understand that the more respected troubleshooter format, which business professionals often consider to better reflect 'real life', in fact seeks to elicit an emotional reaction from viewers by focusing on the impact of the 'journey' experienced by its participants.

Television, Representation and the Audience

We would suggest then that these critical arguments are in fact conflating two different aspects of the mediation process that television brings to every event it covers from news and sports to factual material. Do business entertainment formats offer an accurate representation of business culture? Of course they don't. All television from the supposedly sacrosanct 'observational documentary' through to reality television offers a partial, constructed (and often reconstructed) representation of reality. Television programmes have always taken the form of a heightened mediated reality to a lesser or greater extent depending on the specific genre and the particular codes and conventions of television being mobilized. Business related television content is no different in this respect. It is not that these programmes offer a false representation, although of course at times they may well do, but rather that they offer a selective interpretation of reality. Thus people with experience of a particular business culture are often highly critical of the representations for not reflecting *their* reality while sections of the audience less aware of that culture are more likely to engage with the content to a differing manner. Nevertheless, it is important to note that our research also demonstrated that audiences are often aware of the limits imposed by television on the aspect of business being represented.

Another question considered throughout this book (and one not often raised by those who dislike business entertainment formats), is do these programmes encourage more broadly sections of the audience to become interested in aspects of entrepreneurial culture. We suggest that the answer is yes, as Lord Bilimoria acknowledges in the quote at the beginning of this chapter. As Claire Young (interview with authors, 29 September 2009), a former contestant on *The Apprentice* who has gone on to start her own business, also argues,

> It is a reality TV programme, but it is about business. And I think *The Apprentice* is credible. I think as its popularity has grown it has attracted a different audience, so it has become a bit more tabloid. But I think when people are negative about it, and very rarely people are, they might say 'oh it's not real business' [but] I am like, 'well what is the difference between selling a stock and share in your fancy bank, and actually selling a banana on a market stall? There is no difference'. It is basic business. And as I said, you know, 11 million people watched us, and a significant number of those are under 21. If somebody is actually motivated to do things by programmes like *The Apprentice* and *Dragons' Den* [then] that is good, because there is not enough going on with positive things for the youth of today, so to speak.

Of course we would also suggest that while these programmes promote greater audience awareness of certain business issues, this does not mean that all want to become entrepreneurs. Such programming may however inspire those needing some encouragement to seek out more advice, as one viewer noted: 'I find with a lot of the programmes you learn more about yourself rather than the actual business. I mean, how you feel about business, how you feel you would react in certain situations' (37-year-old general manager, Glasgow).

Audience Studies

What is clear from our research then is that programmes such as *The Apprentice* and *Dragons' Den* do encourage a learning of 'soft skills' amongst audiences and while this may be more pronounced for younger viewers it also resonates across other age groups. A central element in this process is of course what audiences bring to the viewing experience. Thus, where people are in the entrepreneurial cycle helps determine the manner in which they engage with these programmes. This means that there is often an 'active audience' watching the same programme on differing levels, some purely for enjoyment and others for information and entertainment. We also found that many value the importance of 'vocationally skilled' presenters as opposed to 'televisually skilled' and that the issue of the 'celebrity entrepreneur' is an attraction in raising the profile of a programme in the cluttered digital landscape. Programmes that work best however clearly understand the importance of narrative and emotional identification and seek to humanize the business world by encouraging audiences to ask themselves questions such as 'how would I feel?' or 'what would I do?' if placed in a similar situation.

As we have noted, for younger members of the audience in particular these programmes can be inspiring and empowering but again it's important to note that audiences are extremely 'media literate' and acutely aware of the limits and constraints of formatted television. In other words, they understand the constraints of representing reality on television but this does not negate the pleasures they may take in negotiating their way through these discourses and representations.

With regards to the term 'entrepreneur', there are regional and national differences in its usage. We found for example that the term was less popular amongst Scottish based respondents than with those in London and, for many, it has become so synonymous with television that it is in danger of becoming redundant. With regards to how the programmes we looked at in this study represent specific groups in society, it appeared that while most perceived them to offer a broadly positive view of business amongst ethnic minorities, the range of entrepreneurs on television remains narrow with more women needed and different aspects of the worlds of work and business explored because, at present, there is too much emphasis on retail and sales.

As we argued in the previous chapter, these programmes and the media profile they generate for the entrepreneurs who take part helps open political doors and offers them opportunities to become policy shapers, something again recognized by the members of the audience we spoke to. What is crucial in terms of audience engagement is that these forms of popular factual television connect with audiences in a manner that is often more intense than their engagement with business content in news and current affairs. In so doing, business entertainment formats naturalize and offer the possibility of lifestyle change for certain segments of the audience, although this is dependent on their own background and experience. In short we found that audiences can gain basic knowledge from these programmes that facilitate some development in business skills and language, but this cannot be simply read as being significantly likely to alter their behaviour.

Overall, we argue that television remains a compelling medium for constructing emotional identification with its audience through the template of the 'journey', and to this end it is simply mistaken to suggest that entertainment and knowledge are mutually exclusive. Television (with a growing social media dimension) remains to us central in debates about the creation and dissemination of public knowledge. Yet while these programmes, mixing entertainment, information and even at times education appear to have become part of the public service portfolio of content in the digital age of television (the most successful business related programmes tend to appear on the BBC and Channel 4 for example), the core mantra for television producers remains the need to first and foremost entertain the audience.

Endpiece

Dismissing such programmes as offering an unrealistic representation of business in many ways may be to miss the point. Television has always offered a mediated version of reality, even in the supposedly accurate documentary genre, and while *Dragons' Den*, *Gerry's Big Decision* or *The Secret Millionaire*, for example, have to entertain the audience, they also feature entrepreneurs willing to put their own money into potential or actual businesses and community projects (even if this investment happens less than may initially appear from the original programmes). At a time when credit and investment is hard to come by, these programmes offer enough insight into some of the challenges of starting a business to fulfil any remit they have to inform. This is also the case with *Ramsay's Kitchen Nightmares* which, in between the swearing and dramatic confrontations, many entrepreneurs believe puts forward an honest account of some of the immense challenges involved in starting and running a catering business (Parks 2006). It also offers a direct link to the original *Troubleshooter* format created in the late 1980s by producer Robert Thirkell and business guru Sir John Harvey-Jones for BBC2 (Boyle 2008, Kelly and Boyle 2011).

The range of representations around entrepreneurs remains relatively narrow on television and is framed by the needs of the television form and the drive of the medium to entertain as much as educate. For example, the importance of risk and jeopardy is essential to creating dramatic television narratives. Yet, existing research (Slater 2007) suggests that for many real-life entrepreneurs the importance of risk-taking is only prevalent in the second stage of the entrepreneurial cycle when they have an awareness of what they now have to lose. Due to the constraints of the medium, television also concentrates on specific business sectors, such as retail, catering and property, whilst also prioritizing profit-making at the expense of creativity, innovation and wider social issues. As such, the rise of social entrepreneurship (Mawson 2008) is largely absent from the business entertainment format, despite the notion of social responsibility being of great importance to a new generation of entrepreneurs. Even the 2011 BBC1 series *Village SOS*, which is described on its website as 'an exciting initiative by Big Lottery Fund and the BBC to launch a rural revival and inspire people to start community businesses that will breathe new life into their areas and create jobs', strangely plays down this aspect in the onscreen programming, framing the series instead within a template more associated with 'restoration' type reality programmes. However, these gaps do not necessarily lessen television's ability to reinforce or even challenge wider perceptions of entrepreneurial activity.

Luke Johnson, who we mentioned above was Chairman of Channel 4 between 2004 and 2010 and is also an entrepreneur and founder of private equity firm Risk Capital Partners, had a slightly more measured view of business entertainment formats when we spoke to him in 2009. His thoughts to us on the relationship between television and public perceptions of the entrepreneur offer an interesting end point for this article as well as proposing a point of departure for future reflection in this area. On the one hand, Johnson (interview with authors, 20 March 2009) was aware that these programmes often,

> present a caricature, a distortion of what entrepreneurialism and business is really about. And to a degree they play up to, I think, some people in the BBC's preconceived idea of what entrepreneurialism is. You know, it is much more sensible and down to earth, and less vicious than the sort of attitudes you get in *Dragons' Den* and *The Apprentice*.

However, he nevertheless went on to note the agenda-setting possibility of television through the way in which it frames its subject matter:

> By making [the business entertainment format] drama, [producers and broadcasters] make it popular, and therefore it gets higher ratings, which you know, has its positive side .. and on balance I am in favour of those sort of shows because I think they do, at the margin, inspire more people to go and work for themselves and take up a career as an inventor and believe that they can get rich and build a business and things. So I do believe, over society as a whole, there has been a huge cultural shift. Yes, I think entrepreneurs are much more admired, you know, Sir Richard Branson types, than they used to be decades ago.

As a businessperson who participated in Thirkell's *Back to the Floor* series in 2000, it is interesting to chart Johnson's changing perspective on business entertainment formats as they have developed over the years.

In terms of the 'celebritization' of the television entrepreneur, an image which Shane (2008) and Kelsey (2010) argue has little to do with more 'ordinary' forms of entrepreneurship, there is nevertheless an understanding of its potential positive influence on the public. For example, following the riots that took place across England in August 2011, leading City broker Tim Morgan, global head of research at Tullett Prebon, compiled a report on issues facing British society in relation to business, finance and consumerism. Noting how the 'dominant ethos of "I buy, therefore I am" needs to be challenged by a shift in emphasis from material to non-material values', Morgan (cited in Hawkes 2011) went on to suggest that,

> A young person who tries to become the next Alan Sugar or James Dyson is as likely to fall short as if he or she sets out to become the next global superstar. But ... failure to become the next Alan Sugar can still leave a person well equipped for a career in management, finance or accountancy. Failure to emulate James Dyson will leave the aspirant with useful engineering or technological skills.

This clearly suggests that policy debates around the role that the media may or may not play in shaping broader attitudes towards the world of work and its role in society are not about to go away. What we would argue is that the broad format of business entertainment is designed primarily to entertain an audience (even within the public service tradition) but in so doing can, of course, achieve other things and this is heavily shaped by the attitudes and particular demographics that audiences bring to the viewing experience.

What is clear from our research then is that television remains a central element in British popular culture. As we move into an era of digital screens and content and the debate moves to how to get particular content on specific screens, the 'black box' remains an important element of the domestic cultural furniture while its influence spreads well beyond the confines of the home. The challenge for public service television is how to reflect on the diversity of business related experiences and the world of work (and unemployment) for all of its audience, not just those who may share the aspirations of the television professional. We have been interested in this book in the role that the media industries play in the construction of the worlds of business and entrepreneurship and would argue that understanding the continuing role played by television in framing aspects of our political and cultural perceptions of the world around us should remain a central concern, even in the digital age, for those within media and communication studies

Appendix
Research Methods

Sample and Recruitment

A series of semi-structured focus groups were carried out in September 2009 in Glasgow and London to allow for a comparison between a regional (Scottish) audience and one based in Britain's business and financial capital. In total, 96 respondents between the ages of 18 and 60 took part and were divided into 12 groups (six in each location). The Glasgow focus groups took place in an educational setting (University of Glasgow) while in London the focus groups were held in a professional setting (Shoreditch Studios). In each location the focus groups were moderated by Professor Raymond Boyle and Dr Lisa Kelly. The recruitment method used was snowball sampling and quota sampling. In Glasgow, targeted adverts were placed in Business 7 and The List (a local business paper and culture magazine respectively) and flyers were distributed in arts and educational venues, at a Business Gateway conference and via email to the Scottish Women in Business members list. In London, the recruitment company Focus Force was hired to source respondents.

The sample was based on the criteria of age (split into three groups of 18–24 year olds, 25–40 year olds and 41 years and over), gender (mix of male and female), and occupational status (two groups divided into self-defined entrepreneurs/business owners/self-employed and employees/unemployed). Respondents came from a wide range of occupations but social class was not part of the criteria. A diverse ethnic mix was sought across all sessions, although London produced a more varied range of contributors than Glasgow. While the majority of groups were of mixed gender and occupation, one all-male and one all-female group was conducted in each city alongside one group consisting solely of those describing themselves as business owners/entrepreneurs/ self-employed and another of employees or unemployed participants with no business experience. All respondents were required to be familiar with at least one example of a business entertainment format to allow them to draw on their personal viewing experience when taking part in discussions. Their level of engagement with these programmes was left unspecified however; therefore they did not have to be 'fans' of this type of television.

The focus group questions were open-ended and organized around three key topics: the programmes; understanding and knowledge; and the entrepreneur. Television clips from a range of British business entertainment formats were used as visual prompts throughout each session. These were *Dragons' Den*, *The Apprentice*, *Ramsay's Kitchen Nightmares*, *Gerry's Big Decision*, *Mary Queen of Charity Shops*, *Property Snakes and Ladders*, *Mary Queen of Shops*, *The Secret Millionaire*, *The Last Millionaire* and *The Apprentice: You're Fired*. Space was left at the end of each session for respondents to raise any issues that had not been discussed. This tended to involve a consideration of gender as (by design) the final visual prompt, *The Apprentice: You're Fired*, featured a panel of guests discussing the behaviour of a female contestant on the fifth series of the show. The focus groups were audio-recorded and additional notes were taken on general group behaviour and body language. The audio recordings were fully transcribed by Elite Secretarial Services before being coded by the focus group moderators using the qualitative software package NVivo.

Qualitative Research: Focus Group Design

- Semi-structured with medium level of moderator involvement. Standard key topics and visual prompts for all focus groups but probing questions differ according to the age, gender and occupational make up of each group.
- Basic questionnaire detailing name, age and occupational status to be filled in by all respondents, along with consent form.

Introduction

Welcome, summary of research topic and explanation of how material will be used. Distribute questionnaire and ask respondents to state their name for the tape.

Key Topics

1. The Programmes

Visual Prompts: *Dragons' Den*, *The Apprentice*, *Ramsay's Kitchen Nightmares*, *Gerry's Big Decision*, *Mary Queen of Charity Shops*, *Property Snakes and Ladders*

Icebreaker

- Are there any programmes in the clips you are not familiar with?
- Which business entertainment formats do you regularly watch?

Questions

- What do you like or dislike about these programmes?
- How do these programmes differ?
- Would you categorise them as either informative, entertaining or a mixture of both?
- Are these programmes true to life?
- As a Scottish or London-based audience, is there anything you specifically relate to?

2. Understanding and Knowledge

Visual Prompts: *Dragons' Den, Mary Queen of Shops*

- Do these programmes help you understand what being involved in business is like?
- Do they inform or engage you more so than documentaries or current affairs?
- Do you think they influence particular groups in society, such as young people?
- Do these programmes influence how the public think about business and entrepreneurship?
- Has the current financial crisis changed your opinion of business and entrepreneurship?
- Do these programmes provide role models in any way?

3. The Entrepreneur

Visual prompts: *The Secret Millionaire, The Last Millionaire*

- What words do you associate with the term entrepreneur?
- Is television important in shaping this opinion?
- What are the stories you associate with entrepreneurs?
- Do you think entrepreneurs use their media profile for other purposes?

Conclusion/Sum Up

Visual Prompt: *The Apprentice: You're Fired*

- Is there anything else you would like to discuss?

Bibliography

Altmeppen, K-D., Lantzsch, K. and Will, A. 2007. Flowing Networks in the Entertainment Business: Organizing International TV Format Trade. *International Journal on Media Management*, 9(3), 94–104.

Anderson, A., Drakopoulou Dodd, S. and Jack, S. 2009. Aggressors; Winners; Victims and Outsiders: European Schools' Social Construction of the Entrepreneur. *International Small Business Journal*, 27(1), 126–136.

Anderson, C. 2006. *The Long Tail: How Endless Choice is Creating Unlimited Demand*. London: Random House Business.

Austin, T and de Jong, W. 2008. (eds) *Rethinking Documentary: New Perspectives, New Practices*. Berkshire and New York: McGraw-Hill/Open University Press

Baker, R. 2011. Mary Portas Asked to Revive High Street. *Marketing Week*, 17 May.

Bakeryinfo. 2010. [Online] Interview with Angela Maher, July 14. Available at: http://www.bakeryinfo.co.uk/news/fullstory.php/aid/6966/Maher_speaks_ out_about_Mary_Queen_of_Shops_experience.html (Accessed 3 April 2011).

Bannatyne, D. 2006. *Anyone Can Do It: From an Ice Cream Van to Dragons' Den*. London: Orion.

Barber, L. 2007. Duncan Bannatyne: The Interview. *The Observer*, 18 February.

Bazalgette, P. 2005. *Billion Dollar Game: How Three Men Risked it All and Changed the Face of Television*. London: Time Warner.

BBC [Online] The Workings of *The Apprentice*. Available at: http://www.bbc. co.uk/apprentice/series6/workings.shtml (Accessed 11 April 2011).

BBC Press Release. 2004. Sir Alan Sugar Confirmed for BBC Two's *The Apprentice*. 18 May.

Bell, M. 2009. Bafta TV Awards: Toasting TV in Tough Times. *Broadcast*, 22 April.

Bennett, J. 2008. The Television Personality System: Televisual Stardom Revisited after Film Theory. *Screen*, 29(1), Spring, 32–50.

Bennett, J. 2011. *Television Personalities: Stardom and the Small Screen*. London and New York: Routledge.

Bennett, J. and Holmes, S. 2010. The 'Place' of Television in Celebrity Studies. *Celebrity Studies*, 1(1), 65–80.

Binks, M. 2009. *UK Business Barometer Survey Report*. Nottingham: Nottingham University Business School.

Biressi, A. and Nunn, H. 2005. *Reality TV: Realism and Revelation*. London: Wallflower.

Bishop, M. and Green, M. 2008. *Philanthrocapitalism: How the Rich can Save the World and Why We Should Let Them*. London: A&C Black.

Blair, T. 2011. *Tony Blair: A Journey*. London: Arrow Books.

Bonner, F. 2003. *Ordinary Television: Analyzing Popular TV*. London: Sage.

Bonner, F. 2011. *Personality Presenters: Television's Intermediaries with Viewers*. Farnham and Burlington, VT: Ashgate.

Born, G. 2004. *Uncertain Vision: Birt, Dyke and the Reinvention of the BBC*. London: Secker and Warburg.

Botham, R and Graves, A. 2009. *The Grey Economy: How Third Age Entrepreneurs Are Contributing to Growth*. London: NESTA, August.

Bower, T. 2008. *Branson*. London: HarperCollins.

Boyle, R. 2008. From *Troubleshooter* to *The Apprentice*: The Changing Face of Business on British Television. *Media, Culture and Society*, 30(3), 415–24.

Boyle, R. 2009. The Rise of the British Entertainment Format on British Television. Localizing Global TV, in *TV Formats Worldwide*, edited by A. Moran. London: Intellect, 97–112.

Boyle, R. and Kelly, L.W. 2010. The Celebrity Entrepreneur on Television: Profile, Politics and Power. *Celebrity Studies*, 1(3), 334–350.

Boyle, R. and Magor, M. 2008. A Nation of Entrepreneurs? Television, Social Change and the Rise of the Entrepreneur. *International Journal of Media and Cultural Politics*, 4(2), 125–44.

Bradley, I. 2007. *Enlightened Entrepreneurs: Business Ethics in Victorian Britain*. London: Lion Hudson.

Brown, M. 2007. *A Licence to be Different: The Story of Channel 4*. London: BFI.

Brunsdon, C. 2003. Lifestyling Britain: The 8–9 Slot on British Television. *International Journal of Cultural Studies*, 6(1), 5–23.

Brunsdon, C., Johnson, C., Moseley, R. and Wheatley, H. 2001. Factual Entertainment on British Television: The Midlands TV Research Group's '8–9' Project. *European Journal of Cultural Studies*, 4(1), 29–62.

Bruzzi, S. 2000. *New Documentary: A Critical Introduction*. London: Routledge.

Bulkely, K. 2009. Filling *Big Brother*'s Big Boots: Forget Creative Renewal, Channel 4 will still need a Cash Cow to replace BB. *Broadcast*, 9 September.

Burnett, M. 2005. *Jump In! Even If You Don't Know How to Swim*. New York: Ballantine.

Business Sense. Spring 2010. Royal Bank of Scotland.

Caan, J. 2009. *James Caan: The Real Deal*. London: Virgin.

Caesar, E. 2009. Duncan Bannatyne: He breathes fire on his own family. *The Sunday Times*, 15 February.

Carrabine, E. 2008. *Crime, Culture and the Media*. Cambridge: Polity.

Casson, M. 2005. *The Entrepreneur: An Economic Theory*. London: Edward Elgar Publishing.

Chell, E. 2005. *The Entrepreneurial Personality: A Social Construction*. London: Routledge.

Chell, E. 2007. Social Enterprise and Entrepreneurship. *International Small Business Journal*, 25(5), 5–23.

Clark, M. 2009. *The Social Entrepreneur Revolution: Doing Good by Making Money, Making Money by Doing Good*. London: Marshall Cavendish.

Cohen, R. 2008. *The Second Bounce of the Ball: Turning Risk into Opportunity.* London: Phoenix.

Corner, J. 1996. *The Art of Record: A Critical Introduction to Documentary.* Manchester: Manchester University Press.

Corner, J. 1998. *Studying Media: Problems of Theory and Method.* Edinburgh: Edinburgh University Press.

Corner, J. 1999. *Critical Ideas in Television Studies.* Oxford: Clarendon.

Corner, J. 2000. Paper to Viewing Fact or Fiction Conference. Voice of the Viewer and Listener in association with the centre for communication and Information Studies at the University of Westminster, 27 June.

Corner, J. 2009. Public Knowledge and Popular Culture: Spaces and Tensions. *Media, Culture & Society* 31(1), 141–149.

Couldry, N. 2010. *Why Voice Matters: Culture and Politics after Neoliberalism.* London, California, New Delhi and Singapore: Sage.

Couldry, N. 2009. Teaching Us to Fake It: The Ritualized Norms of Television's 'Reality' Games, in *Reality TV: Remaking Television Culture,* edited by S. Murray and L. Ouellette. New York and London: New York University Press, 82–99.

Couldry, N. and Littler, J. 2008. The Work of Work: Reality TV and the Negotiation of Neo-liberal Work in *The Apprentice,* in *Rethinking Documentary: New Perspectives, New Practices,* edited by T. Austin and W. De Jong. Berkshire and New York: McGraw-Hill/Open University Press, 258–267.

Couldry, N. and Markham, T. 2007. Celebrity Culture and Public Connection: Bridge or Chasm. *International Journal of Cultural Studies,* 10(4), 403–421.

Dahlgren, P. 2005. Television, Public Spheres and Civic Cultures, in *A Companion to Television,* edited by J. Wasko. Malden, MA, Oxford and Victoria: Blackwell, 411–432.

Darlow, M. 2004. *Independents Struggle: The Programme Makers Who Took on the TV Establishment.* London: Quartet.

Davidson, A. 2001. Alan Sugar. *Management Today,* 1 May.

Davidson, A. 2002. Richard Branson. *Management Today,* 1 August.

Davidson, A. 2009. Fun-lover Deborah Meaden is no dragon. *The Sunday Times,* 5 April.

Davies, N. 2008. *Flat Earth News.* London: Chatto and Windus.

Davis, A. 2007. *The Mediation of Power.* London: Routledge.

Davis, A. and Seymour, E. 2010. Generating Forms of Media Capital Inside and Outside a Field: The Strange Case of David Cameron. *Media, Culture and Society.* 32(5), 739–759.

Day, J. 2006. *Apprentice* Promoted to BBC1. *Media Guardian,* 25 August.

De Solier, L. 2005. TV Dinners: Culinary Television, Education and Distinction. *Continuum: Journal of Media and Cultural Studies,* 19(1), 465–482.

Dovey, J. 2000. *Freakshow: First Person Media and Factual Television.* London: Pluto Press.

Dovey, J. 2008. Simulating the Public Sphere, in *Rethinking Documentary: New Perspectives, New Practices*, edited by T. Austin and W. De Jong. Berkshire: Open University Press, 246–257.

Down, S. 2006. *Narratives of Enterprise: Crafting Entrepreneurial Self-identity in a Small Firm*. London: Edward Elgar.

Down, S. 2010. *Enterprise, Entrepreneurship and Small Business*. London, California, New Delhi and Singapore: Sage.

Drake, P and Miah, A. 2010. The Cultural Politics of Celebrity. *Cultural Politics*, 6(1), 49–64.

Dyer, R. 1973. *Light Entertainment*. London: BFI.

Dyer, R. 1979. *Stars*. London: BFI.

Dyke, G. 2004. *Greg Dyke: Inside Story*. London, New York, Toronto and Sydney: Harper Perennial.

Dyson, J. 2010. *Ingenious Britain: Making the UK the Leading High Tech Exporter in Europe*. Conservative Party: London.

The Economist. 2009. Special Report: Entrepreneurship, 12 March.

Eisner, S.P. 2006. *Apprentice* Watch: Learning Through Reality TV. *Journal of College Teaching and Learning*, 3(9), 19–37.

Elnaugh, R. 2009. *Business Nightmares: Hitting Rock Bottom and Coming out on Top*. London: Crimson Publishing.

Enterprise UK. 2009. *The Untapped Potential Report*. Northwest Regional Development Agency and Enterprise UK, November.

European Commission. 2007. *Promoting Entrepreneurship on TV and in Other Audio-visual Media*. Brussels: European Commission, December.

Factual Commissioning Forum. 2002. London: The Barbican Centre, 11 March.

Fairclough, N. 2000. *New Labour, New Language?* London: Routledge.

Ferguson, N. 2008. *The Ascent of Money: A Financial History of the World*. New York: Penguin Press.

Friedman, J. 2002. (ed.) *Reality Squared: Televisual Discourse on the Real*. New Brunswick. NJ and London: Rutgers University Press.

Frith, S. 2000. The Black Box: The Value of Television and the Future of Television Research, *Screen* 41(1), Spring, 33–50.

Gavin, N.T. (ed.) 2000. *Economy, Media and Public Knowledge*. Leicester: Leicester University Press.

Geraghty, C. 2000. Re-examining Stardom: Questions of Text, Bodies and Performance, in *Reinventing Film Studies*, edited by C. Gledhill and L. Williams. London: Arnold, 182–201.

Gladwell, M. 2008. *Outliers: The Story of Success*. London: Allen Lane.

Guthey, E., Clark, T. and Jackson, B. 2009. *Demystifying Business Celebrity*. London and New York: Routledge.

Gwyther, M. and Saunders, A. 2006. The MT 40 Interview: Sir John Harvey-Jones. *Management Today*, 1 September.

Hall, D. 1999. *In the Company of Heroes: An Insider's Guide to Entrepreneur's at Work*. London and Dover, NH: Kogan.

Hang, M. and van Weezel, A. 2005. *Media and Entrepreneurship: A Survey of the Literature Relating Both Concepts.* Paper presented at the 18th Scandinavian Academy of Management Meeting (NFF), Aarhus School of Business, Denmark, 18–20 August.

Hargreaves, I. 2003. *Journalism: Truth or Dare.* Oxford: Oxford University Press.

Harvey-Jones, J. 1992. *Troubleshooter 2: The Sequel to Britain's Business Bestseller.* London: Penguin.

Harvey-Jones, J. 1994. *Making it Happen: Reflections on Leadership.* London: HarperCollins.

Harvey-Jones, J. 1996. *Troubleshooter Returns.* London: Penguin and BBC Books.

Harvey-Jones, J. and Massey, A. 1990. *Troubleshooter.* London: BBC Books.

Hashemi, S. and Hashemi, B. 2002. *Anyone Can Do It: Building Coffee Republic from our Kitchen Table.* Chichester: Capstone.

Hawkes, A. 2011. UK Riots were product of consumerism and will hit economy, says City broker. *The Guardian*, 22 August.

Hendershot, H. 2009. Belabored Reality: Making it Work on The Simple Life and Project Runway, in *Reality TV: Remaking Television Culture*, edited by S. Murray and L. Ouellette. New York and London: New York University Press, 243–259.

Henderson, R. and Robertson, M. 2000. Who Wants to be an Entrepreneur? Young Adult Attitudes to Entrepreneurship as a Career. *Career Development International*, 5(6), 279–287.

Hill, A. 2005. *Reality TV: Audiences and Popular Factual Television.* London and New York: Routledge.

Hill, A. 2007. *Restyling Factual TV: The Reception of News, Documentary and Reality Genres.* Abingdon and New York: Routledge.

Hill, A. 2008. Documentary Modes of Engagement, in *Rethinking Documentary: New Perspectives, New Practices*, edited by T. Austin and W. de Jong. Maidenhead and New York: Open University Press, 217–231.

Hill, A., Weibull, L. and Nilsson, A. 2007. Public and Popular: British and Swedish Audience Trends in Factual and Reality television. *Cultural Trends*, 16(1) 17–44.

Hoag, A. and Seo, S. 2005. *Media Entrepreneurship: Definition, Theory and Context.* Paper presented at the NCTA Academic Seminar, San Francisco, April.

Holmes, S. 2008. *The Quiz Show.* Edinburgh: Edinburgh University Press.

Holmes, S and Jermyn, D. 2004. (eds) *Understanding Reality Television.* London: Routledge.

Horton, D. and Wohl, R. 1956. Mass Communication and Parasocial Interaction. *Psychiatry*, 19(3), 215–229.

Jenkins, H. 2008. *Convergence Culture: Where Old and New Media Collide.* New York: New York University Press.

Jensen, K. 1987. News as Ideology: Economic Statistics and Political Ritual in Television Network News. *Journal of Communication* 37(1), 8–27.

Johansson, A.W. 2004. Narrating the Entrepreneur. *International Small Business Journal*, 22(3), 273–291.

Johnson, L. 2011. A loathsome show, a panto villain host and an insult to business. *Daily Mail*, 11 May.

Journal of the Royal Society for the Promotion of Health. 2008. Bully for Reality TV, 128(2), 52.

Kelly, L.W. 2008. [Online] TV Tears: Learning Through Emotion in Popular Factual Entertainment. *Flow*, 9(2). Available at: http://flowtv.org/2008/11/tv-tears-learning-through-emotion-in-popular-factual-entertainment-lisa-w-kelly-university-of-glasgow/ (Accessed 13 May 2011).

Kelly, L.W. 2010. Public Personas, Private Lives and the Power of the Celebrity Comedian: A Consideration of the Ross and Brand 'Sachsgate' Affair. *Celebrity Studies*. 1(1), 115–117.

Kelly, L.W. and Boyle, R. 2011. Business on Television: Continuity, Change, and Risk in the Development of Television's 'Business Entertainment Format'. *Television and New Media*, 12(3), 228–247.

Kelsey, R. 2010. *What's Stopping You? Why Smart People Don't Always Reach their Potential and How you Can*. Chichester: Capstone.

Kilborn, R., Hibberd, M. and Boyle, R. 2001. The Rise of the Docusoap: The Case of *Vets in Practice*. *Screen*, 42(4), 382–395.

Kirk, S. 2004. [Online] Interview with Jane Root. *University of Sussex*. Available at: http://www.sussex.ac.uk/alumni/notablealumni/interviews/janeroot (Accessed 26 July 2011).

Landes, D.S. 1999. *The Wealth and Poverty of Nations: Why Some Are So Rich and Some So Poor*. London: Abacus.

Langer, J. 1998. *Tabloid Television: Popular Journalism and the 'Other' News*. London: Routledge.

Langer, J. 2006. Television's Personality System, in *The Celebrity Culture Reader*, edited by P.D. Marshall. London and New York: Routledge, 181–195.

Lansley, S. and Forrester, A. 2006. *Top Man: How Philip Green Built his High Street Empire*. London: Aurum.

Levie, J., Hart, M. and Karim, M.S. 2010. Impact of Media on Entrepreneurial Intentions and Actions. *Global Entrepreneurship Monitor*. London: BIS/Aston Business School.

Lewis, T. (ed.) 2008. *TV Transformations: Revealing the Makeover Show*. London and New York: Routledge.

Lichter, S.R., Lichter, L.S. and Rothman, S. 1994. *Prime Time: How TV Portrays American Culture*. Washington, D.C.: Regnery.

Littler, J. 2007. Celebrity CEOs and the Cultural Economy of Tabloid Intimacy, in *A Reader in Stardom and Celebrity*, edited by S. Holmes and S. Redmond. London: Sage.

Lury, K. 1995. Television Performance: Being Acting and 'Corpsing.' *New Formations*, 26, 114–131.

Lusted, D. 1998. The Popular Culture Debate and Light Entertainment on Television, in *The Television Studies Book*, edited by C. Geraghty and D. Lusted. London: Arnold, 175–190.

Marr, A. 2008. *A History of Modern Britain*. London: Pan Books.

Marshall, P.D. (ed.) 2006. *The Celebrity Culture Reader*. London and New York: Routledge.

Marshall, P.D. 2010. The Promotion and Presentation of the Self: Celebrity as Marker of Presentational Media. *Celebrity Studies*, 1(1), 35–48.

Matthews, V. 2006. Docu-soap Can Get in your Eyes. *Management Today*, 7 February, 40–45.

Mawson, A. 2008. *The Social Entrepreneur: Making Communities Work*. London: Atlantic Books.

McGuigan, J. 2008. Apprentices to Cool Capitalism. *Social Semiotics* 18(3), 309–319.

McMurria, J. 2009. Global TV Realities: International Markets, Geopolitics, and the Transcultural Contexts of Reality TV, in *Reality TV: Remaking Television Culture*, edited by S. Murray and L. Ouellette. New York and London: New York University Press.

Meaden, D. 2009. *Common Sense Rules: What you Really Need to Know about Business*. London: Random House Business.

Media Management and Transformation Centre. 2007. *The Promotion of Entrepreneurship in the Audio-visual Media (especially TV)*. Jonkoping: Jonkoping International Business School, Jonkoping University.

Miller, D. and Dinan, W. 2008. *A Century of Spin: How PR Became the Cutting Edge of Corporate Power*. London: Pluto.

Mittell, J. 2001. A Cultural Approach to Television Genre Theory. *Cinema Journal*, 40(3), 3–24.

Mittell, J. 2004. *Genre and Television: From Cop Show to Cartoons in American Culture*. New York and London: Routledge.

Moran, A. 1998. *Copycat Television: Globalisation, Program Formats and Cultural Identity*. Luton: University of Luton.

Morgan, P. 2005. *The Insider: The Private Diaries of a Scandalous Decade*. London: Ebury Press.

Murdock, G. 1994. Money Talks: Broadcasting Finance and Public Culture, in *Behind the Screens: The Structure of British Broadcasting in the Nineties*, edited by S. Hood. London: Lawrence and Wishart.

Murray, S. and Ouellette, L. 2009. Second Edition. *Reality TV. Reality TV: Remaking Television Culture*. New York and London: New York University Press.

Neale, S. 1990. Questions of Genre. *Screen*, 31(1) Spring, 45–66.

Nelson, R. 1997. *TV Drama in Transition: Forms, Values and Cultural Change*. Maidenhead: Palgrave.

Nichols, B. 1991. *Representing Reality: Issues and Concepts in Documentary*. Bloomington: Indiana University Press.

Nicholson, L. and Anderson, A.R. 2005. News and Nuances of the Entrepreneurial Myth and Metaphor: Linguistic Games in Entrepreneurial Sense-Making and Sense-Giving. *Entrepreneurship Theory and Practice*, March, 153–172.

Oborne, P. 2008. *The Triumph of the Political Class*. London: Pocket Books.

Ofcom. 2005. *Communications Market Report*. London: Ofcom.

Ouellette, L. and Hay, J. 2008. *Better Living Through Reality TV: Television and Post-Welfare Citizenship*. Walden, MA and Oxford: Blackwell.

Owen, J. 2011. 'You're Fired,' entrepreneurs tell Lord Sugar. *The Independent on Sunday*, 1 May.

Parks, S. 2006. *How to be an Entrepreneur: The Six Secrets of Self-Made Success*. Harlow: Prentice Hall.

Peston, R. 2008. *Who Runs Britain? How the Super-Rich Are Changing Our Lives*. London: Hodder and Stoughton.

Philo, G. 1995. (ed.) *Glasgow University Media Reader, Vol. 2: Industry, Economy, War and Politics*. London: Routledge.

Pinseler, J. 2010. Punitive Reality TV: Televising Punishment and the Production of Law and Order, in *Trans-Reality Television: The Transgression of Reality, Genre, Politics and Audience*, edited by S. Van Bauwel and N. Carpentier. Lanham, Maryland: Lexington, 125–147.

Potter, I. 2008. *The Rise and Rise of The Independents: A Television History*. Guerilla Books.

Powell, H. and Prasad, L. 2010. 'As seen on TV.' The Celebrity Expert: How Taste is Shaped by Lifestyle Media. *Cultural Politics*, 6(1), 111–124.

Quimby, K. 2005. Negotiating [Gay] Marriage on Prime-Time Television. *The Journal of Popular Culture*. 38(4), 713–731.

Radio Times. 2011. Revealed: Secrets of *The Apprentice*. 16–22 July, 26–27.

Radu, M. and Redien-Collot, R. 2008. The Social Representation of Entrepreneurs in the French Press: Desirable and Feasible Models? *International Small Business Journal*, 26(3), 259–298.

Raphael, C. 2009. The Political Economic Origins of Reali-TV, in *Reality TV: Remaking Television Culture*, edited by S. Murray and L. Ouellette. New York and London: New York University Press, 123–140.

Rees-Mogg, M. 2008. *Dragons or Angels? An Unofficial Guide to* Dragons' Den *and Business Investment*. Richmond: Crimson.

Rehn, A. 2008. Pop (Culture) Goes the Organization: On Highbrow, Lowbrow and Hybrids in Studying Popular Culture Within Organizational Studies. *Organization*, 15(5), 765–783.

Resource: The Newsletter of Scotland's National Academy. 2011. Interview with Ralf Klinnert, 32, Summer.

Richardson, K. 1998. Signs and Wonders: Interpreting the Economy through Television, in *Approaches to Media Discourse*, edited by A. Bell and P. Garrett. Oxford: Blackwell.

Ross, D. 2009. Why the real Deborah Meaden is not such an old dragon after all. *Daily Mail*, 18 June.

Rouse, L. 2003. Are Imports on the Slide? *Broadcast*, 5 October, 38–39.

Sandbrook, D. 2006. *Never Had it so Good: A History of Britain from Suez to The Beatles*. London: Abacus.

Sampson, A. 1989. *The Midas Touch: Money, People and Power From West to East*. London, Sydney, Auckland and Toronto: Hodder and Stoughton.

Sampson, A. 1996. *Company Man: The Rise and Fall of Corporate Life*. London: HarperCollins.

Sampson, 2008. *The Anatomist: the Autobiography of Anthony Sampson*. London: Politico Publishing.

Scannell, P. 1996. *Radio, Television and Modern Life*. London: Blackwell.

Schlesinger, P. 2007. Creativity: From Discourse to Doctrine? *Screen* 48(3), 377–387.

Schlesinger, P. and Tumber, H. 1995. *Reporting Crime*. Oxford: Oxford University Press.

Schumpeter, J.A. 1934. *The Theory of Economic Development: An Inquiry into Profits, Capital, Credit, Interest, and the Business Cycle*. London: H. Milford.

Schumpeter, J.A. 2010. *Capitalism, Socialism and Democracy*. London: Routledge.

Seale, C. 2002. *Media and Health*. London: Sage.

Shane, S.A. 2008. *The Illusions of Entrepreneurship: The Costly Myths that Entrepreneurs, Investors and Policy Makers Live By*. New Haven and London: Yale University Press.

Shane, S. and Venkataraman, S. 2000. The Promise of Entrepreneurship as a Field of Research. *The Academy of Management Review*, 25(1), 217–226.

Skeggs, B., Thumim, N. and Wood, H. 2008. 'Oh goodness, I am watching reality TV': How methods make class in audience research. *European Journal of Cultural Studies*, 11(1), 5–24.

Slater, D. 2007. *The Changing Face of UK Entrepreneurism*. London: Shell Livewire and London School of Economics, June.

Social Enterprise UK. [Online] Case Studies: Fifteen. Available at: http://www. socialenterprise.org.uk/pages/fifteen.html. (Accessed 1 September 2011).

Sparks, C. 1994. Independent Production: Unions and Casualization, in *Behind the Screens: The Structure of British Broadcasting in the Nineties*, edited by S. Hood. London: Lawrence and Wishart, 133–153.

Stangler, D. 2009. *The Coming Entrepreneurship Boom*. Kansas City: Ewing Marion Kauffman Foundation, June.

Stanyer, J. 2007. *Modern Political Communication: Mediated Politics in Uncertain Times*. Oxford: Polity.

Steemers, J. 2004. *Selling Television: British Television in the Global Marketplace*. London: BFI.

Steemers, J. 2010. *Creating Preschool Television: A Story of Commerce, Creativity and Curriculum*. Basingstoke and New York: Palgrave Macmillan.

Sugar, A. 2011. *What You See is What You Get: My Autobiography*. London: Macmillan.

Teather, D. 2000. New Post Signals Pro-Business Switch by BBC. *The Guardian,* 7 November.

Temko, N. 2006. Brown outlines his vision for an 'X Factor' Britain. *The Observer,* 5 November

Theberge, L. J. 1981. *Crooks, Conmen and Clowns: Businessmen in TV Entertainment.* Washington, D.C., Media Institute.

Thirkell, R. 2010. *C.O.N.F.L.I.C.T. An Insider's Guide to Storytelling in Factual/ Reality TV and Film.* London: Methuen.

Tolson, A., 2001. 'Being yourself': The Pursuit of Authentic Celebrity. *Discourse Studies,* 3, 443–457.

Tumber, H. 2000. *Media Power, Professionals and Policies.* London: Routledge.

Turner, G. 2010. Approaching Celebrity Studies. *Celebrity Studies,* 1(1), 11–20.

Ursell, G. 2000. Turning a way of life into a business: An account and critique of the transformation of British television from public service to commercial enterprise. *Critical Perspectives on Accounting,* 11, 741–764

Van Zoonen, L. 2005. *Entertaining the Citizen: When Politics and Popular Culture Converge.* Lanham, MD: Rowman and Littlefield.

Virr, C. and Young, V. 2009. Deborah Meadon and Her Sisters. *Women and Home.* March.

Waisbord, S. 2004. McTV: Understanding the Global Popularity of Television Formats. *Television and New Media,* 5, 359–383.

Waller, D. 2011. Managers Not so Sweet on Sugar. *Management Today,* 9 May.

Weber, B.R. 2000. *Makeover TV: Selfhood, Citizenship and Celebrity.* Durham and London: New York University Press.

Wernick, A. 1991. *Promotional Culture.* London: Sage.

Wilson, J.F. 1995. *British Business History, 1720–1994.* Manchester: Manchester University Press.

Williams, H. 2006. *Britain's Power Elites: The Rebirth of a Ruling Class.* London: Constable.

Williams, J. 2004. *Entertaining the Nation: A Social History of British Television.* Stroud: Sutton Publishing Ltd.

Wollaston, S. 2011. TV Review: *Dragons' Den. The Guardian,* 31 July.

Yiannopoulos, M. 2011. The pernicious cult of the 'celebrity' entrepreneur. *The Daily Telegraph,* 5 January.

Young, Lord. 1990. *The Enterprise Years: A Businessman in the Cabinet.* London: Headline.

Index